103-3- $8.00	136-5- $20.00	152-39-$45.00	172- $300.00(R)	247- $4.00
104-1- $12.00	137-6- $12.00	153-40-$50.00	173- $300.00(R)	248- $4.00
104-2- $35.00(S)	137-7- $20.00	153-41-$25.00	174- $300.00(R)	249- $4.00
104-3- $25.00(S)	137-8- $20.00	153-42-$40.00	175- $380.00(R)	250- $4.00
105- $12.00	137-9- $20.00	153-43-$25.00	176- $380.00(R)	251- $4.00
106- $14.00	137-10-$18.00	153-44-$45.00	177- $380.00(R)	252- $4.00
107- $14.00	138-11-$18.00	154-45-$60.00	178- $350.00(R)	253- $4.00
108- $14.00	138-12-$18.00	154-46-$60.00	179- $225.00(R)	254- $4.00
109- $14.00	138-13-$18.00	154-47-$60.00	180- $225.00(R)	255- $4.00
110- $14.00	138-14-$18.00	154-48-$150.00(R)**	181- $250.00(R)	256- $12.00
111- $14.00	138-15-$18.00	155-1- $3.50	182- $250.00(R)	257- $10.00
112- $30.00	139-1- $5.00	155-2- $3.50	183- $225.00(R)	258- $10.00
113-1- $20.00	139-2- $10.00	155-3- $3.50	184- $225.00(R)	259- $20.00
113-2- $20.00	139-3- $5.00	155-4- $3.50	185- $250.00(R)	260- $20.00
113-3- $20.00	140-1- $12.00(S)	155-5- $3.50	186- $225.00(R)	261- $20.00
113-4- $20.00	140-2- $24.00(S)	156-6- $7.50	187- $225.00(R)	262- $20.00
113-5- $20.00	140-3- $12.00(S)	156-7- $7.50	188- $225.00(R)	263-1- $12.00
114-6- $20.00	141-1- $6.00	156-8- $7.50	189- $20.00	263-2- $7.50
114-7- $20.00	141-2- $6.00	156-9- $3.50	190- $20.00	263-3- $3.50
114-8- $25.00*	141-3- $12.00	156-10- $3.50	191- $12.00	263-4- $10.00
114-9- $25.00	141-4- $8.00	157-11- $3.50	192- $12.00	263-5- $15.00
114-10-$32.00*	141-5- $6.00	157-12- $3.50	193- $18.00	263-6- $7.50
115-11-$25.00	142-6- $8.00	157-13- $3.50	194- $12.00	263-7- $18.00
115-12-$36.00*	142-7- $6.00	157-14- $3.50	195- $7.00	263-8- $15.00
115-13-$25.00	142-8- $12.00	157-15- $3.50	196- $7.00	263-9- $10.00
115-14-$40.00	142-9- $12.00	158-16- $3.50	197- $7.00	263-10- $4.00
115-15-$25.00	142-10-$12.00	158-17- $7.50	198- $8.00	264-1- $12.00
116-16-$40.00	143-11-$12.00	158-18- $3.50	199- $6.00	264-2- $12.00
116-17-$45.00	143-12-$12.00	158-19- $3.50	200- $7.00	264-3- $14.00
116-18-$100.00(S)*	143-13-$12.00	158-20-$10.00	201- $7.00	264-4- $12.00
116-19-$45.00	143-14- $8.00	159-21- $3.50	202- $5.00	264-5- $12.00
116-20-$125.00(S)*	143-15- $8.00	159-22- $7.50	203- $5.00	264-6- $14.00
117-1- $5.00	144-16- $8.00	159-23- $3.50	204- $4.00	264-7- $12.00
117-2- $10.00	144-17-$14.00	159-24- $7.50	205- $8.00	264-8- $14.00
117-3- $5.00	144-18- $8.00	159-25- $3.50	206- $8.00	264-9- $12.00
118-1- $5.00	144-19- $8.00	160-26- $3.50	207- $8.00	264-10-$14.00
118-2- $10.00	144-20- $8.00	160-27- $3.50	208- $8.00	265-1- $12.00
118-3- $5.00	145-1- $25.00	160-28-$10.00	209- $8.00	265-2- $12.00
119-1- $5.00	145-2- $35.00	160-29-$10.00	210- $5.00	265-3- $12.00
119-2- $10.00	145-3- $25.00	160-30- $7.50	211- $8.00	265-4- $12.00
119-3- $5.00	145-4- $35.00	161-31- $3.50	212- $14.00	265-5- $12.00
120-1- $5.00	145-5- $25.00	161-32- $7.50	213- $5.00	265-6- $12.00
120-2- $10.00	146-6- $55.00	161-33- $7.50	214- $8.00	265-7- $12.00
120-3- $5.00	146-7- $40.00	161-34- $7.50	215- $5.00	265-8- $12.00
121-1- $5.00	146-8- $70.00	161-35- $7.50	216- $4.00	266-1- $12.00
121-2- $10.00	146-9- $30.00	162-36-$10.00	217- $20.00	266-2- $8.00
121-3- $5.00	146-10-$70.00	162-37-$12.00	218- $7.00	266-3- $14.00
122-1- $5.00	147-11-$25.00	162-38-$12.00	219- $12.00	266-4- $8.00
122-2- $10.00	147-12-$55.00	162-39- $7.50	220- $4.00	266-5- $12.00
122-3- $5.00	147-13-$50.00	162-40- $7.50	221- $15.00	266-6- $8.00
123-1- $5.00	147-14-$25.00	163-41-$15.00	222- $20.00	266-7- $8.00
123-2- $10.00	147-15-$25.00	163-42-$15.00	223- $4.00	266-8- $12.00
123-3- $5.00	148-16-$50.00	163-43- $7.50	224- $26.00	267-1- $5.00
124-1- $5.00	148-17-$60.00	163-44- $7.50	225- $20.00	267-2- $5.00
124-2- $10.00	148-18-$25.00	163-45-$15.00	226- $5.00	267-3- $12.00
124-3- $5.00	148-19-$25.00	164-46-$10.00	227- $5.00	267-4- $12.00
125-1- $6.00	148-20-$45.00	164-47- $3.50	228- $5.00	267-5- $12.00
125-2- $12.00	149-21-$35.00	164-48- $7.50	229- $5.00	267-6- $12.00
125-3- $6.00	149-22-$45.00	164-49-$15.00	230- $5.00	267-7- $12.00
126-1- $6.00	149-23-$50.00	164-50- $3.50	231- $5.00	267-8- $12.00
126-2- $12.00	149-24-$45.00	165-51- $7.50	232- $5.00	268-1- $12.00
126-3- $6.00	150-25-$40.00	165-52- $7.50	233- $5.00	268-2- $12.00
127- $75.00	150-26-$35.00	165-53-$18.00	234- $5.00	268-3- $14.00
128- $75.00	150-27-$35.00	165-54- $3.50	235- $5.00	268-4- $12.00
129- $75.00	150-28-$25.00	165-55- $7.50	236- $5.00	268-5- $12.00
130- $95.00(S)	150-29-$25.00	166-56-$15.00	237- $5.00	268-6- $16.00
131- $75.00	151-30-$45.00	166-57-$15.00	238- $5.00	268-7- $16.00
132- $25.00	151-31-$45.00	166-58-$15.00	239- $5.00	268-8- $16.00
133- $25.00	151-32-$25.00	166-59-$10.00	240- $5.00	269-9- $12.00
134- $25.00	151-33-$25.00	166-60-$10.00	241- $4.00	269-10-$12.00
135- $25.00	151-34-$50.00	167- $350.00(R)	242- $4.00	269-11-$16.00
136-1- $20.00	152-35-$30.00	168- $300.00(R)	243- $4.00	269-12-$10.00
136-2- $20.00	152-36-$25.00	169- $300.00(R)	244- $4.00	269-13-$12.00
136-3- $12.00	152-37-$25.00	170- $300.00(R)	245- $4.00	269-14-$16.00
136-4- $12.00	152-38-$30.00	171- $300.00(R)	246- $4.00	269-15-$16.00

THE WORLD OF WADE: Collectable Porcelain and Potte

by Ian Warner and Mike Posgay

Suggested Price Guide 1993

The suggested prices in this Price Guide are representative of price averages in the United States of America and Canada. Due to the many differences in prices of similar i various parts of the U.K., U.S.A. and Canada, no attempt has been made to give a high and low range, rather an overall average of prices is suggested. All prices are for items in mint condition, i.e. no chips, cracks, scratches, crazing or faded decorations.

The collector should realize that a price paid at an auction, flea market, antique show or store is not always the true value of a particular item. Auction prices vary greatly due to competition between bidders, and flea market, antique show or store prices more often than not reflect dealer knowledge, or lack thereof, of the collector market.

Collectors should remember, however, that this is a guide only and it is the buyer who must ultimately decide the value of any particular item.

Certain items have been identified with a letter or letters following the suggested price. They are (S) scarce, (R) rare and (VR) very rare.

No. 263-7 pg.43 (Tom Smith Party Cracker 1976-77) shows a white Polar Bear on a blue base instead of the correct beige colored Polar Bear on a blue base.

* Items marked thus refer to the original issue Nursery Favourites.

** Items marked thus refer to the original Wade figurines. Beware of recent reproductions of the early Whimsie Swan and Shire Horse.

*** Items marked thus denote prices for full and boxed decanters. Empty, unboxed decanters command approximately 50% less than suggested list price.

† Items marked thus refer to the original 1970's - 1986 Wade Ireland issue. This set was re-issued in 1992 with the Seagoe Ceramics ink backstamp.

†† Items marked thus refer to the original 1962 - 1986 Wade Ireland issue. This set was re-issued in 1992 with the Seagoe Ceramics backstamp.

The authors and publisher assume no liability for any losses that may occur from consulting this guide.

To contact the authors please write to: P.O. BOX 93022, 499 Main Street South, BRAMPTON, Ontario Canada L6Y 4V8.

****

No.	Price	No.	Price	No.	Price	No.	Price	No.	Price
1-	$275.00(R)	23-	$20.00	45-	$40.00	67-	$50.00	89-	$20.00
2-	$300.00(R)	24-	$18.00	46-	$50.00(S)	68-	$35.00	90-	$16.00
3-	$175.00(R)	25-	$200.00(S)	47-	$60.00(S)	69-	$75.00	91-	$30.00
4-	$140.00(S)	26-	$100.00(S)	48-	$60.00(S)	70-	$75.00	92-	$35.00
5-	$140.00(S)	27-	$100.00(S)	49-	$50.00	71-	$35.00	93-	$45.00
6-	$125.00(S)	28-	$100.00(S)	50-	$55.00	72-	$160.00(S)	94-	$16.00
7-	$115.00(S)	29-	$100.00(S)	51-	$55.00	73-	$30.00	95-	$25.00
8-	$115.00(S)	30-	$100.00(S)	52-	$30.00	74-	$28.00	96-	$16.00
9-	$100.00(S)	31-	$100.00(S)	53-	$50.00	75-	$50.00	97-	$30.00
10-	$95.00(S)	32-	$100.00(S)	54-	$25.00	76-	$20.00	98-	$150.00(S)
11-	$95.00(S)	33-	$50.00	55-	$25.00	77-	$20.00	99-	$120.00(S)
12-	$95.00(S)	34-	$30.00	56-	$25.00	78-	$60.00	100-1-	$8.00
13-	$95.00(S)	35-	$30.00	57-	$25.00	79-	$100.00(S)	100-2-	$6.00
14-	$95.00(S)	36-	$50.00(S)	58-	$6.00	80-	$50.00	100-3-	$6.00
15-	$95.00(S)	37-	$30.00	59-	$8.00	81-	$50.00(S)	101-1-	$20.00
16-	$95.00(S)	38-	$50.00	60-	$4.00	82-	$150.00(R)	101-2-	$12.00
17-	$160.00(VR)	39-	$75.00	61-	$50.00(S)	83-	$30.00	101-3-	$12.00
18-	$85.00	40-	$30.00	62-	$40.00(S)	84-	$20.00	102-1-	$8.00
19-	$145.00(S)	41-	$40.00	63-	$90.00(S)	85-	$50.00	102-2-	$4.00
20-	$160.00(S)	42-	$40.00	64-	$90.00(S)	86-	$30.00	102-3-	$4.00
21-	$160.00(S)	43-	$40.00	65-	$90.00	87-	$25.00	103-1-	$8.00
22-	$195.00(S)	44-	$40.00	66-	$90.00	88-	$20.00	103-2-	$8.00

625- $12.00	701- $12.50	752- $20.00	828- $4.00	FIG. 84-3- $120.00(R)
626- $12.00	702- $17.00	753- $20.00	829- $4.00	FIG. 84-4- $95.00(S)
627- $12.00	703- $8.00	754- $27.50	830- $4.00	FIG. 84-5- $80.00
628- $5.00	704- $10.00	755- $27.50	831- $4.00	FIG. 84-6- $60.00
629- $10.00	705- $35.00	756- $20.00	832- $4.00	FIG. 85- $95.00(R)
630- $10.00	706- $22.00	757- $20.00	833- $135.00	FIG. 86- $30.00
631- $10.00	707- $38.00	758- $27.50	834- $135.00	FIG. 87- $40.00 set
632- $10.00	708- $45.00	759- $27.50	835- $135.00	FIG. 89- $30.00
633- $10.00	709- $10.00	760- $28.00	836- $135.00	FIG. 104- $60.00
634- $5.00	710- $30.00	761- $30.00	837- $12.00	FIG. 105- $15.00
635- $5.00	711- $25.00	762- $30.00	838- $125.00***	FIG. 108- $450.00(VR)
636- $5.00	712- $32.50	763- $28.00	FIG. 17-A- $150.00(S)	FIG. 109- $25.00(S)
637- $5.00	713- $10.00	764- $15.00	FIG. 17-B- $100.00(S)	FIG. 110- $22.00
638- $5.00	714- $12.00	765- $20.00	FIG. 17-C- $160.00(S)	FIG. 111- $30.00
639- $5.00	715- $12.00	766- $20.00	FIG. 17-D- $115.00(S)	FIG. 112- $45.00(R)
640- $5.00	716- $35.00	767- $20.00	FIG. 17-E- $115.00(S)	FIG. 113- $25.00
641- $14.00	717- $6.00	768- $27.50	FIG. 17-F- $160.00(S)	FIG. 114- $25.00
642- $14.00	718- $10.00	769- $27.50	FIG. 18- $95.00(S)	FIG. 115- $32.50
643- $14.00	719- $10.00	770- $15.00	FIG. 19- $80.00(S)	FIG. 123
644- $6.00	720- $12.00	771- $40.00	FIG. 23- $25.00	Blue- $12.00 each
645- $6.00	721- $12.00	772- $27.50	FIG. 24- $45.00	Green- $12.00 each
646- $5.00	722- $30.00†	773- $27.50	FIG. 25-A- $140.00	Yellow- $18.00 each
647- $10.00	723- $28.00†	774- $25.00	FIG. 25-B- $150.00	Beige- $28.00 each
648- $10.00	724- $40.00†	775- $25.00	FIG. 25-C- $180.00(S)	FIG. 124
649- $6.00	725- $28.00†	776- $18.00	FIG. 25-D- $150.00	Cottage- $30.00
650- $6.00	726- $28.00†	777- $20.00	FIG. 25-E- $160.00	Pig- $50.00
651- $6.00	727- $55.00†	778- $20.00	FIG. 30- $450.00(boxed)	Elephant- $50.00
652- $6.00	728- $85.00†	779- $50.00***	FIG. 31- $90.00	FIG. 125
653- $10.00	729- $28.00†	780- $20.00	FIG. 33- $20.00 each	Acorn- $25.00
654- $5.00	730- $28.00†	781- $28.00	FIG. 36- $100.00 each	Rabbit- $50.00
655- $5.00	731- $35.50	782- $20.00	FIG. 38	Pig- $35.00
656- $5.00	732- $35.50	783- $40.00(S)	Lady- $180.00	FIG. 126- $55.00
657- $5.00	633- $26.50	784- $32.50	Tramp- $260.00	FIG. 128- $15.00
658- $6.00	734- $35.00	785- $50.00(S)	Bambi- $120.00	FIG. 129- $35.00(S)
659- $12.00	735- $12.00	786- $15.00	Scamp- $150.00	FIG. 130- $13.00
660- $12.00	736- $12.00	787- $10.00	FIG. 39	FIG. 131- $20.00
661- $55.00	737- $12.00	788- $26.00	Jock- $250.00	FIG. 135-A- $12.00
662- $200.00(S)***	738- $30.00	789- $28.00	Dachie- $360.00	FIG. 135-B- $12.00
663- $160.00(S)***	739- $18.50	790- $12.00	Thumper- $310.00	FIG. 135-C- $12.00
664- $160.00(S)***	740- $18.50	791- $10.00	Trusty- $150.00	FIG. 135-D- $12.00
665- $95.00(VR)	741- $16.00	792- $18.00	Si- $120.00	FIG. 135-E- $12.00
666- $300.00(VR)	742- $12.00	793- $22.00	Am-$120.00	FIG. 135-F- $12.00
667- $85.00	743- $12.00	794- $24.00	FIG. 40-A- $8.00	FIG. 135-G- $16.00
668- $85.00	744- $12.00	795- $27.50	FIG. 40-B- $16.00	FIG. 135-H- $16.00
669- $80.00	745- $16.00	796- $12.00	FIG. 40-C- $14.00	FIG. 135-J- $16.00
670- $30.00	746- $14.00	797- $15.00	FIG. 40-D- $18.00	FIG. 136- $130.00(S)
671- $18.00	747- $14.00	798- $12.00	FIG. 40-E- $18.00	FIG. 137- $150.00(S)
672- $18.00	748- $18.00	799- $22.50(S)	FIG. 41- $200.00(R)**	FIG. 138- $150.00(S)
673- $35.00(S)	749-C346-$25.00	800- $20.00	FIG. 53- $60.00	FIG. 139- $190.00(R)
674- $15.00	C345- $25.00	801- $15.00	FIG. 59- $8.00 each	FIG. 140- $25.00
675- $15.00	749-C347-$35.00	802- $15.00	FIG. 60- $100.00(S)	FIG. 141- $20.00
676- $15.00	749-C348-$55.00	803- $14.00	FIG. 66- $200.00(S)	FIG. 142- $12.00
677- $20.00	749-C360-$20.00	804- $15.00	FIG. 67- $30.00 each	FIG. 143- $27.50(S)
678- $35.00	749-C350-$30.00	805- $19.00	FIG. 72- $18.50	FIG. 144- $60.00(S)
679- $50.00 pair	749-C351-$18.00	806- $12.00	FIG. 73- $22.00	FIG. 145- $38.50(S)
680- $28.00	749-C352-$25.00	807- $20.00	FIG. 74- $15.00	FIG. 146- $18.00
681- $55.00	749-C353-$40.00	808- $10.00	FIG. 75- $15.00	FIG. 147- $20.00
682- $35.00	749-C354-$18.00	809- $15.00	FIG. 76- $70.00	FIG. 148- $14.00
683- $14.50	749-C355-$60.00	810- $12.00	FIG. 77- $5.00	FIG. 149- $25.00
684- $18.50	749-C356-$28.00	811- $45.00(S)	FIG. 78- $8.00	FIG. 150- $35.00
685- $25.00	749-C357-$25.00	812- $25.00	FIG. 79- $60.00	FIG. 151- $20.00
686- $90.00	749-C358-$14.00	813- $25.00	FIG. 80- $170.00(R)	FIG. 152- $55.00(S)
687- $45.00	749-C359-$14.00	814- $25.00	FIG. 83-1- $75.00	FIG. 153- $55.00
688- $20.00	749-C349-$30.00	815- $15.00	FIG. 83-2- $65.00	FIG. 154- $45.00
689- $25.00	750-1-$125.00††	816- $18.00	FIG. 83-3- $75.00	FIG. 155- $45.00
690- $28.00	750-2-$125.00††	817- $14.00	FIG. 83-4- $65.00	FIG. 156- $40.00
691- $25.00	750-3-$125.00††	818- $15.00	FIG. 83-5- $110.00(S)	FIG. 157- $15.00
692- $20.00	750-4-$125.00††	819- $28.00	FIG. 83-6- $130.00(R)	FIG. 158-A- $25.00
693- $22.50	750-5-$125.00††	820- $28.00	FIG. 83-7- $65.00	FIG. 158-B- $25.00
694- $22.50	750-6-$125.00††	821- $15.00	FIG. 83-8- $65.00	FIG. 158-C- $25.00
695- $15.00	750-7-$125.00††	822- $20.00	FIG. 83-9- $130.00(R)	FIG. 158-D- $25.00
696- $40.00(S)	750-8-$125.00††	823- $20.00	FIG. 83-10- $55.00	
697- $30.00(S)	750-9-$190.00††	824- $20.00	FIG. 83-11- $90.00(S)	
698- $36.00(S)	750-10-$190.00††	825- $20.00	FIG. 83-12- $70.00	
699- $32.00(S)	750-11-$190.00††	826- $4.00	FIG. 84-1- $60.00	
700- $16.00	751- $18.00	827- $4.00	FIG. 84-2- $50.00(S)	

269-16-$40.00	325- $18.00	400- $28.00	475- $27.50	550- $15.00
270-17-$10.00	326- $18.00	401- $95.00(S)	476- $30.00	551- $18.50
270-18-$16.00	327- $18.00	402- $60.00	477- $6.00	552- $18.50
270-19-$16.00	328- $18.00	403- $60.00(R)	478- $8.00	553- $15.00
270-20-$35.00	329- $12.00	404- $6.00	479- $40.00 set	554- $15.00
270-21-$12.00	330- $12.00	405- $30.00(S)	480- $14.00	555- $18.50
270-22-$12.00	331- $12.00	406- $50.00(S)	481- $42.50(S)	556- $15.00
270-23-$18.00	332- $15.00	407- $28.00	482- $20.00	557- $18.50
270-24-$16.00	333- $12.00	408- $45.00	483- $30.00	558- $40.00
271-25-$18.00	334- $12.00	409- $45.00	384- $14.00	559- $180.00(R)
271-26-$12.00	335- $22.50	410- $45.00	485- $90.00(S)	560- $80.00
271-27-$18.00	336- $22.50	411- $30.00	486- $20.00	561- $80.00
271-28-$16.00	337- $22.50	412- $75.00(S)	487- $90.00(S)	562- $65.00
271-29-$16.00	338- $18.50	413- $75.00(S)	488- $18.00	563- $60.00
271-30-$16.00	339- $18.50	414- $75.00(S)	489- $38.00	564- $60.00
271-31-$18.00	340- $25.00	415- $75.00(S)	490- $10.00	565- $110.00(S)
271-32-$20.00	341- $28.00	416- $75.00(S)	491- $20.00	566- $25.00(S)
272-1- $50.00	342- $28.00	417- $75.00(S)	492- $100.00(S)	567- $90.00(S)
272-2- $50.00	343- $35.00	418- $15.00	493- $18.00	568- $90.00(S)
272-3- $50.00	344- $40.00	419- $15.00	494- $35.00	569- $175.00
272-4- $50.00	345- $22.00	420- $8.00	495- $12.00	570- $200.00
272-5- $50.00	346- $10.00	421- $30.00	496- $8.00	571- $14.00
272-6- $50.00	347- $60.00(S)	422- $32.50	497- $14.00	572- $14.00
273- $10.00	348- $6.00	423- $47.50(S)	498- $6.00	573- $14.00
274- $17.50	349- $6.00	424- $12.50	499- $8.00	574- $14.00
275- $8.00	350- $6.00	425- $12.50	500- $27.50	575- $14.00
276- $8.00	351- $8.00	426- $18.00	501- $8.00	576- $14.00
277- $17.50	352- $30.00	427- $12.50	502- $14.00	577- $14.00
278- $20.00	353- $50.00	428- $32.50	503- $20.00	578- $14.00
279- $10.00	354- $55.00	429- $18.00	504- $18.00	579- $14.00
280- $6.00	355- $60.00	430- $25.00(R)	505- $20.00	580- $14.00
281- $24.00	356- $65.00	431- $32.50	506- $40.00	581- $14.00
282- $20.00	357- $60.00(S)	432- $10.00	507- $35.00	582- $14.00
283- $24.00	358- $60.00(S)	433- $15.00	508- $30.00	583- $14.00
284- $9.00	359- $160.00(S)	434- $125.00	509- $40.00	584- $12.00
285- $30.00	360- $140.00(S)	435- $27.50	510- $30.00	585- $12.00
286- $24.00	361- $160.00(S)	436- $15.00	511- $30.00	586- $14.00
287- $24.00	362- $75.00	437- $45.00	512- $60.00	587- $12.00
288- $27.50	363- $75.00	438- $65.00(VR)	513- $40.00	588- $12.00
289- $5.00	364- $25.00	439- $25.00	514- $35.00	589- $12.00
290- $5.00	365- $30.00	440- $20.00	515- $30.00	590- $12.00
291- $20.00(S)	366- $25.00	441- $10.00	516- $80.00(S)	591- $6.00
292- $50.00(S)	367- $180.00	442- $8.00	517- $40.00	592- $14.00
293- $8.00	368- $30.00	443- $15.00	518- $30.00	593- $10.00
294- $10.00	369- $25.00	444- $8.00	519- $75.00(S)	594- $14.00
295- $8.00	370- $160.00(S)	445- $8.00	520- $22.50	595- $12.00
296- $20.00	371- $150.00(S)	446- $8.00	521- $15.50	596- $10.00
297- $20.00	372- $30.00	447- $10.00	522- $18.50	597- $10.00
298- $12.00 set	373- $80.00	448- $38.00	523- $10.00	598- $6.00
299- $12.00	374- $80.00	449- $35.00	524- $12.50	599- $10.00
300- $15.00	375- $50.00	450- $30.00	525- $22.50	600- $10.00
301- $12.00	376- $50.00	451- $35.00	526- $18.50	601- $10.00
302- $12.00	377- $40.00	452- $20.00	527- $40.00	602- $14.00
303- $20.00	378- $45.00	453- $18.00	528- $45.00	603- $12.00
304- $15.00	379- $50.00	454- $18.00	529- $42.50	604- $18.00
305- $25.00	380- $160.00	455- $100.00(S)	530- $30.00	605- $18.00
306- $18.00	381- $20.00	456- $27.50	531- $32.50	606- $18.00
307- $50.00	382- $25.00	457- $32.50	532- $30.00	607- $18.00
308- $25.00	383- $30.00	458- $10.00	533- $25.00	608- $10.00
309- $10.00	384- $25.00	459- $35.00	534- $25.00	609- $10.00
310- $10.00	385- $30.00	460- $50.00(VR)	535- $25.00	610- $10.00
311- $20.00	386- $145.00	461- $10.00	536- $20.00	611- $15.00
312- $40.00	387- $80.00	462- $40.00	537- $8.00	612- $15.00
313- $40.00	388- $80.00	463- $20.00	538- $28.00	613- $15.00
314- $40.00	389- $80.00	464- $25.00	539- $15.50	614- $15.00
315- $40.00	390- $80.00	465- $18.00	540- $18.50	615- $15.00
316- $50.00	391- $50.00	466- $10.00	541- $18.50	616- $15.00
317- $50.00	392- $50.00	467- $8.00	542- $15.00	617- $15.00
318- $24.00(S)	393- $50.00	468- $6.00	543- $15.50	618- $15.00
319- $24.00(S)	394- $20.00	469- $14.00	544- $18.50	619- $15.00
320- $24.00	395- $28.00	470- $35.00	545- $12.00	620- $15.00
321- $24.00	396- $20.00	471- $60.00(R)	546- $16.00	621- $15.00
322- $18.00	397- $15.00	472- $18.00	547- $14.00	622- $14.00
323- $18.00	398- $90.00(S)	473- $14.00	548- $15.00	623- $14.00
324- $18.00	399- $75.00	474- $16.00	549- $15.00	624- $14.00

DATING WADE PRODUCTS BY THE USE OF BACKSTAMPS.

It has been the policy of Wade Potteries to keep production records for a period of only seven years. Whilst both present and past employees of the company have been most helpful in searching through their memories and records (both personal and company owned) that have been retained, it has been somewhat of a problem giving exact production dates of items made prior to the late 1940's.

In some cases, backstamps referred to as Mark Type in the text have been made available by the pottery and, in other cases, production dates of many items have been obtained from illustrations shown in the Pottery Gazette and Glass Trade Review. As many of the backstamps overlapped in use, this is by no means an exact way of dating items as, in some cases, old molds were reused and given the current backstamp. It is, therefore, possible to find one particular item with as many as four different backstamps, but, by referring to the following list of "Mark Types," it will be possible for the collector to obtain a general time period of production for many pieces made during the 1930's, late 1940's through the 1950's. This applies largely to the tableware made by Wade Heath & Company Ltd.

Two of the earlier Wade backstamps, Mark Types 1A and 2A, refer to a type of decoration, ORCADIA, which was in production for a short time only, approx. three years. It should be noted that all pieces of ORCADIA ware were "individual" as the exact combination of "color running" could never be repeated.

The words "Flaxman" or "Flaxmanware," which refers to a type of Matt Glaze finish or Decorated Matt Glaze finish, is often included in a Wade Heath backstamp. These words were taken from the name of the A.J. Wade Ltd. factory, Flaxman Tile Works, when both Wade Heath & Company Ltd. and A.J. Wade Ltd. shared the same premises. With the move of Wade Heath to the Royal Victoria Pottery in 1938, the words "Flaxman" and "Flaxmanware" were dropped from the backstamp.

During the war years of 1939-1942, Wade Heath used only one backstamp (Mark Type 3) which was used on white ware produced for home consumption only and on decorated ware produced for export. Other backstamps were used only on a particular line where the name of the finish of a mold shape was incorporated into the backstamps e.g. Mark Type 9.

A new style of lettering for the word "Wade" was introduced starting with Mark Type 10 when the word "Heath" was dropped from the backstamps. The word "Wade" went through a number of variations until the introduction of the transfer type backstamp, Mark Type 19, which was then also used by George Wade & Son Ltd.

Backstamps for George Wade & Son Ltd. are easier to date as decorative ware was limited in production during the 1930's, most of which was marked. When decorative ware was reintroduced by George Wade in the 1950's, most pieces were either mold marked or had a black and gold label affixed to the base. It is these latter items, when the paper labels have been detached, that can cause a collector to overlook an otherwise unmarked Wade item. Luckily, the memories of Wade employees are still quite clear regarding this era and information for this time period is more readily available.

The majority of backstamps used by Wade (Ireland) Ltd. stayed in use for the length of production of various items even though new backstamps were introduced during these periods; however, some backstamps were used for a particular line, e.g. Mark Type 34 and others were specifically designed for a particular distributor, e.g. Mark Type 39.

During the years between 1950-1970, when Wade Heath in association with Reginald Corfield (Sales) Ltd. were producing large amounts of advertising items, their backstamps went through a number of changes. The first backstamp (Mark Type 42) was revised circa 1957 to a backstamp of similar size but with heavier lettering (Mark Type 43). Circa 1962 the backstamp with the heavier lettering was reduced slightly in size (Mark Type 44). From observations and available records, it would appear that Mark Type 43 and Mark Type 44 overlapped in use for a number of years in the early 1960's. In 1970, when Wade (PDM) Ltd. was created, a completely new backstamp was introduced (Mark Type 46) which was later revised to the current backstamp (Mark Type 47) which shows the three letters: PDM separated.

WADE GROUP OF POTTERIES
MARKS & BACKSTAMPS

WADE & CO.

WADES
ENGLAND

Mark Type 1
Mid 1920's-1927
Ink Stamp

WADES
ORCADIA
WARE
BRITISH MADE

Mark Type 1A
Mid 1920's-1927
Ink Stamp

WADE HEATH & CO. LTD.

WADEHEATH
ENGLAND

Mark Type 2
1928-1937
Ink Stamp

WADEHEATH
ORCADIA
WARE
BRITISH MADE

Mark Type 2A
1928-1934
Ink Stamp

WADEHEATH
B
ENGLAND

Mark Type 3
1939-1942
Ink Stamp

Flaxman Ware
Hand Made Pottery
BY WADEHEATH
ENGLAND

Mark Type 4
Circa 1936
Ink Stamp

Wadeheath
Ware
England

Mark Type 5
Circa 1937
Ink Stamp

FLAXMAN
WADE
HEATH
ENGLAND

Mark Type 6
Circa 1937-1938
Ink Stamp

WADE
HEATH
ENGLAND

Mark Type 7
Circa 1938-1950
Ink Stamp

WADE
HEATH
ENGLAND

Mark Type 8
Circa 1938-1950
Ink Stamp

"GOTHIC"
WADE
HEATH
ENGLAND

Mark Type 9
Circa Late 1930's-1950
Ink Stamp

WADE
ENGLAND

Mark Type 10
Circa Late 1940's
Ink Stamp

WADE
ENGLAND
"GOTHIC"

Mark Type 11
Circa 1948-1954
Ink Stamp

WADE
Bramble
ENGLAND

Mark Type 12
Circa 1950-1955
Ink Stamp

"HARVEST"
WARE
WADE
ENGLAND

Mark Type 13
Circa 1947-Early 1950's
Ink Stamp

WADE
ENGLAND

Mark Type 14
Circa 1947-Early 1950's
Ink Stamp

WADE
ENGLAND

Mark Type 15
Circa 1947-1953
Ink Stamp

WADE
MADE IN
ENGLAND
HAND PAINTED

Mark Type 16
Circa 1953+
Transfer

Mark Type 17
Circa 1953+
Transfer

WADE
"FESTIVAL"
ENGLAND

Mark Type 18
Circa 1953+
Transfer

WADE
ENGLAND

Mark Type 19
Circa 1953+
Transfer
(George Wade & Son Ltd.
Also Used This Mark
From Circa 1953 On.)

Mark Type 20
1985+
Transfer

GEORGE WADE & SON LTD.

Mark Type 21
Circa Early 1930's-Late 1930's
Ink Stamp

Mark Type 22
Circa Early 1930's-Late 1930's
Hand Painted Ink

Mark Type 23
Circa 1939
Ink Stamp

WADE
Porcelain
Made in England

Mark Type 24
1958+
Molded

WADE
PORCELAIN
MADE IN ENGLAND

Mark Type 25
1957-1981
Molded

WADE
MADE IN
ENGLAND

Mark Type 26
1959+
Molded

WADE
MADE IN ENGLAND

Mark Type 27
1958+
Molded

WADE (IRELAND) LTD.

Mark Type 28
1953+
Impressed

Mark Type 29
Mid 1954+
Impressed

Mark Type 30
Mid 1954
Transfer

Mark Type 31
Mid 1950's+
Molded

Mark Type 32
1955
Impressed

Mark Type 33
1962
Molded

Mark Type 34
Mid 1960's
Molded

Mark Type 40
1977+
Molded

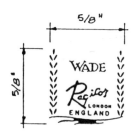

Mark Type 44
1962-1968
Transfer

Mark Type 35
1970
Impressed

Mark Type 41
1980+
Molded
&
Transfer

Mark Type 45
1968-1970
Transfer

Mark Type 36
1973
Impressed

WADE HEATH & CO. LTD.
&
REGINALD CORFIELD (SALES) LTD.

Mark Type 37
1970+
Transfer

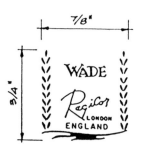

Mark Type 42
1950-1957
Transfer

WADE (PDM) LTD.

Mark Type 46
1970-1980
Transfer

Mark Type 38
Mid 1970's
Impressed

Mark Type 39
1965-1968
Impressed

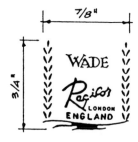

Mark Type 43
1957-1966
Transfer

(NOTE: MARK 43 SIMILAR TO
MARK 42 BUT HEAVIER
LETTERING.)

Mark Type 47
1980+
Transfer

Figurines,

Flowers

and

Animal Figures

by

George Wade & Son Ltd.

and

Wade Heath & Company Ltd.

FIGURINES *by GEORGE WADE & SON LTD. CIRCA 1927-1937.*

Up until the late 1920's, industrial ceramics had been the primary product of George Wade & Son Ltd. at their Manchester Pottery. This limited field of products was felt, by the late Sir George Wade, to make the pottery vulnerable to the ever changing needs of the market. In 1927, with diversification in mind and an interest in a new type of material called "cellulose" used for finishing earthenware etc., George Wade decided to introduce their first range of moderately priced figurines and wall masks made of earthenware using the cellulose finish. The cellulose was applied over the colored decoration forming a type of underglaze finish. Unfortunately the cellulose finish turned yellow over a period of time disintegrating and peeling off the surface of the figurine. Needless to say this type of finish was discontinued along with the majority of the figurines from the range by the mid to late 1930's.

The majority of these slip cast figurines were modeled by Jessica Van Hallen, a descendant, through marriage, of Henry Hallen. She was head designer for Wade at the time. Her style was very distinct with her figures having a decidedly "Art Deco" appearance. Due to the unfortunate failing of the cellulose finish, the "Van Hallen" figurines are extremely hard to find in mint condition and are now highly sought after by collectors.

The figurines are usually marked with Mark Type 21 along with the name of the figurine. In some cases, the "leaping deer" above the words "Made in England" is omitted. Due to lack of records, the exact number of figurines produced is not known; however, FIG. 1, FIG. 2 and FIG. 3 illustrate the majority of figurines produced with the cellulose finish.

Helga 10in.	Cherry 10ins.	Grace 9¼in.	Ginger 9½in.	Carole 8½in.	Dawn 8¼in.	Conchita 8¾in.
Zena 8⅞in.	Rhythm 9¾in.	Carmen 9¼in.	Daisette 10in.	Argentina 9½in.	Joy 9¼in.	Blossoms 7¾in.	Springtime 9in.
Madonna and Child 13½in.	Hille Bobbe 10in.	Christina 11in.	Colorado 10in.	Alsatian 10¼in. high 18in. length		Sadie 13½in.

FIG. 1.

FIG. 1. FIGURINES CIRCA 1927 — LATE 1930's (Cellulose Finish).

A. Helga . . . . .10″ high	K. Daisette . . . . .10″ high
B. Cherry . . . . .10″ high	L. Argentina . . . . .9½″ high
C. Grace . . . . .9¼″ high	M. Joy . . . . .9¼″ high
D. Ginger . . . . .9½″ high	N. Blossoms . . . . .7¾″ high
E. Carole . . . . .8½″ high	O. Springtime . . . . .9″ high
F. Dawn . . . . .8¼″ high	P. Madonna and Child . . . . .13½″ high
G. Conchita . . . . .8¾″ high	Q. Hille Bobbe . . . . .10″ high
H. Zena .8⅞″ high	R. Christina . . . . .11″ high
I. Rhythm . . . . .9¾″ high	S. Colorado . . . . .10″ high
J. Carmen . . . . .9¼″ high	T. Alsatian . . . . .10¼″ high by 18″ long
	U. Sadie . . . . .13½″ high

FIG. 2.

FIG. 2. FIGURINES CIRCA 1927-LATE 1930's
(Cellulose Finish).

A. Queenie	4″ high	M. Humoresque	8¼″ high
B. Cynthia	5″ high	N. Anton	5¾″ high
C. Tony	4½″ high	O. Gloria	5¾″ high
D. Jose	4½″ high	P. Alsatian	4¾″ high by 8¾″ long
E. Betty	5″ high	Q. Jean	6¾″ high
F. Strawberry Girl	5¼″ high	R. Barbara	8½″ high
G. Elf	4″ high	S. Pompadour	6″ high
H. Zena	4″ high	T. Curtsey	5″ high
I. Pavlova	4½″ high	U. Harriet	8″ high
J. Tessa	5″ high	V. Spaniel	2½″ high by 5½″ long
K. Alice	5½″ high	W. Joyce	7¼″ high
L. Sunshine	6½″ high	X. Peggy	6¾″ high

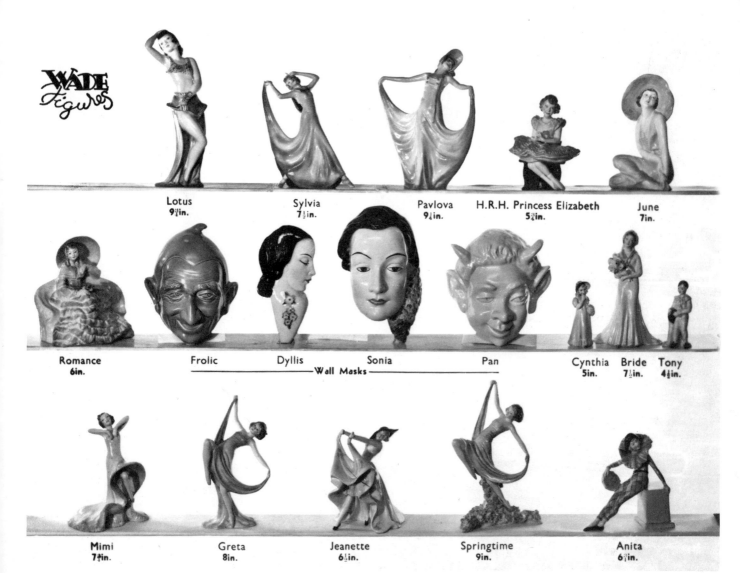

Lotus
9⅞in.

Sylvia
7½in.

Pavlova
9¼in.

H.R.H. Princess Elizabeth
5¾in.

June
7in.

Romance
6in.

Frolic

Dyllis

Sonia

Wall Masks

Pan

Cynthia
5in.

Bride
7½in.

Tony
4½in.

Mimi
7¾in.

Greta
8in.

Jeanette
6½in.

Springtime
9in.

Anita
6⅞in.

FIG. 3.

FIG. 3. FIGURINES CIRCA 1927-LATE 1930's
(Cellulose Finish).

A. Lotus . . . . .9¾" high
B. Sylvia . . . . .7½" high
C. Pavlova . . . . : . . . . .9¼" high
D. H.R.H. Princess Elizabeth . . . . .5¾" high
E. June . . . . .7" high
F. Romance . . . . .6" high
G. Frolic (Wall Mask)
H. Dyllis (Wall Mask)

I. Sonia (Wall Mask)
J. Pan (Wall Mask)
K. Cynthia . . . . .5" high
L. Bride . . . . .7½" high
M. Tony . . . . .4½" high
N. Mimi . . . . .7¾" high
O. Greta . . . . .8" high
P. Jeanette . . . . .6½" high
R. Springtime . . . . .9" high
S. Anita . . . . .6¾" high

THE WORLD OF WADE

Collectable Porcelain and Pottery.

by

IAN WARNER

with

MIKE POSGAY

This book is dedicated to the memory of
The late Sir George Wade, M.C.,
and
The late G. Anthony J. Wade, M.C.

TABLE OF CONTENTS

PAGES

Foreword..v

How to use this book vi

Acknowledgments vii

The World of Wade. Introduction 1

Mark Types and Backstamps 6

Figurines, Flowers and Animal Figures by George Wade & Son Ltd. and Wade Heath & Company Ltd. 9

Whimsies 1953-1959 and 1971-1984
"The World of Survival" & "The Connoisseurs Collection" by George Wade & Son Ltd. 89

Premiums & Promotional Items by George Wade & Son Ltd. 95

Whimsey-On-Why Village Sets by George Wade & Son Ltd. and
Miscellaneous Items by George Wade & Son Ltd. and Wade Heath & Company Ltd. 105

Decorative Pitchers by Wade Heath & Company Ltd. 119

Tableware by Wade Heath & Company Ltd. 125

Tankards & Souvenirs by Wade Heath & Company Ltd. and Wade (Ireland) Ltd. 147

Royal Commemoratives by George Wade & Son Ltd., Wade Heath & Company Ltd. and Wade (Ireland) Ltd. 152

Wade (Ireland) Ltd. 156

Wade (PDM) Ltd. 167

Miscellaneous Items by The Wade Group of Companies 179

FOREWORD

Some time ago, Nora Koch, editor and publisher of the "Daze Inc." of Otisville, Michigan, suggested I write an article on Red Rose tea figurines made by Wade of England. I was familiar with these miniature figurines but was unaware that they had become collectable. Always interested in researching something new in the field of glass or pottery, I began to look into the subject. The further involved I became, the more my interest in Wade developed. After much correspondence over the past several years with the helpful staff of George Wade & Son Ltd. and Wade Heath & Company Ltd. I soon realized that the field of "Wade collecting" was by no means limited to the tea figurines.

In no time at all my research turned me into a full fledged "Wade collector" and both Nora and I soon recognized there was a need for a book to cover this rather extensive field of collectable pottery. As my information and collection increased I decided that not only was a research trip to England in order but also, due to the amount of work involved in producing the book, I would need the help of a co-author. My good friend and business partner, Mike Posgay, came to my rescue and I extend to him my sincere thanks.

This book you, as a collector, are about to peruse is the result of Mike's and my collaboration along with the help of a very friendly computer. I trust Wade collectors will find this book an informative and helpful addition to their libraries.

Ian Warner

Brampton, Ontario. 1988.

HOW TO USE THIS BOOK

In order to assist the reader to more easily use this book as a source of reference, the following comments might be in order.

The book is divided into sections as noted in the list of contents which is self explanatory. Whilst many products of the Wade Group of Potteries have been shown or indicated, it is impossible to include all the products from the potteries over the 1927 to 1987 period, the period about which this book is written.

To help the reader in locating items illustrated in the color section it should be noted that all pieces are numbered. These numbers are in sequence in the text section of the book. This should enable the reader to find the written reference to any particular item more easily. Where a series of items, issued in sets, are listed e.g. The Whimsies, each set is given a single number denoting the items location in the text and/or the color section. This number is followed by another number giving the items position in the series e.g. No. 145-1 LEAPING FAWN etc. Series that were issued over a period of years, in sets of five for example, each set of five is given a new item number followed by its sequence number in the set e.g. No. 146-6 BULL.

Interspersed amongst the numbered items in the text are: FIG. numbers which refer to the black and white illustrations, line drawings, and reproductions of trade literature. These illustrations are located in close proximity to the FIG. number in the text.

As a general rule, the term "lithograph" decoration as noted in the book refers to pre WWII production and "silk-screen" decoration refers to post WWII production. In the early 1950's George Wade & Son Ltd. formed their own silk-screen department and supplied both Wade Heath and themselves with all silk-screen designs.

Hopefully information presented in this book regarding pattern numbers and pattern names will help establish common ground for collectors and dealers.

For dates of production the reader should refer to the section: Mark Types and Backstamps.

ACKNOWLEDGMENTS

Writing acknowledgments is synonymous with accepting an Academy Award with the many thanks that are usually stated on such occasions. To quote one well-known actress who, on accepting her Academy Award, said: "I would like to thank everyone I have ever known in my whole life." Whilst a similar quote would be an easy way of thanking the many people whose help has made this book a reality, it would not be, by any means, an adequate "thank you." So if readers will bear with us we would like to give our heartfelt thanks to the following people:

First of all we would like to extend our sincere thanks to D.L.J. Dawe, Admn. Sales Manager for George Wade & Son Ltd. Without Derek Dawe's interest and continued help searching out records, dates and numerous items of vital information along with lending us many items of trade literature from his personal files, this book could never have been written. Our many letters to Derek Dawe have always been full of questions and requests for information to the point where we became embarrassed; however, our letters were always met with a quick and helpful reply, usually including additional information that Mr. Dawe had found in his search to answer our original question. We also extend our gratitude to Derek Dawe for the time he spent reviewing and correcting errors to this book whilst in its manuscript form. We would also like to express our gratitude to Claud Rowley, Marketing Director, Wade Heath & Co. Ltd., who assisted with information regarding the Wade Heath & Company Ltd. and Wade (PDM) Ltd. divisions of the Wade Group of Potteries and for the items of trade literature and company records with which he supplied us for our information. Our thanks go to John A. Stringer, Managing Director of Wade (Ireland) Ltd., George V. Bennett, former Director, Wade (PDM) Ltd., and Terence C. Cox, Managing Director, Wade (PDM) Ltd. The assistance these gentlemen gave us, helping to date many pieces as well as backstamps and reviewing the manuscript is greatly appreciated. We are also grateful to the many staff members of the Wade Potteries in Burslem, who not only helped search out old records but talked of their experiences, memories and also took time to show us around both the Manchester Pottery and the Royal Victoria Pottery.

A special word of thanks must go to Straker and Iris Carryer whose experience with Wade (Ireland) Ltd., in its early years, gave us a greater understanding of the development of that Division of the Wade Group. The memories expressed to us by Iris Carryer of the talks with her father, the late Sir George Wade, and the development of the products at the Manchester Pottery in the 1920's and the 1930's was not only helpful but of immense interest.

Another lady to whom we extend our gratitude is Georgina Lawton who worked as a designer at the Royal Victoria Pottery from the mid 1940's through the late 1960's. Mrs. Lawton gave up many hours of her time to talk with us and assist in dating early post-war Wade Heath products and confirm the reissue of many pre war molds. We also thank Mrs. Lawton for lending us her only copy of an early Wade Heath catalog for reproduction in the book.

J. Vernon Shields, nephew of the late Sir George Wade, deserves a special mention. We are deeply grateful for the help he gave by lending us personal legal documents to confirm dates of the various mergers and take-overs of the Wade Group of Potteries. Also for lending us photographs of the Wade Heath pottery and a number of its employees. Mr. Shields also gave us the benefit of his memories of the Wade potteries from his thirty two years of service from 1924 to 1956, culminating as joint managing director of Wade Heath & Co. Ltd. and director of George Wade & Son Ltd. We also extend our thanks to Audrey O. Shields for the time spent typing up the answers to our many questions.

Our grateful thanks to the following:

Nora Koch, whose idea it was to write this book.

John G. Rigg, President & Chief Operating Officer, Redco Foods Inc. who had more than a passing interest in the Red Rose Tea figurines.

Leslie Routhier, Product Manager, Red Rose Tea, Thomas J. Lipton Inc.

F.J. Tabenor, Bass Public Limited Company.

B. Beanland, Company Secretary, Guinness Breweries.

David J. Curry, former General Manager, Pusser's Ltd.

Valerie Moody and Carole Murdock, Collector's Corner, Colorado, for their aid and excellent advice.

Osborne Collection, Toronto, Ontario.

William Heacock, for his ideas, interest and encouragement.

Phyllis Warner, for her understanding and putting up with our comings and goings during our research trip to England.

Betty and Bill Newbound, whose friendship and understanding were there when most needed.

Elizabeth Ballentine, for being the friend she is.

Our thanks are also due the following:

William Brethour, Greta Capps, Tina Carter of "Hot Tea", California; Iris Chute, Sue Cobbing, Mimi David of Anador Trading, Inc., Ontario; Virginia Ellison, Louis Federspiel, Edith Hacking, Heather McArthur, Margo McCann, Sharon Milne, James Provine of James Provine Company, Illinois; Jeanne and Ken Sheridan, Fran and Peter Sperring, Liba Smykal, Harold Temple, Fay Thompson, Muriel Trouton, Portadown, Northern Ireland; and Fred Wilkins.

Finally we would like to use an expression which we believe has never been used before: "Last but by no means least!" We would like to thank David Richardson, President, Richardson Printing Corporation, for his help, advice, patience and for his guidance during the long photography sessions and his continued belief in the worth of this book. Thanks also go to Deana Tullius, staff photographer for helping to make the photography sessions seemingly effortless. Our apologies for closeting her in the attic at regular intervals to load film. We also thank Nancy Laughery, art director, and Ronda Ludwig for the ardous task of designing the layout and pasting-up this book.

The World of Wade.

Introduction.

INTRODUCTION

The Wade Group of Potteries, as we know it today, originally consisted of individually owned potteries whose owners were either members or friends of the Wade family. With the passing years the various potteries gradually, by one means or another, began to amalgamate until they were all formed into a public company in the mid 1950's under the name of "The Wade Group of Potteries."

Probably the best known of the Wade potteries is George Wade and Son Ltd. whose home is the Manchester Pottery on Greenhead Street (formerly High Street) in Burslem, a suburb of Stoke-on-Trent (the works became so named as so many of its original products were produced for the textile industry and were shipped to Manchester). The origins of George Wade & Son Ltd. started in 1810, with a small pottery, consisting of a small workshop with a single bottle oven, owned by Henry Hallen, a distant relative or friend of George Wade, the grandfather of the late chairman, Mr. Anthony Wade. During the early days of Henry Hallen, the main items produced were bottles and related pottery items. Records also show that mixing dishes and paint pots were made for the well-known British artists' color manufacturer, Winsor and Newton.

In the early part of the 19th century, the textile industry was in full swing and Henry Hallen saw the potential demand for the specialized items that would be needed for the large mills that were being developed in the North of England. Hallen realized that every shuttle needed a pottery "eye," which prevented the yarn from cutting into the wooden part of the shuttle. Also the spinning machinery required "creels" that turned in hard glazed cuplike bearings called "creel steps" plus other specialized shapes in pottery that would be used as "guides" in the textile machines. Gradually Hallen's production of "ordinary pottery" dropped off, giving way to an increased production of the more profitable needs of the textile mills.

In the second half of the 19th century when Henry Hallen's pottery was in full production of commercial type ceramic ware, a new pottery was formed in 1867, by George Wade and known simply as the George Wade pottery. After the death of Henry Hallen, his business was subjected to strenuous competition by George Wade, who ultimately bought the Henry Hallen pottery and ran it as a separate concern for a number of years. At the beginning of the 20th century, the Hallen pottery ceased to trade under the name of Henry Hallen and was absorbed by the George Wade pottery located at the Manchester Pottery, High Street, Burslem.

The George Wade pottery continued to specialize in thread guides for the spinning industry along with other ceramic items needed to meet the growing demand for industrial ceramics. These types of ceramic items were the major products

Royal Victoria Pottery. Circa 1951

of George Wade right up to and after World War I. Luckily, for Wade, the pottery had developed an extra hard brand of porcelain needed to meet the requirements of the developing industries. When gas was introduced for domestic lighting, Wade was able to supply the first burners and then, when gas was replaced by electricity, the company was able to "quick change" to the manufacture of the early insulators.

On June 24, 1919, the George Wade pottery was incorporated as a private limited company under the name of George Wade & Son Ltd. which continued to manufacture pottery fittings for textile machinery, gas burners, bottle stoppers, electrical porcelain insulators, and other porcelain articles used for industrial purposes which had been carried on by the late George Wade at the Manchester Pottery.

Whilst George Wade was fully occupied with his company, George Wade & Son Ltd., his brother, Albert J. Wade, was operating his own business, J.&W. Wade & Co., which in June 1927, was formed into a private limited company under the name of A.J. Wade Ltd. This company was the manufacturer of glazed tiles and faience fireplace surrounds. Albert J. Wade also had an interest in another pottery, operating under the name Wade & Co. which, in December 1927, also became a separate private company under the name of Wade, Heath & Co. Ltd. The company, at this time, was manufacturing Rockingham teapots, jugs, etc. with the typical red body and dark brown glaze. George Heath was a life-long friend of Albert Wade, and they were partners until Heath's untimely death. At this time, Albert Wade took controlling interest in both, A.J. Wade Ltd. and Wade, Heath & Co. Ltd. until his death in January 1933.

With the death of A.J. Wade, Colonel G.A. Wade, son of George Wade, inherited control of both A.J. Wade Ltd. and Wade, Heath & Co. Ltd., forming the two companies, along with North Road Mill Co., into a public company called Wade Potteries Ltd. in October 1935. This did not include George Wade and Son Ltd. at the Manchester Pottery which Colonel G.A. Wade had been given control of in 1926/28. Prior to World War II, George Wade and Son Ltd. continued with the manufacture of Electro-Technical Porcelain, stoppers for non-refillable bottles and a small art department. This small art department which opened up around 1927, supplemented the technical side of production with the development of a range of moderately priced figurines which had a, then quite new, cellulose finish. The figurines were beautifully designed, many in the Art Deco style, and sold so well that a range of animals was also added to the line. Unfortunately the cellulose finish proved to be short lasting as the finish tended to turn yellow and peel off with age. Thus this type of finish was soon discontinued, and it is, therefore, a lucky collector who finds one of these cellulose finished figurines or animals in good condition nowadays. Some of the models were reintroduced in the late 1930's with a high gloss, underglaze finish, along with a range of small to large size animals. Many of these larger animals and birds were of high quality and very expensive with the molds taken from wood carvings carved by a man named Faust Lang. These figurines, although marketed before the war, were not marketed seriously until after the war. At the onset of World War II, production of all nonessential items ceased and the Manchester Pottery

directed all its capabilities to the war effort including the production of ammunition. Parts of the pottery were also used purely for storage.

Over at A.J. Wade Ltd., production continued with the manufacture of glazed tiles and fireplace surrounds with Wade, Heath & Co. Ltd., who took over the Royal Victoria Pottery in 1938, concentrating on the production of earthenware tableware, decorative pitchers and eventually figurines when they acquired the franchise to produce Walt Disney characters. Much of this production ended with World War II. All production of figurines ceased and, as with George Wade and Son Ltd., all production was directed toward the war effort except for a minimal production of plain, undecorated "utility" dinner and tea ware.

In 1946, Colonel G.A. Wade, later knighted becoming Sir George Wade, who had now become Chairman of the British Electrical Ceramic Manufacturer's Association, was asked by the government to increase production by creating new facilities to be located in "depressed" areas and not in the high-employed areas such as Stoke-on-Trent. Colonel Wade asked his son-in-law Major H.S. Carryer to find such a location.

After what H.S. Carryer described as a "reconnaissance in depth" throughout England, Scotland, Wales and Northern Ireland, an old linen mill was located in Portadown, Northern Ireland. The mill was an ideal site for a new pottery. Not only were there 150,000 square feet of buildings but also plenty of labor willing to retrain in a new industry and good transport facilities along with financial incentives from the government of Northern Ireland. In 1946, George Wade & Son Ltd. acquired and converted the linen mill, which had a long lease hold of 842 years dating from 1853, so obtained the residue of a term of 204 years from May 1, 1947. On January 2, 1950, a private limited company known as Wade (Ulster) Ltd. was incorporated and started producing die pressed insulators needed to fill the numerous orders for this type of product The company also introduced High Alumina manufacturing at the same time as George Wade & Son Ltd. and in 1986 introduced another technical ceramic product—Fused Silica. In November 1966, the name Wade (Ulster) Ltd. was changed to Wade (Ireland) Ltd.

In 1958, A.J. Wade, Wade Heath & Co. Ltd., George Wade and Son Ltd. and Wade (Ulster) Ltd. combined. They formed a public company, to be known, as they are today, The Wade Group of Potteries.

When demand for decorative items dropped to a low point in 1965, most giftware production was stopped. George Wade and Son Ltd. carried on with a small range of giftware items such as the tortoise sets and ashbowl but concentrated on its production of gas refractories and a completely new range of High Alumina Bodies which have a host of uses in the mechanical, chemical, micro-electronic and nuclear engineering fields. By the early 1970's, the demand for giftware once again increased so George Wade and Son Ltd. returned to combining their production of industrial products with giftware items and do so to this day.

Wade Heath & Co. Ltd. also carried on with a small production of giftware, but its new direction was to be in the production of special orders or "contract" orders for a large number of clients from breweries and distilleries to tobacco

Left to right. Sir George Wade, Chairman of Wade Potteries Ltd., Chairman and Joint Managing Director of George Wade & Son Ltd. and Joint Managing Director of Wade Heath & Co. Ltd.

Mr. E.L. Nickels, Sales Director of Wade Heath & Co. Ltd.

J. Vernon Shields, Director of George Wade & Son Ltd. and Joint Managing Director of Wade Heath & Co. Ltd. Circa 1951.

manufacturers, etc. Wade Heath & Co. Ltd. had its own design and modeling team, and, since the early 1950's, used decorative transfers produced by George Wade & Son Ltd. With the resources of the Wade Group of Potteries behind it, the client's requirements can be met from the most suitable manufacturing processes which includes casting, pressing, throwing or turning. The items can also be chosen in a wide range of glazes and colors from a one or two-color printing to the most complicated multi-colored design.

For a number of years, the distribution and order of promotional items was the result of a collaboration between Wade Heath & Co. Ltd. and Reginald Corfield (Sales) Ltd. In 1969, this collaboration came to an end, and a new company was formed by the Wade Group to deal with the design and marketing of their promotional items. This new company, incorporated in August 1969, was named Wade (PDM) Limited, the PDM standing for "Point of Sale, Design and Marketing."

Wade (PDM) Ltd. does not restrict itself to pottery for its advertising commissions. The company is also involved with the production of items made of glass, plastic, and tin, and is, therefore, affiliated with other companies who specialize in materials other than pottery and ceramics. These companies include Avon Tin Printers, Nazeing Glassworks, Diamond Injection Moulders, Stewart Plastics, Interprint Associates and Vista Ties.

For a short time between the mid 1970's and 1982, Wade bought and renovated the Govancroft Pottery in Scotland. The purpose of this pottery was to produce the hand thrown pots so often required by the Scottish Whisky Distillers. However, demand dropped off considerably for this type of container so the pottery was closed in 1982. There are still a few clients of Wade who require their containers to be "hand thrown" so one of the potters from Govancroft, an expert in throwing pots, was persuaded to relocate to Burslem and can be seen today plying his trade at the Manchester Pottery.

Thus, from its start with Henry Hallen in 1810, to the present day, the Wade Group of Potteries is still in full production as a public company. Hopefully, it will be so for many years to come.

ANIMAL FIGURES
by GEORGE WADE & SON LTD.

From the late 1920's, to the early days of World War II, George Wade & Son Ltd. supplemented their production of industrial ceramics and cellulose finished figurines with a line of cellulose finished, medium-sized animals.

FIG. 4. DOG MODELS (CELLULOSE FINISH).

FIG. 4. DOG MODELS CIRCA 1927-EARLY 1930's (Cellulose Finish).

Min. Alsatian	4¾" high by 8¾" long
Setter	6" high by 9¾" long
Airedale	7" high by 8" long
Spaniel	5½" high by 5" long
Scottie	4¾" high by 6¼" long
Spaniel (Playful Puppy)	2½" high by 5½" long
Borzoi	12" high by 12½" long
Alsatian	10¼" high by 18" long
Dalmation	8¾" high by 11½" long
Terrier	7" high by 8" long

Similar to the cellulose-finished figurines, the animal figures with this type of finish soon lost their popularity and were replaced, in the early 1930's, with a new line of slip cast, porcelain animal models with an underglaze finish, ranging from miniature rabbits to large size rabbits, ducks and dogs. Many of these miniature animal figures were marked by hand-written ink marks similar to Mark Type 22. These marks vary according to the size of the model and also due to the fact that they are handwritten by the decorators. In some cases, the models have the mark omitted.

13

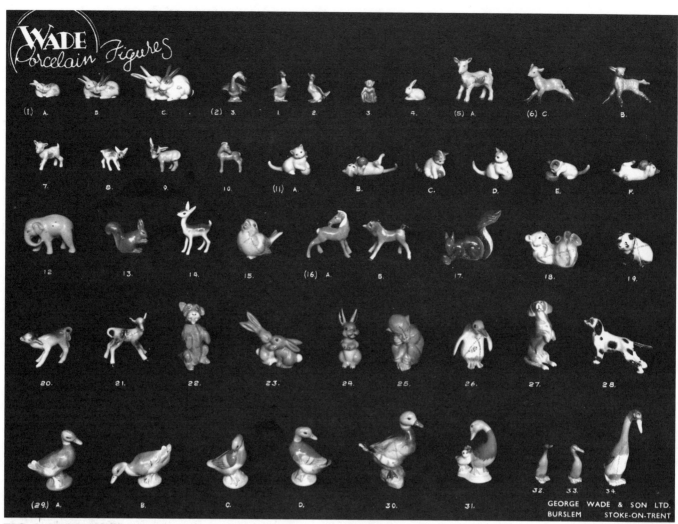

FIG. 5. MINIATURE ANIMAL FIGURES (UNDERGLAZE FINISH).

FIG. 5. MINIATURE ANIMAL FIGURES
CIRCA EARLY 1930's-1939 (Underglaze finish).

1. **Double Bunnies A** . . . . ⅞″ high by 1″ long
   B . . . . . 1¼″ high by 1¾″ long
   C . . . . 1⅝″ high by 2¾″ long
2. **Flying Ducks 3** . . . . 1⅝″ high by 1¾″ long
   1 . . . . 1½″ high by 1¼″ long
   2 . . . . 1½″ high by 1¾″ long
3. **Min. Monkey** . . . . 1⅛″ high by ¾″ long
4. **Min. Bunny** . . . . ⅞″ high by 1⅛″ long
5. **Large Lamb A** . . . . 2⅛″ high by 2″ long
6. **Playful Lambs C** . . . . 2″ high by 2⅜″ long
   B . . . . 2″ high by 2⅜″ long
7. **Min. Lamb** . . . . 1½″ high by 1¼″ long
8. **Min. Deer** . . . . 1⅛″ high by 1¼″ long
9. **Min. Donkey** . . . . 1⅞″ high by 1½″ long
10. **Min. Fowl** . . . . 1½″ high by 1¼″ long
11. **Cats A** . . . . 1½″ high by 2⅛″ long
    B . . . . 1⅛″ high by 2⅞″ long
    C . . . . 1¼″ high by 1¾″ long
    D . . . . 1½″ high by 2⅛″ long
    E . . . . 1″ high by 2¾″ long
    F . . . . 1″ high by 2¾″ long
12. **Elephant** . . . . 2″ high by 2½″ long
13. **Small Squirrel** . . . . 1⅝″ high by 2⅛″ long

14. **Large Deer** . . . . 2½″ high by 1¾″ long
15. **Chick** . . . . 1¾″ high by 2⅓″ long
16. **Foals A** . . . . 2½″ high by 2½″ long
    B . . . . 2″ high by 2¼″ long
17. **Squirrel** . . . . 2½″ high by 2½″ long
18. **Bear** . . . . 1⅝″ high by 2½″ long
19. **Baby Panda** . . . . 1½″ high by 2¼″ long
20. **Calf** . . . . 2⅜″ high by 1¼″ long
21. **Ibex** . . . . 2¼″ high by 2¼″ long
22. **Dog** . . . . 3⅛″ high by 1¾″ long
23. **Double Rabbits** . . . . 2½″ high by 2¾″ long
24. **Single Rabbit** . . . . 2⅝″ high by 1⅜″ long
25. **Monkey** . . . . 2½″ high by 2″ long
26. **Penguin** . . . . 2¾″ high by 2¼″ long
27. **Dachshund** . . . . 3⅛″ high by 1½″ long
28. **Min. Setter** . . . . 3½″ high by 2¼″ long
29. **Ducks A** . . . . 2¾″ high by 2⅛″ long
    B . . . . 1¾″ high by 3⅛″ long
    C . . . . 3″ high by 3⅛″ long
    D . . . . 3″ high by 2⅛″ long
30. **Mallard** . . . . 3⅝″ high by 3½″ long
31. **Drake and Daddy** . . . . 3⅛″ high by 2″ long
32. **Longnecked Duck—Head up** . . . 2″ high by ⅞″ long
33. **Longnecked Duck—Head down** . 2″ high by ¾″ long
34. **Large Longnecked Duck** . . . . 3¾″ high by 1⅜″ long

In approximately 1935, George Wade introduced a new line of underglaze porcelain figurines, using both new molds and reintroducing a small number of molds previously used for the cellulose finished figurines. The new molds also included a number of animal figurines of very high quality. These models, which were in production until 1939, were expensive and quite exquisite, and many were based on molds taken from wood carvings made by designer Faust Lang.

Most of the large underglaze figurines were marked "Wade England" along with the name of the figurine and sometimes the year of production. See FIG. 6.

Forty-seven of the known large underglaze figurines are illustrated in FIG. 7, FIG. 8 and FIG. 9.

FIG. 6.

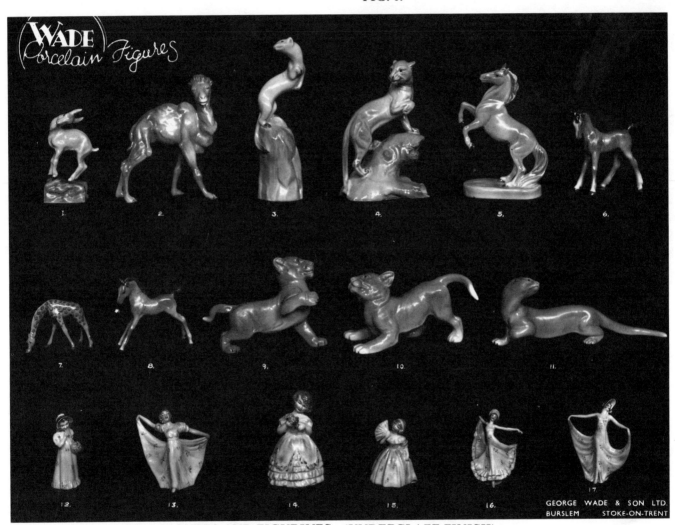

FIG. 7. LARGE ANIMAL FIGURES AND FIGURINES. (UNDERGLAZE FINISH)

FIG. 7. LARGE ANIMAL FIGURES AND FIGURINES CIRCA 1935-1939 (Underglaze Finish).

1. **Chamois Kid** . . . . .5¼″ high by 3¼″ long
2. **Camel** . . . . .7¾″ high by 6¾″ long
3. **Ermine** . . . . .9½″ high by 3″ long
4. **Panther** . . . . .8″ high by 5″ long
5. **Horse** . . . . .7¾″ high by 6¾″ long
6. **Large Dartmoor Pony** . . . . . .4⅞″ high by 4¼″ long
7. **Giraffe** . . . . .3″ high by 4″ long
8. **Medium Dartmoor Pony** . . . . . .4″ high by 4″ long

9. **Lion Cub Paw up** . . . . .5¼″ high by 7¼″ long
10. **Lion Cub Paw down** . . . . . . .5¼″ high by 7¼″ long
11. **Otter** . . . . .4″ high by 10¾″ long
12. **Cynthia** . . . . .5″ high
13. **Jose** . . . . .4½″ high
14. **Betty** . . . . .5″ high
15. **Queenie** .3⅝″ high
16. **Min. Zena** .4″ high
17. **Min. Pavlova** . . . . .4½″ high

15

FIG. 8. LARGE ANIMAL FIGURES AND FIGURINES.
    (UNDERGLAZE FINISH)

FIG. 8. LARGE ANIMAL FIGURES AND FIGURINES
CIRCA 1935-1939 (Underglaze Finish).

A. Ermine . . . . 9½″ high by 3″ long
B. Choir Boy . . . . 7⅜″ high
C. Joy . . . . 9¼″ high
D. Juliette . . . . 9¼″ high
E. Panther . . . . 8½″ high
F. Horse . . . . 7¾″ high by 6¾″ long
G. Camel . . . . 7¾″ high by 6¾″ long
H. Chamois Kid . . . . 5¼″ high by 3¼″ long
I. Lion Cub Paws Up . . . . 5¼″ high by 7¼″ long
J. Otter . . . . 4″ high by 10¾″ long
K. Lion Cub Paws Down . . . . . . 5¼″ high by 7¼″ long

L. Cockatoo . . . . 5¾″ high
M. Double Budgerigar . . . . 7¾″ high
N. Stag . . . . 8¾″ high
O. Capuchin . . . . 10″ high
P. Old Nanny . . . . 9″ high
Q. Grebe . . . . 9¼″ high
R. Single Budgerigar . . . . 6¾″ high
S. Parrot . . . . 10¼″ high
T. Brown Bear . . . . 9½″ high
U. Madonna and Child . . . . 13½″ high
V. Aqua Vase and Base . . . . 10¼″ high
W. Polar Bear . . . . 7¼″ high

FIG. 9. BIRDS (UNDERGLAZE FINISH).

FIG. 9. BIRDS LATE 1930's — MID 1950's
(Underglaze Finish).

In the late 1930's, a set of seven birds, also based on carvings by Faust Lang, were introduced but not marketed seriously until after WW II when the molds were taken over by Wade Heath who produced and marketed them until the mid 1950's.

1. Goldfinch (wings open)..................4" high
2. Goldfinch (wings closed) ....4" high
3. Pelican (Nut Dish or Ash Tray) ....5" high
4. Woodpecker ....6" high
5. Budgerigar............................8" high
6. Cockatoo ....6" high
7. Heron.................................7" high

WADE FLOWERS
CIRCA 1930-1939.

Along with the figurines and animals in the years prior to World War II, George Wade & Son Ltd. also produced a large range of earthenware and china flower arrangements, all with an underglaze finish. Numbers 1 through 65 shown in FIG. 10, FIG. 11 and FIG 12 are all earthenware.

Illustrations of numbers 66 through 79 are missing from Wade's records. Numbers 80 through 109 shown in FIG. 13, are all china.

These flower arrangement models are hard to find in mint condition. The majority of the models have a handwritten Mark Type 22 along with the model number and name. Some models are mold marked "British Made" including the handwritten marks.

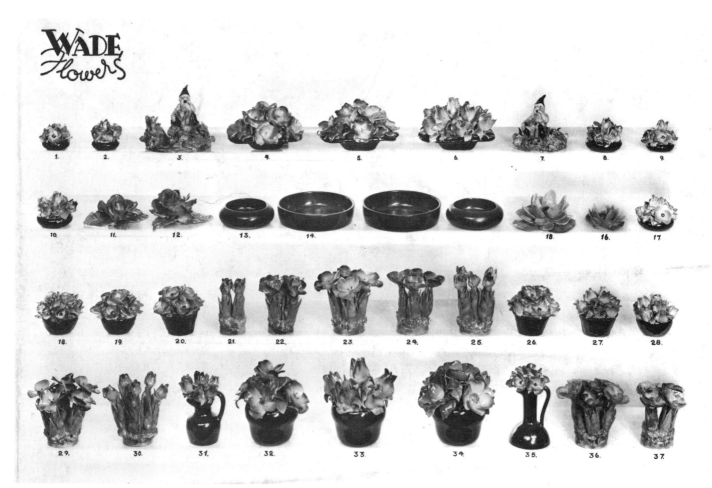

FIG. 10. EARTHENWARE FLOWERS.

FIG. 10. EARTHENWARE FLOWERS.
1. Posy Pot, G. Wild Rose
2. Posy Pot, G. Tulips
3. Large Rock Gardens
4. Wicker Baskets. Wild Rose
5. Wicker Basket. Pansy
6. Wicker Basket. Tulip
7. Small Rock Garden
8. Posy Pot, E. Tulips
9. Posy Pot, G. Assorted
10. Posy Pot, E. Assorted
11. Small Rose Menu Holder
12. Large Rose Menu Holder
13. Black Bowl for Medium and Small Size Centres
14. Black Bowl for Large Size Centre
15. Large Lily Menu Holder
16. Small Lily Menu Holder
17. Posy Pot, E. Wild Rose
18. Posy Pot, D. Assorted
19. Posy Pot, D. Wild Rose
20. Posy Pot, SB. Wild Rose
21. Small Centre Tulip
22. Small Centre Wild Rose
23. Medium Centre Pansy
24. Medium Centre Wild Rose
25. Medium Centre Tulip
26. Posy Pot, SB. Assorted
27. Posy Pot, SB. Tulip
28. Posy Pot, D. Tulip
29. Centre, Six Flowers, Pansy
30. Centre, Six Flowers, Tulips
31. Short-Necked Jugs, Tulips
32. Vulcan, Pansy
33. Vulcan, Tulip
34. Vulcan, Poppy
35. Long-Necked Jugs, Wild Rose
36. Centre, Six Flowers, Wild Rose
37. Medium Witchbowl, Centre Poppy

FIG. 11. EARTHENWARE FLOWERS.

FIG. 11. EARTHENWARE FLOWERS.

38. Min. Loose Centre Anemones and Bowl
39. Ajax Bowl, Anemone
40. Ajax Bowl, Tulips
41. Ajax Bowl, Pansy
42. Min. Loose Centre, Anemones, Roses and Bowl
43. Centre, 6″ x 5″ Wild Rose and Bowl
44. Large Centre Pansy and Bowl
45. Large Centre Poppy

46. Large Centre Tulip
47. Large Centre Delphinium
48. Large Centre Anemones
49. No Name Available
50. Loose Centre Anemones and Bowl
51. Streamline Jug, Assorted Flowers
52. Brick, Assorted Flowers
53. Globe Bowl, Assorted Flowers

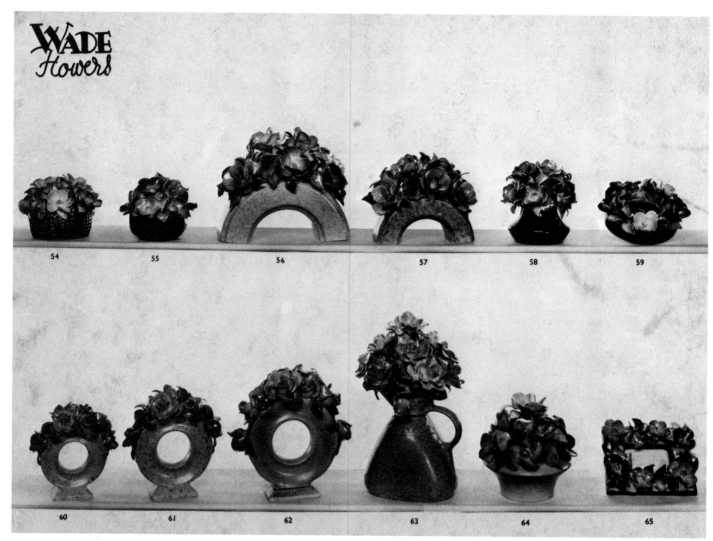

FIG. 12. EARTHENWARE FLOWERS.

FIG. 12. EARTHENWARE FLOWERS.

54. Posy Basket
55. Octagonal Bowl
56. Medium Arch
57. Small Arch
58. Temple
59. Posy Pansy Ring

60. Small Saturn
61. Medium Saturn
62. Large Saturn
63. Roman Jug
64. Binnie
65. Square (table decoration)

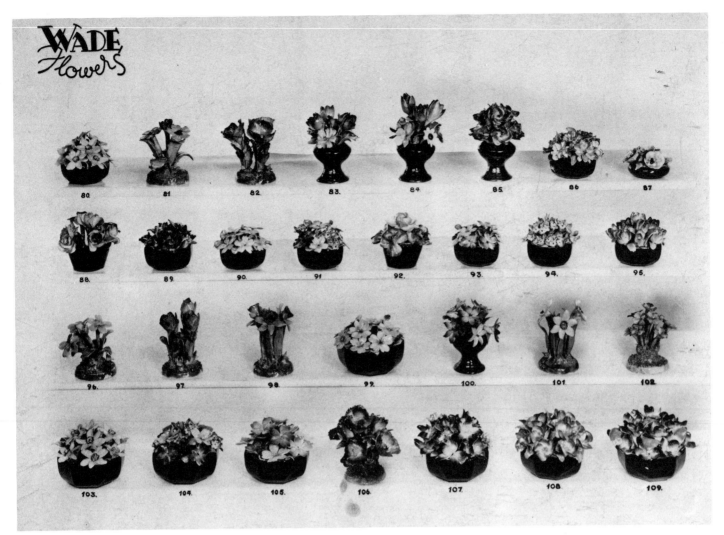

FIG. 13. CHINA FLOWERS.

FIG. 13. CHINA FLOWERS.

80. J. 5 Bowl Narcissus
81. H. 1 Centre Primula
82. H. 2 Centre Poppy
83. Small Vase C.T. Carnation, Tulip
84. Small Vase D.V.T. Daisy, Violet, Tulip
85. Small Vase, Oleander
86. J. 18 Bowl Carnation
87. E. Bowl Anemone
88. S.B. Basket Roses
89. J.V.F. Bowl, Violet, Forget-me-not
90. J. 4 Bowl, Primrose
91. J.P.F. Bowl, Primula, Forget-me-not
92. S.B. Basket, Assorted
93. J. 1 Bowl, Primula
94. J. 6 Bowl, Forget-me-not

95. J. 3 Bowl, Tulip
96. H. 4 Centre Primrose
97. H. 3 Centre Tulip
98. H. 8 Centre Daffodil
99. K. 4 Bowl, Primrose
100. Small Vase, Hibiscus
101. H. 5 Centre, Narcissus
102. Centre, Shamrock
103. K. 5 Bowl, Narcissus
104. K.P.F. Bowl, Primula, Forget-me-not
105. K. 1 Bowl, Primula, Forget-me-not
106. Small Cluster Anemones with Bowl
107. K.V.F. Bowl, Violet, Forget-me-not
108. K. Bowl, Buttercup
109. K. 16 Bowl, Violets

ANIMAL FIGURES
by WADE HEATH & COMPANY LIMITED CIRCA 1937-LATE 1950's.

During the late 1930's, Wade Heath expanded its lines of tableware with the production of a small range of large size, slip cast, realistic and comic animal figures. These figures had a single color underglaze finish and were backstamped with Mark Type 6. Production of these animal figures ceased in 1939, and there are no records of the molds being reused after WW II.

With the gradual relaxing of restrictions imposed by the British Government on decorative, ornamental items produced during WW II., Wade Heath began to introduce such items to their lines in the late 1940's.

These ornamental pieces included many of the animal figures previously manufactured by George Wade & Son Ltd. at the Manchester Pottery in the 1930's. The George Wade molds were transferred to Wade Heath at the Royal Victoria Pottery, allowing George Wade & Son Ltd. to continue, in the early post-war years, the production of the much needed industrial ceramic ware.

The pre-war George Wade molds were complimented by new molds made by Wade Heath. Many of these products can be seen in pictures taken at the 1954 British Industries Fair. The post-war figures can be identified by the backstamps. Figures made in the late 1940's, to early 1950's, are backstamped with Mark Types 10 or 15, and those made in the mid to late 1950's are marked with Mark Type 19.

FIG. 14. ANIMAL FIGURES CIRCA 1937-1939.
(Underglaze Finish).

1. Squirrel
2. Laughing Rabbit (small)
3. Laughing Rabbit (medium)
4. Laughing Rabbit (large)
5. Cheeky Duckling
6. Rabbit (miniature)
7. Rabbit (small)
8. Rabbit (medium)
9. Rabbit (large)
10. Terrier
11. Pongo (large)
12. Pongo (medium)
13. Pongo (small)
14. Walking Scottie
15. Jumbo
16. Sitting Scottie
17. Crouching Rabbit
18. Old Buck

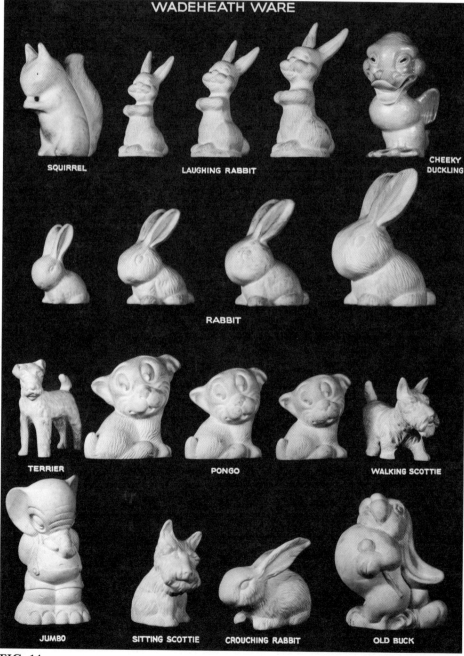

FIG. 14.

FIG. 15. ANIMAL FIGURES AND FIGURINES.

FIG. 15. ANIMAL FIGURES and FIGURINES
CIRCA LATE 1940's-LATE 1950's. (Underglaze Finish).

1. Seagull . . . . .1" high
2. Cat (George Wade mold) . . . . .1½" high
3. Cat (George Wade mold) . . . . .1½" high
4. Cat (George Wade mold) . . . . .1½" high
5. Cat (George Wade mold) . . . . .1½" high
6. Cat (George Wade mold) . . . . .1½" high
7. Squirrel (George Wade mold) . . . . .1½" high

The Duck Family
8. Mrs. Duck . . . . .2½" high
9. Dilly . . . . .1½" high
10. Mr. Duck .2½" high
11. Dack . . . . .1½" high
12. Elephant .2" high
13. Single Rabbit . . . . .2½" high

The Penguin Family
14. Mrs. Penguin . . . . .3" high
15. Penny . . . . .2" high
16. Benny . . . . .2" high
17. Mr. Penguin . . . . .3½" high
18. Cheerful Charlie . . . . .3½" high
19. Doleful Dan . . . . .3½" high
20. Drake and Daddy (George Wade mold) . . .3⅛" high

21. Setter (George Wade mold) . . . . .3½" high
22. Calf (George Wade mold) . . . . .2⅜" high
23. Long Necked Ducks (George Wade molds) . .2" high
24. Long Necked Duck (George Wade mold) . . .2" high

The Rabbit Family
25. Mrs. Rabbit . . . . .3½" high
26. Fluff . . . . .2" high
27. Puff . . . . .2" high
28. Mr. Rabbit . . . . .3½" high
29. Lamb (George Wade mold) . . . . .2" high
30. Lamb (George Wade mold) . . . . .2" high
31. Double Rabbits . . . . .2½" high
32. Double Bunnies (small size)
(George Wade mold) . . . . .⅞" high
33. Min. Bunny (George Wade mold) . . . . . . .⅞" high
34. Double Bunnies (large size)
(George Wade mold) . . . . .1⅝" high

Babies with Flowers
35. I've a Bear Behind . . . . .2½" high
36. Blynken . . . . .2" high
37. Nod . . . . .2½" high
38. Wynken . . . . .2½" high

(The Babies were supplied with or without flowers on the base.)

23

ANIMAL MINIATURES
BY WADE HEATH CIRCA LATE 1950's.

A selection of slip cast creatures captured the charm of animal grace and were decorated in delicate underglaze colors. The set featured a Puppy, Miniature Deer, Dartmoor Ponies, Foals and a revival of the pre-war George Wade mold of the Single Rabbit.

Animal Miniatures

FIG. 16.

FIGURINES *BY GEORGE WADE & SON LTD. AND WADE HEATH & COMPANY LTD.* *(Refer to the color section).*

FIGURINES
BY GEORGE WADE & SON LTD. 1927-1940.

As noted at the beginning of this section, George Wade & Son Ltd. experimented with figurines finished with the then, new cellulose finish. The first two figurines in the color section illustrate examples of this type of model. The third figurine illustrated, "Betty," although first produced with the cellulose finish, was reintroduced in the late 1930's with an underglaze finish. Additional figurines reintroduced with an underglaze finish are noted in FIG. 7, and FIG. 8.

No. 1. CARNIVAL—with cellulose type finish and Mark Type 21 without the "leaping deer". The figurine is 7" high.

No. 2. JEANETTE—with cellulose type finish and Mark Type 21. The figurine is 6½" high.

No. 3. BETTY—with underglaze decoration and marked "WADE ENGLAND." The figurine is 5" high.

NURSERY RHYME FIGURINES
BY WADE HEATH & COMPANY LTD.
CIRCA 1949-1958.

Between 1939 and the late 1940's, no figurines were produced by either George Wade & Son Ltd. or Wade Heath & Co. Ltd. After the end of WWII, much rebuilding was required, and there was a need for industrial ceramics. It fell upon George Wade & Son Ltd., at the Manchester Pottery, to supply the necessary ceramic items needed for the rebuilding of the bombed out industrial plants. By the late 1940's, Wade Heath was back into the manufacture of decorative tableware, and, as restrictions eased, non-essential items such as ornamental figurines were beginning to make a comeback.

As the Manchester Pottery was still occupied with the production of industrial ceramics, it fell upon Wade Heath at the Royal Victoria Pottery to produce a new line of figurines that would appeal to the public. This line was based on popular nursery rhyme characters designed by both Nancy Greatrex and the then art director, Robert Barlow, who designed the Tinker, Tailor etc. series.

The series comprised of the following sets:

SET 1.

No. 4. BLYNKEN—measures 2" high with Mark Type 10.

No. 5. NOD—measures 2½" high with Mark Type 10.

Others in the set were: WYNKEN and I'VE A BEAR BEHIND (the figurine is holding a Teddy Bear behind his back). The figurines were made with or without flowers on the base. Figurines made in the early years of production are backstamped with Mark Type 10, and those produced after 1954, are backstamped with Mark Type 19. The name of the figurine was stamped alongside the marks.

SET 2.

No. 6. GOLDILOCKS—measures 4" high with Mark Type 19.

No. 7. BABY BEAR—measures 1¾" high with Mark Type 19.

Others in the set were: MOTHER BEAR and FATHER BEAR. (See FIG. 17). Each figurine is marked, on the base, with the name of the character.

SET 3.

No. 8. BUTCHER—measures 3¼" high with Mark Type 19.

Others in the set were: BAKER and CANKLESTICK MAKER. The figurines may be found double backstamped with Mark Types 19 and 15 as is the Butcher figurine illustrated. Each model has the name of the character marked on the base.

SET 4.

No. 9. LITTLE JACK HORNER—measures 2½" high and is unmarked.

The other character in this set is LITTLE MISS MUFFET. (See FIG. 17).

NURSERY RHYME *figures*

FIG. 17. (A) LITTLE MISS MUFFET, (B) LITTLE JACK HORNER,
(C) FATHER BEAR, (D) GOLDILOCKS,
(E) BABY BEAR, (F) MOTHER BEAR

SET 5.

No. 10. TINKER—measures 2½" high with Mark
Type 15.

No. 11. TAILOR—measures 2½" high with Mark
Type 15.

FIG. 18. SOLDIER—measures 3" high with Mark
Type 15.

No. 12. SAILOR—measures 3" high with Mark
Type 15.

No. 13. RICH MAN—measures 3" high with Mark
Type 15.

No. 14. POOR MAN—measures 3" high with Mark
Type 15.

No. 15. BEGGAR MAN—measures 2½" high with
Mark Type 15.

No. 16. THIEF—measures 3" high with Mark Type 15.

Figurines in this set made after 1955, were backstamped
with Mark Type 19. Each model has the name of the character
marked on the base.

FIG. 18.

FIGURINES *BY GEORGE WADE & SON LTD. 1956-1987.*

By the mid 1950's, Wade Heath began to decrease their production of figural items to concentrate on the manufacture of tableware and advertising lines.

The demand for interesting and colorful figurines was still strong so George Wade & Son Ltd. once again started to manufacture this type of item at the Manchester Pottery. Since the early 1950's, George Wade & Son Ltd. had been gradually getting back into the production of ornamental ware, mainly with single color, simple posy bowl type articles. It was an obvious step to further develop this type of ware by introducing new figural lines.

SNIPPETS *1956-1958.*

The two sets of "Snippets," three figurines in each set, were based on famous ships and the nursery rhyme, Hansel and Gretel. The bright enamel-colored figurines (front only) are flat with an extension on the base to support the figurine in a vertical position. This type of modelling can be compared to the paper cut-on type of figures.

The first set consisted of three ships, THE MAYFLOWER, THE SANTA MARIA and THE REVENGE.

The second set consisted of HANSEL, GRETEL and BEAR.

FIG. 19. GRETEL—measures 2¼" high by 1½" across the base. The figurine is transfer marked "WADE 'SNIPPET' NO. 5 'GRETEL' REAL PORCELAIN MADE IN ENGLAND."

FIG. 19.

MABEL LUCIE ATTWELL CHARACTERS *1959.*

The set consisted of two figurines based on characters from illustrations by Mabel Lucie Attwell. Her drawings

of small children with blue eyes, chubby rosy cheeks, stubby legs and plump tummies appeared in numerous magazines, books and hundreds of colored picture postcards.

"Sam" and "Sarah" have the special appeal of all Mabel Lucie Attwell characters. These charming studies are decorated in attractive under-glaze and on-glaze colours and cost **6/11d. each**

Copyright Mabel Lucie Attwell 1959

FIG. 20.

No. 17. SAM—measures 3⅛" high by 3" long and is mold marked "WADE PORCELAIN—MABEL LUCIE ATTWELL © MADE IN ENGLAND". A companion piece is SARAH, a figurine of a small girl and puppy in a similar pose to Sam.

Copyright for the above illustration is owned by the "Mabel Lucie Attwell Estate".

CHILD STUDIES *1962.*

The set consisted of four figurines representing Scottish and Welsh children in national costumes.

FIG. 21.

BISTO-KIDS *CIRCA MID 1970's.*

A pair of salt and pepper shakers were modeled in the image of the "BISTO-KIDS," popular advertising characters used for promoting the "BISTO" product made by The Rank, Hovis McDougall Foods Company. The two figurines were modeled by George Wade & Son Ltd. in Burslem but were manufactured by their associates, Wade (Ireland) Ltd.

No. 18. BISTO-KID pepper shaker measures 4″ high and marked "© RHM FOODS LTD. & Applied Creativity—WADE Staffordshire." The salt shaker, companion piece to the above item, was similar in design but in the form of a girl.

THE BRITISH CHARACTER SET
CIRCA 1959.

A set of four figurines were based on typical characters, merchants and professionals found in the city and east end of London. The figurines have applied, circular black/gold labels marked "Genuine WADE Porcelain MADE IN ENGLAND".

FIG. 22.

No. 19. PEARLY QUEEN—measures 2⅞″ high by 1½″ base.
No. 20. PEARLY KING—measures 2¾″ high by 1″ base.
No. 21. FISHMONGER—measures 3⅛″ high by 1″ base.
No. 22. LAWYER—measures 2⅞″ high by 1″ base.

AQUARIUM SET CIRCA 1975-1980.

A set of six porcelain articles were produced for distribution to various pet shop suppliers with the intention that the items would be used as decorative ornaments to be placed in aquariums. The five items were all mold marked, around the edge of the base, "WADE ENGLAND."

No. 23. MERMAID—measures 2½″ high by 2¼″ long.
No. 24. DIVER—measures 2¾″ high by 1″ diameter base.

FIG. 23. LIGHTHOUSE—measures 3″ high by 1¾″ diameter base.

FIG. 23.

FIG. 24. BRIDGE—measures 2¾″ high by 3⅝″ wide.

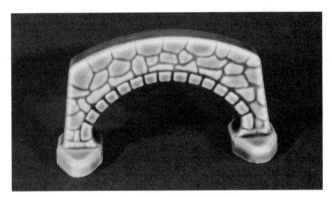

FIG. 24.

The fifth and sixth items in this set were a model of a SNAIL and a SEAHORSE.

SNOW WHITE AND THE SEVEN DWARFS 1981-1986.

This set of colorful underglaze slip cast figurines were first introduced in late 1981, and withdrawn from production in December 1986. Each figurine has a transfer mark on the base reading: "WADE ENGLAND © Walt Disney Productions."

No. 25. SNOW WHITE—measures 3¾″ high by 4¾″ overall base.
No. 26. SLEEPY—measures 3″ high by 1½″ diameter base.
No. 27. DOC—measures 3″ high by 1¾″ across the base.
No. 28. HAPPY—measures 3¼″ high by 1½″ diameter base.
No. 29. BASHFUL—measures 3¼″ high by 1½″ across the base.

No. 30. GRUMPY—measures 3″ high
by 1¾″ across the base.
No. 31. SNEEZY—measures 3¼″ high
by 1½″ diameter base.
No. 32. DOPEY—measures 3¼″ high
by 1¾″ diameter base.

ANIMAL FIGURES *BY WADE HEATH & COMPANY LTD. AND GEORGE WADE & SON LTD. MID 1930's—1960.*
(Refer to the color section.)

This page of the color section shows illustrations of animal figures made by Wade Heath & Company Ltd. in the 1930's, and figures made in the 1940's-1950's, from pre-war George Wade molds. Also illustrated are George Wade figures and figurines made by the company in the 1930's, and the 1950's to 1960.

No. 33. PLAYFUL LAMB—made by Wade Heath from
a pre-war George Wade mold and is stamped
with Mark Type 15.
No. 34. CAT—made by George Wade in the mid 1930's
and has Mark Type 22 on the base.
(Also made by Wade Heath after WW II).
No. 35. CAT—made by Wade Heath from a pre-war
George Wade mold and is stamped with transfer
Mark Type 19.
No. 36. BABY PANDA—produced by George Wade in
the 1930's and is not known to have been
reproduced after WW II.
No. 37. SINGLE RABBIT—made by Wade Heath from
a pre-war George Wade mold and is
backstamped "Made in England".
No. 38. DACHSHUND—made by George Wade in the
mid 1930's and has Mark Type 22 on the base.
(Not known to have been reproduced after
WW II but remaining figures, made prior to
the war by George Wade, were used as posy
bowl composites by Wade Heath in the
late 1940's).
No. 39. DOLEFUL DAN—made by Wade Heath and has
Mark Type 15 on the base.
No. 40. SQUIRREL—made by Wade Heath from a
prewar George Wade mold and has transfer
Mark Type 19 on the base.

During the war years, a relatively large number of animal figures produced by George Wade & Son Ltd. in the 1930's but not marketed, were put into storage. With the end of hostilities, these figures were taken over by Wade Heath. By attaching the animal figures to a base, along with an open mustard bowl from either the "Bramble" or early "Basket Ware decoration No.U.4804" lines of tableware, and were decorated with small porcelain flowers around the rim and marketed as posy bowls. The "animal/mustard bowl" composites were all marked with colored ink (usually brown or green) backstamps Mark Type 10.

No. 41. DUCK POSY BOWL—with "Bramble" mustard
bowl measuring 3¼″ high by 4″ long.
No. 42. MONGREL POSY BOWL—with "Basket Ware"
mustard bowl measuring 3¼″ high by 4″ long.
No. 43. ROOSTER POSY BOWL—with "Bramble"
mustard bowl measuring 3¾″ high by 4¼″ long.
No. 44. DACHSHUND POSY BOWL—with "Bramble"
mustard bowl measuring 3½″ high by 3½″ long.
No. 45. MALLARD POSY BOWL—with "Bramble"
mustard bowl measuring 3¼″ high by 4″ long.
No. 46. KITTEN—believed to have been produced by
Wade Heath in the mid 1950's. The figure
measures 1¾″ high by 2½″ long and has Mark
Type 19 on the base.

NOVELTY ANIMAL FIGURES
1955-1960.

A set of five comical animals, made by George Wade & Son Ltd., consisting of "A" BERNIE and POO, "B" KITTEN on the KEYS, "C" JONAH and the WHALE, "D" DUSTBIN CAT and "E" JUMBO JIM.

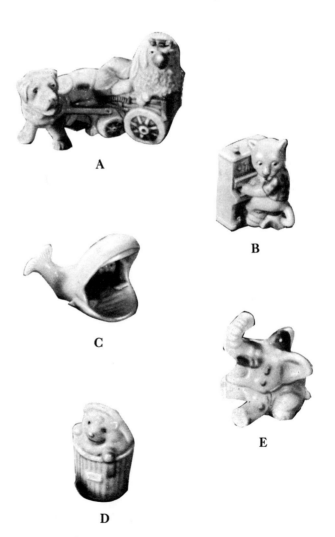

FIG. 25. NOVELTY ANIMAL FIGURES.

DRUM BOX SERIES *1956-1959*

A set of five animals playing musical instruments forming an "animal band" produced by George Wade & Son Ltd. The figurines in this set are unmarked but may originally have had paper labels.

FIG. 26.

No. 47. CLARA—the cello playing cow
measuring 2" high.
No. 48. JEM—the tuba playing bulldog
measuring 2" high.

Others in the set were: "HARPY," a harp playing dog, "TRUNKY," a drum playing elephant and "DORA," the donkey singer of the group.

FIG. 27.

NODDY SET *1958-1960.*

A series of four figurines based on characters from the popular Enid Blyton series of children's books. This set was produced by George Wade & Son Ltd. The figurines in this set are unmarked but may originally have had paper labels.

No. 49. MISS FLUFFY CAT—measures 2½" high
by 1½" across the base.

Others in the set were: "NODDY," an elf with a blue pointed hat; "BIG EARS," an older elf with a red pointed hat and "MR. PLOD," the policeman. See FIG 27. "© Darrell Waters Ltd."

WADE HEATH ANIMALS
1937-1959.

For illustration of the range of large animals see FIG. 14.

No. 50. RABBIT—medium size, measuring 6" high
with Mark Type 6 on the base.
No. 51. LAUGHING RABBIT—medium size,
measuring 7" high with
Mark Type 6 on the base.

FIGURINES, ANIMAL FIGURES AND ASHTRAYS *BY GEORGE WADE & SON LTD. 1956-1987.*

TORTOISE ASHBOWLS
1965-1984.

Due to popularity of the tortoise figurines, Wade decided to introduce an ashtray, or ashbowl, as referred to by Wade, utilizing the figurines as decoration to add interest to the bowls. Two sizes of bowls were made, the smaller one having the baby tortoise applied to the inside of the bowl, and the larger bowl having the mid-size tortoise applied as decoration. Both bowls were produced in the Scintillite finish described under "The Tortoise Family."

No. 52. SMALL TORTOISE ASHBOWL—issued in
1976, and withdrawn from production in 1984.
This bowl measures 5¾" diameter by 1⅝" high
and is mold marked "WADE MADE IN
ENGLAND" on the underside of the base.
See Mark Type 27.
No. 53. LARGE TORTOISE ASHBOWL—this ashbowl
was actually issued prior to the small bowl but
due to problems with the large size mold was
replaced by the smaller bowl. The large
Tortoise Ashbowl was made between 1965-1975,
and measures 7¼" diameter by 2" high.
The mark "WADE PORCELAIN MADE IN
ENGLAND" is impressed into the underside of
the base. See Mark Type 25.

Minikins

SERIES A.

FIG. 28.

SERIES B.

Minikins

MINIKINS SETS *1956-1959.*

The Minikin series were issued in three sets over a three year period. From records available, the first set in the series (Series "A") consisted of four shapes and for each of these shapes there were two different pairs of eyes and expressions, and two different styles of decoration. This gives an overall selection of sixteen animals. The other two sets (Series "B" and "C") were made up of four figurines each. The figurines were made in both a white and beige finish with various motifs and colorful highlights applied to the body. The tiny figurines have smooth bases and are not marked.

SERIES "A" *1956.*

No. 54. CAT—measures 1¼″ high by 1¼″ overall. The figurines in this series were a variety of cats and rabbits some only highlighted with shading and well defined eyes and ears whilst others had highlighting along with line decoration.

SERIES C.

FIG. 29.

SERIES "B" 1957.

No. 55. KITTEN—measures 1″ high by 1″ overall.

No. 56. PELICAN—measures 1⅛″ high by ⅞″ overall. The figurines in this series comprised of a pelican, dog, donkey and a fawn. The figurines were decorated with bright colors and motifs such as anchors and flowers with the eyes well defined.

SERIES "C" 1958.

No. 57. BULL—measures ⅞″ high by 1⅛″ overall. The figurines in this series were a cat, rabbit, bull and cow. They were decorated either with areas of shading applied to the beige body or with flowers, hearts and arrows or musical notes.

"TREASURES"— THE ELEPHANT CHAIN 1956.

First set in a series which was to be developed over a number of years but never materialized. The set consists of five elephants graduated in size and most perfectly modelled and decorated.

FIG. 30. TREASURES.

THE TORTOISE FAMILY
1958-TO DATE
(Unless noted otherwise).

This series of various size tortoises, from the tiny baby figurine to the large jumbo size tortoise, were extremely popular as gift items and had a long production run. With the introduction of the "Papa" tortoise in 1958, a new type of glaze finish was also introduced by Wade and given the name "Scintillite". It is believed that the name of this new finish was derived from the word "Scintillating" as the finish gave a sparkling effect. The effect was achieved by using a soluble blue color under an amber glaze. This type of finish was to be used on a number of giftware items.

In 1964/1965 a few thousand of both sizes of the Baby Tortoise (No. 58 and No. 60) were issued in a green glaze finish.

No. 58. BABY TORTISE—introduced in 1960, this figurine measures 3″ from head to tip of tail by 2⅛″ wide at the feet by 1¼″ high and is mold marked "WADE PORCELAIN MADE IN ENGLAND" on the base.

No. 59. LARGE TORTOISE—introduced in 1958, and referred to as "Papa" in Wade literature as "Papa is an ashtray." This larger size figurine has a removable lid in the form of its shell exposing a shallow ashtray. The complete figurine measures 4″ from head to tail by 2¾″ wide at the feet by 1⅝″ tall. It has an impressed mold mark "WADE PORCELAIN MADE IN ENGLAND" along with a figure 1 which would indicate the mold number.

No. 60. BABY TORTOISE—introduced in 1960, along with its companion, but slightly larger, baby tortoise. This tiny figurine measures 2″ from head to tail by 1½″ wide at the feet by ⅞″ high and is mold marked "WADE PORCELAIN MADE IN ENGLAND" on the base.

No. 61. "SLOW FE" BABY TORTOISE—produced circa 1969-1970. This figurine is from a similar mold as No. 58 but with the addition of an extra piece in the top tool to emboss the words "Slow Fe" which then appeared in a rectangular recess on the top of the shell. All measurements and mold marks are similar to "Baby Tortoise" No. 58. "Slow Fe" was introduced as a promotional item for a pharmaceutical company.

No. 62. JUMBO TORTOISE—introduced to the tortoise line in 1973, the largest of all the figurines in the tortoise series is modeled to resemble a sea turtle rather than a tortoise, but Wade literature refers to it by the name "Tortoise." The shell forms a removable lid exposing a good-sized dish. The overall size with the shell/lid in place measures 6″ from head to tail by 4″ wide by 2⅜″ high and is mold marked "WADE PORCELAIN MADE IN ENGLAND" on the base. See Mark Type 25.

HANNA-BARBERA CARTOON CHARACTERS CIRCA 1959-1960.

The cartoon character Huckleberry Hound, along with his cartoon companions Yogi Bear and Mr. Jinks, (not shown) have long been favorites with children of all ages. With this in mind, Wade produced three decorative figurines based on these characters. The figurines have fine parallel molded ridges on the underside of the base and are unmarked. It is most probable that the figurines were originally issued with paper labels.

No. 63. HUCKLEBERRY HOUND—measures 2⅜″ high on 1⅛″ diameter base.

No. 64. YOGI BEAR—measures 2½″ high on 1⅛″ diameter base.

(cont. on pg. 81.)

THE WORLD OF WADE

COLOR PLATES

NURSERY RHYME FIGURINES
(4-16)

1   2   3   4   5   6   7

8   9   10   11   12   13   14   15   16   17

BRITISH CHARACTER SET
(19-22)

SNOW WHITE
AND THE
SEVEN DWARFS
(25-32)

18   19   20   21   22   23   24   25

26   27   28   29   30   31   32

33   34   35   36   37   38   39   40

41   42   43

44   45   46

50   47 48 49   51

"MINIKINS"

52   54   55   56   57   53

TORTOISE FAMILY
(58-62)

58   59   60   61   62

TV PETS
(65-68)

"TOM
AND
JERRY"
(69-70)

63   64   65   66   67   68   69   70

SPIRIT
CONTAINERS
(71-73)

71   72   73

DISNEY MINIATURE FIGURINES
(74-97)

74   75   76   77   78   79   80   81   82

83   84   85   86   87   88   89   90   91   92

93   94   95

96   97

DISNEY "BLOW-UPS"
(98-99)

98   99

(Disney Characters © The Walt Disney Company.)

DOGS AND PUPPIES
(100-1 to 104-3)

CAT DISH
(105)

100-1   100-2   100-3   101-1   101-2   101-3   102-1   102-2   102-3

105

PUPPY DISHES
(106-112)

103-1   103-2   103-3   104-1   104-2   104-3   106   107

108   109   110   111   112

"NURSERY FAVOURITES"
(113-1 to 116-20)

| 113-1 | 113-2 | 113-3 | 113-4 | 113-5 | 114-6 | 114-7 | 114-8 | 114-9 | 114-10 |

| 115-11 | 115-12 | 115-13 | 115-14 | 115-15 | 116-16 | 116-17 | 116-18 | 116-19 | 116-20 |

"HAPPY FAMILIES"
(117-1 to 126-3)

117-2 118-2 119-2 120-2 121-2 122-2

117-3 118-1 118-3 119-1 119-3 120-1 120-3 121-1 121-3 122-1 122-3

117-1

124-2 125-2 126-2

123-1 123-2 123-3 124-1 124-3 125-1 125-3 126-1 126-3

37

CHAMPIONSHIP DOGS
(127-131)

DOG PIPE RESTS
(132-135)

127   128   129   130   131   132

"WHOPPAS"
(136-1 to 138-15)

133   134   135   136-1   136-2   136-3   136-4

136-5   137-6   137-7   137-8   137-9   137-10   138-11   138-12   138-13   138-14   138-15

HORSE SETS
(139-1 to 140-3)

139-1   139-2   139-3   140-1   140-2   140-3

WHIMSIE-LAND (141-1 to 144-20)

141-1 141-2 141-3 141-4 141-5

142-6 142-7 142-8 142-9 142-10

143-11 143-12 143-13 143-14 143-15

144-16 144-17 144-18 144-19 144-20

"WHIMSIES" 1953-1959
(145-1 to 154-48)

145-1 145-2 145-3 145-4 145-5 146-6 146-7 146-8 146-9 146-10

147-11 147-12 147-13 147-14 147-15 148-16 148-17 148-18 148-19 148-20

149-21 149-22 149-23 149-24 150-25 150-26 150-27 150-28 150-29

151-30 151-31 151-32 151-33 151-34 152-35 152-36 152-37 152-38 152-39

153-40 153-41 153-42 153-43 153-44 154-45 154-46 154-47 154-48

"WHIMSIES" 1971-1984
(155-1 to 166-60)

155-1   155-2   155-3   155-4   155-5   156-6   156-7   156-8   156-9   156-10   157-11   157-12

157-13   157-14   157-15   158-16   158-17   158-18   158-19   158-20   159-21   159-22   159-23

159-24   159-25   160-26   160-27   160-28   160-29   160-30   161-31   161-32   161-33   161-34   161-35

162-36   162-37   162-38   162-39   162-40   163-41   163-42   163-43   163-44   163-45   164-46   164-47   164-48

164-49   164-50   165-51   165-52   165-53   165-54   165-55   165-56   166-57   166-58   166-59   166-60

WORLD OF SURVIVAL
(167-178)

167   168   169

170   171   172

CONNOISSEUR'S COLLECTION
(179-188)

173

179   180

40

174

175

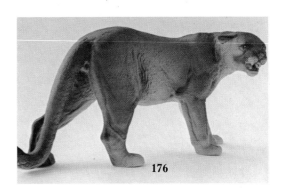

176

177

178

181

182

183

184

185

186

187

188

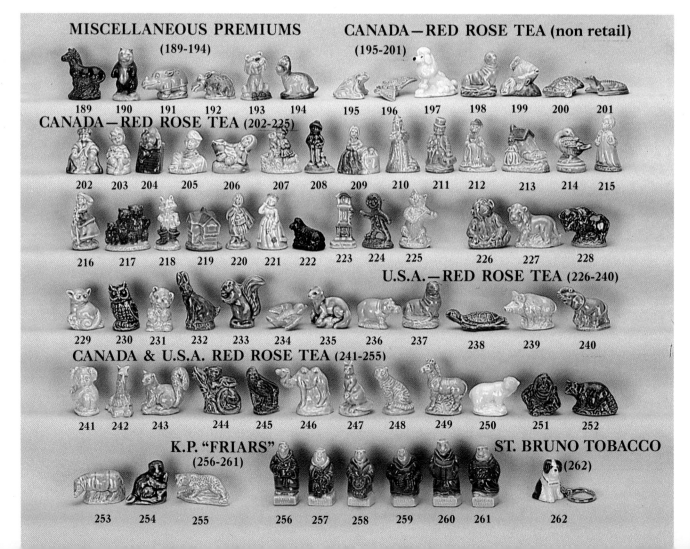

MISCELLANEOUS PREMIUMS
(189-194)

189 190 191 192 193 194

CANADA—RED ROSE TEA (non retail)
(195-201)

195 196 197 198 199 200 201

CANADA—RED ROSE TEA (202-225)

202 203 204 205 206 207 208 209 210 211 212 213 214 215

216 217 218 219 220 221 222 223 224 225 226 227 228

U.S.A.—RED ROSE TEA (226-240)

229 230 231 232 233 234 235 236 237 238 239 240

CANADA & U.S.A. RED ROSE TEA (241-255)

241 242 243 244 245 246 247 248 249 250 251 252

K.P. "FRIARS"
(256-261)

ST. BRUNO TOBACCO
(262)

253 254 255 256 257 258 259 260 261 262

"PARTY CRACKER FIGURINES"
(263-1 to 267-8)

263-1 263-2 263-3 263-4 263-5 263-6 263-7 263-8 263-9 263-10

264-1 264-2 264-3 264-4 264-5 264-6 264-7 264-8 264-9 264-10

265-1 265-2 265-3 265-4 265-5 265-6 265-7 265-8

266-1 266-2 266-3 266-4 266-5 266-6 266-7 266-8

267-1 267-2 267-3 267-4 267-5 267-6 267-7 267-8

"WHIMSEY-ON-WHY"
(268-271)

268-1 268-2 268-3 268-4 268-5 268-6 268-7 268-8

269-9 269-10 269-11 269-12 269-13 269-14 269-15 269-16

270-17 270-18 270-19 270-20 270-21 270-22 270-23 270-24

271-25 271-26 271-27 271-28 271-29 271-30 271-31 271-32

"SAN FRANCISCO MINI MANSIONS"
(358-1 to 358-6)

272-1 272-2 272-3 272-4 272-5 272-6

273   274   275   276   277

278   279   280   281   282   283

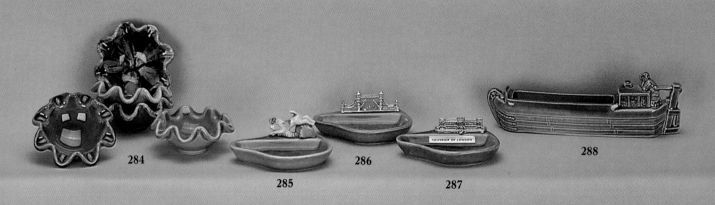

284   285   286   287   288

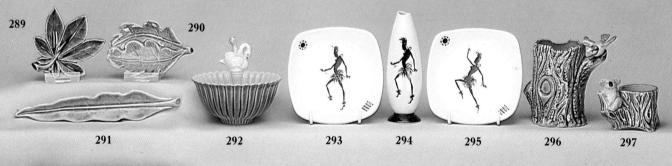

289   290   291   292   293   294   295   296   297

298   299   300   301   302   303   304   305

306   307   308   309   310   311

312 313 314 315

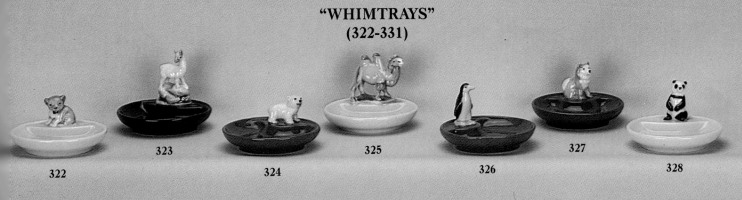

"VILLAGE STORES"
(312-321)

316 317 318 319 320 321

"WHIMTRAYS"
(322-331)

322 323 324 325 326 327 328

"BOULDRAY" TRAYS
(332-333)

"PEERAGE"
TRAY
(334)

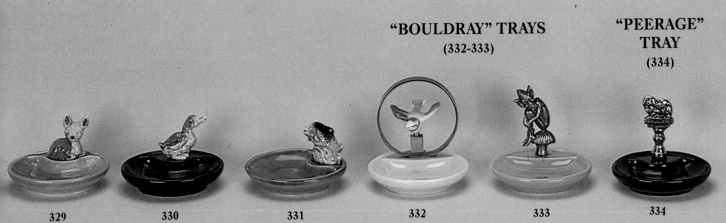

329 330 331 332 333 334

ADDIS SHAVING MUGS
(335-339)

335 336 337 338 339

WESTMINSTER PIGGY BANK FAMILY
(340-344)

340 341 342 343 344

351

345 346 347 348 349 350 352

THOMAS THE TANK ENGINE AND FRIENDS
(353-356)

353 354 355 356 357 358

WADE HEATH PITCHERS
(359-397)

359

360

361

362

363

364

365

366

367

368

369

370

371

372

373   374   375   376

377   378   379   380

381   382   383   384   385

386   387   388   389

390   391   392   393

394   395   396   397

PEONY
(398-399)

398

399

GOTHIC
(400-402)

400

401

402

403

404

405

406

407

408

409

410

50

411   412   413   414   415

416   417

418   419

420   421   422   423

424   425   426   427   428

"GRAPE" DECORATION
(430, 431, 433-438)

429 430 431 432

433 434 435 436

437 438 439 440

"BASKET WARE"
(429, 432, 439-448)

441
442 443 444 445 446 447 448

52

449

450

481

452

453

454

455

456

457

458

459

460

461

462

463

464

"BRAMBLE WARE"
(465-505)

465

466

467

468

469

470

471

472

473

474

475

476

477

478

479

480

481

482

483

54

484   485   486   487   488

489   490   491   492   493   494

495   496   497   498   499   500

501   502   503   504   505

506   507   508   509   510

511   512   513   514   515

516   517   518   519

520   521   522   523   524   525   526

527 528 529

530 531

532 533 534 535 536 537

538 540 541 543 544 546 547
539 542 545

548 549 551 552 555 557
550 553 554 556

WADE HEATH TEAPOTS
(558-570)

558   559   560   561

562   563   564   565

566   567   568   569   570

571   572   573   574

575   576   577   578

579   580   581   582

583   584   585   586

587

588

589

590

591

592

593

594

595

596

597

598

599

600

601

602

603

60

TANKARDS By WADE ENGLAND

1 Barrel, 2 Tavern, 3 Plymouth,
4 Veteran Car, 5 Rugby Football,
6 Beer Drinkers, 7 Golfers,
8 9 10 11 Countrymen.

SOUVENIRS
(604-660)

| 604 | 605 | 606 | 607 | 608 | 609 | 610 |

| 611 | 612 | 613 | 614 | 615 | 616 | 617 |

| 618 | 619 | 620 | 621 |

61

622   623   624

625   626

627   628   629   630   631   632   633

634   635   636   637   638   639   640

641   642   643

644   645   646

647   648   649   650   651   652   653

654   655   656   657   658   659   660

661

662

663

664

665

666

667

668

669

670

671

672

673

674

675

676

677

678

679

IRISH PORCELAIN
(680-749)

680 681 682 683 684 685

686 687 688 689 690 691

692 693 694 695

"COUNTRYWARE"
(696-699)

696 697 698 699

64

700   701   702   703   704   705   706

707   708   709   710   711   712

713   714   715   716   717   718   719

"IRISH CHARACTER FIGURES"
(722-730)

720   721

722   723   724   725   726   727   728   729   730

731   732   733   734   735   736   737   738   739   740

"BALLY-WHIM VILLAGE"
(741-748)

741   742   743   744   745   746   747   748

"MOURNE" RANGE

C.346 C.345 C.347 C.348 C.360 C.350 C.351 C.352 C.353 C.354 C.355 C.356 C.357 C.358/9 C.349

made in Ireland...

**BELFAST -
COLERAINE - DUNGANNON
TRILLICK - DONAGHADEE
KILKEEL...**

*Just as the mere saying of
names like these conjure
up the time-honoured
images of Ireland, so then
does WADE (Ireland) LTD.
symbolize the ultimate in
value, quality and beauty
in Irish Porcelain.*

*If it's a touch of
the "auld sod" you're after
or a gift for someone that
will be appreciated for years
to come, Irish Porcelain from
WADE (Ireland) LTD.
is the answer.*

*The superb workmanship,
the exquisite colours and
designs combine to produce
porcelain worthy of
any setting...*

749

IRISH PORCELAIN
SONG FIGURES

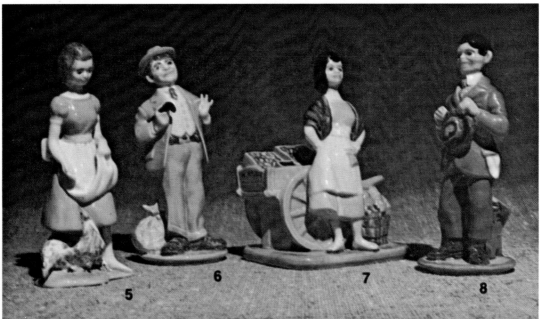

751 752 753 754 755

756 757 758 759

760 761 762 763 764

765 766 767 768 769

770

771

772

773

774

775

776

777

778

779

780

781

782

783

784

785

786

787

788

789

790

791

69

792

793

794

795

796

797

798

799

800

801

802

803

804

805

806

807

808

809

810

GILBEY'S WINE BARRELS
(811-814, 822-825)

811

812

813

814

816

BASS PROMOTIONAL ITEMS
(816-821)

815

817

818

819

820

821

822

823

824

825

BOTTLE POURERS
(826-832)

GUINNESS FIGURINES
(833-836)

826

827

828

829

830

831

832

833

834

835

836

837

Original Designs From The
Wade Heath & Co. Ltd. Design Book

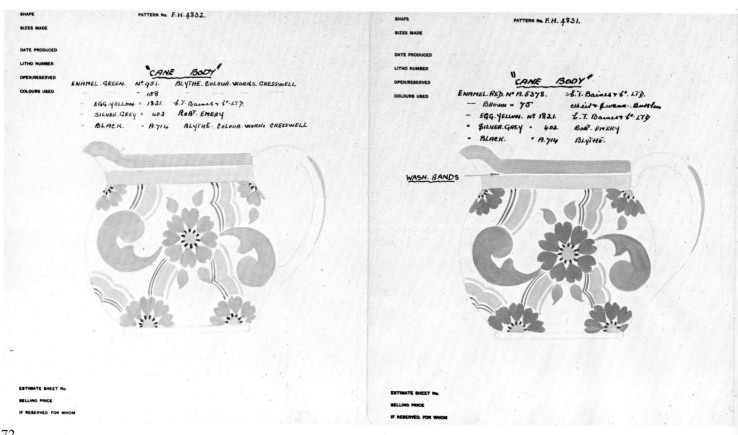

SHAPE

SIZES MADE

DATE PRODUCED

LITHO NUMBER

OPEN/RESERVED

COLOURS USED

PATTERN No. 5078.   COPPER LUSTRE:- RESIST.
FREE-HAND ulg.

PINK:- C.65X189. HARR.
MAUVE- 116 HARR.
GREEN:- 2164 M. SWANN.
YELLOW- 15117. BLYTHE
BROWN- 3607. BLYTHE

ESTIMATE SHEET No.

SELLING PRICE

IF RESERVED, FOR WHOM

SHAPE

SIZES MADE

DATE PRODUCED

LITHO NUMBER

OPEN/RESERVED

COLOURS USED

PATTERN No. 5075.   COPPER LUSTRE
FREE-HAND. ulg.

PINK:- C.65X189 HAR.
GREEN:- DRAKE NECK MAYER
BROWN:- 3607. BLYTHE

ESTIMATE SHEET No.

SELLING PRICE

IF RESERVED, FOR WHOM

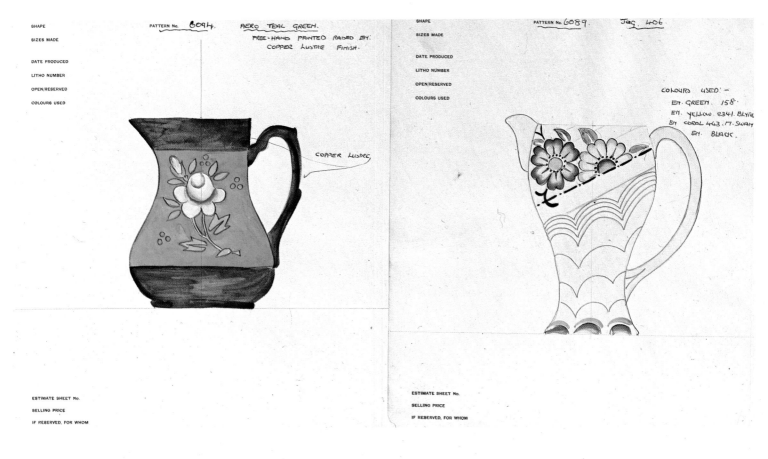

SHAPE

SIZES MADE

DATE PRODUCED

LITHO NUMBER

OPEN/RESERVED

COLOURS USED

PATTERN No. 6094.   AERO TEAL GREEN.
FREE-HAND PAINTED RAISED EN:
COPPER LUSTRE FINISH.

COPPER LUSTRE

ESTIMATE SHEET No.

SELLING PRICE

IF RESERVED, FOR WHOM

SHAPE

SIZES MADE

DATE PRODUCED

LITHO NUMBER

OPEN/RESERVED

COLOURS USED

PATTERN No. 6089.   Jug. 406.

COLOURS USED:-
EN. GREEN. 158.
EN. YELLOW 2341. BLYTHE
EN CORAL 463. M. SWAN
EN. BLACK.

ESTIMATE SHEET No.

SELLING PRICE

IF RESERVED, FOR WHOM

73

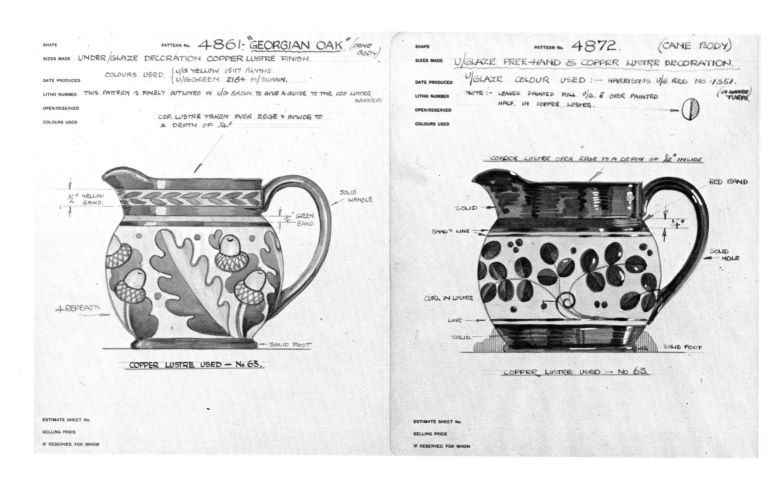

SHAPE

PATTERN No. 4861: "GEORGIAN OAK" (CANE BODY)

SIZES MADE UNDER/GLAZE DECORATION COPPER LUSTRE FINISH.

DATE PRODUCED COLOURS USED. { U/G YELLOW 15117 BLYTHE.
{ U/G GREEN. 2184 M/SWANN.

LITHO NUMBER THIS PATTERN IS FINELY OUTLINED IN U/G BROWN TO GIVE A GUIDE TO THE COP LUSTRE WORKERS

OPEN/RESERVED

COLOURS USED COP. LUSTRE TAKEN OVER EDGE & INSIDE TO A DEPTH OF 1/4"

1/2" YELLOW BAND.

1/4" GREEN BAND.

SOLID HANDLE

4 REPEATS

SOLID FOOT

COPPER LUSTRE USED — No 63.

ESTIMATE SHEET No.

SELLING PRICE

IF RESERVED, FOR WHOM

SHAPE PATTERN No. 4872. (CANE BODY)

SIZES MADE U/GLAZE FREE-HAND & COPPER LUSTRE DECORATION.

DATE PRODUCED U/GLAZE COLOUR USED :— HARRISONS U/G RED NO. 1351.

LITHO NUMBER NOTE :— LEAVES PAINTED FULL U/G. & OVER PAINTED (IN WATER TURPS)

OPEN/RESERVED HALF. IN COPPER LUSTRE.

COLOURS USED

COPPER LUSTRE OVER EDGE TO A DEPTH OF 1/2" INSIDE

RED BAND

SOLID

BAND & LINE

1/4"

SOLID HDLE

CURL IN LUSTRE

LINE

SOLID

SOLID FOOT

COPPER LUSTRE USED :— No 63.

ESTIMATE SHEET No.

SELLING PRICE

IF RESERVED, FOR WHOM

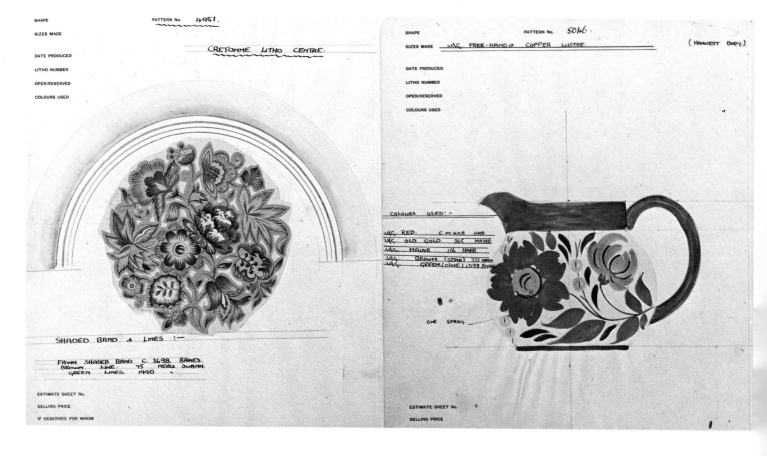

SHAPE PATTERN No. 4951.

SIZES MADE

DATE PRODUCED

LITHO NUMBER

OPEN/RESERVED

COLOURS USED

CRETONNE LITHO CENTRE.

SHADED BAND & LINES :—

FAWN SHADED BAND C. 3698. BAINES.
BROWN LINE 75 MEIRA SWANN.
GREEN LINES 1990

ESTIMATE SHEET No.

SELLING PRICE

IF RESERVED, FOR WHOM

SHAPE PATTERN No. 5046.

SIZES MADE U/G. FREE-HAND & COPPER LUSTRE. (HARVEST BODY.)

DATE PRODUCED

LITHO NUMBER

OPEN/RESERVED

COLOURS USED

COLOURS USED :—

U/G. RED.	C.M. x65 HARR.
U/G. OLD GOLD.	265 MAYER
U/G. MAUVE	116 HARR.
U/G. BROWN (SEPIA)	372 HARR.
U/G. GREEN (OLIVE)	17/98 BLYTHE.

ONE SPRAY.

ESTIMATE SHEET No.

SELLING PRICE

74

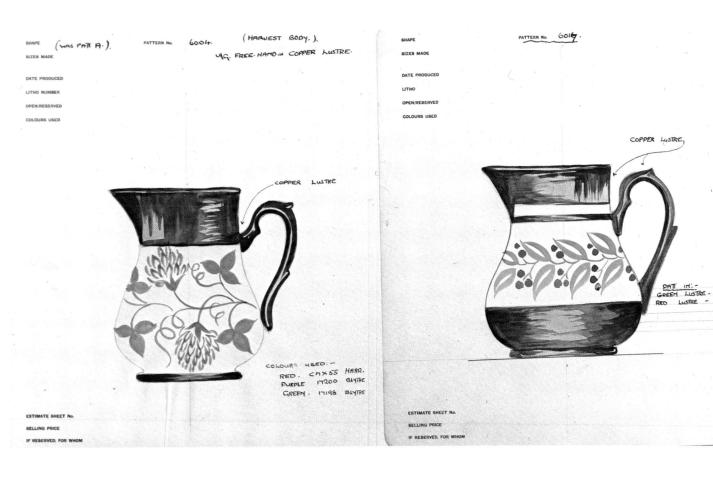

SHAPE (WAS PATT A.)   PATTERN No. 6004   (HARVEST BODY.)
SIZES MADE   W.G. FREE-HAND & COPPER LUSTRE.

DATE PRODUCED
LITHO NUMBER
OPEN/RESERVED
COLOURS USED

COPPER LUSTRE

COLOURS USED:-
RED. CMX55 HARR.
PURPLE 17200 BLYTHE
GREEN. 17198 BLYTHE

ESTIMATE SHEET No.
SELLING PRICE
IF RESERVED, FOR WHOM

SHAPE   PATTERN No. 6017.
SIZES MADE

DATE PRODUCED
LITHO
OPEN/RESERVED
COLOURS USED

COPPER LUSTRE,

PATT IN:-
GREEN LUSTRE.
RED LUSTRE.

ESTIMATE SHEET No.
SELLING PRICE
IF RESERVED, FOR WHOM

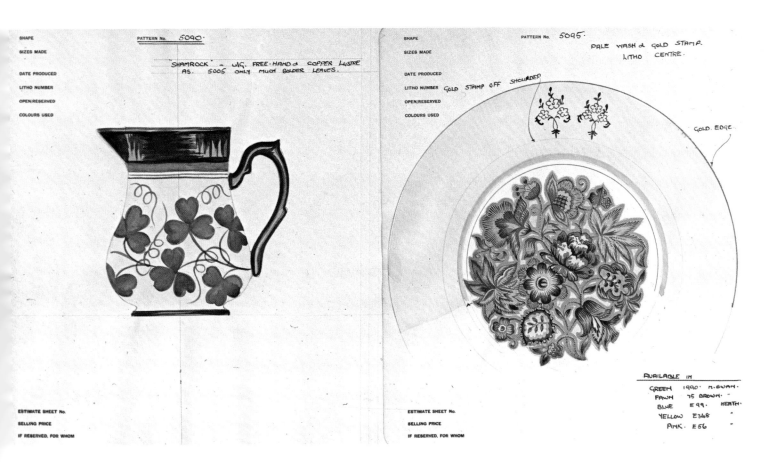

SHAPE   PATTERN No. 5090.
SIZES MADE

DATE PRODUCED   SHAMROCK - W.G. FREE-HAND & COPPER LUSTRE
LITHO NUMBER   AS. 5005 ONLY MUCH BOLDER LEAVES.
OPEN/RESERVED
COLOURS USED

ESTIMATE SHEET No.
SELLING PRICE
IF RESERVED, FOR WHOM

SHAPE   PATTERN No. 5095.
SIZES MADE   PALE WASH & GOLD STAMP.
                                          LITHO CENTRE.
DATE PRODUCED
LITHO NUMBER GOLD STAMP OFF SHOULDER
OPEN/RESERVED
COLOURS USED

GOLD EDGE

AVAILABLE IN

GREEN 1990 H.SWAN.
FAWN 75 BROWN.
BLUE E99. HEATH.
YELLOW E348
PINK. E56

ESTIMATE SHEET No.
SELLING PRICE
IF RESERVED, FOR WHOM

75

SHAPE DANDY. PATTERN No. 4842.

SIZES MADE DECORATED UNDER. GLAZE. AND FINISHED IN COP. LUSTRE (CANE BODY.)

DATE PRODUCED U.G. COLOURS {YELLOW 15117 BLYTHE.
LITHO NUMBER USED. {PINK. 1133 HARRISONS
{MAUVE 116 "
OPEN/RESERVED {GREEN. 2164. M<u>c</u> SWANN.
{OLIVE GREEN 120 BLYTHE.
COLOURS USED

COPPER LUSTRE

ESTIMATE SHEET No.

SELLING PRICE

IF RESERVED, FOR WHOM

SHAPE DANDY. PATTERN No. 4843.

SIZES MADE

DATE PRODUCED AS 4842 BUT OLIVE GREEN NOT USED

LITHO NUMBER

OPEN/RESERVED

COLOURS USED

BANDED IN PINK →

ESTIMATE SHEET No.

SELLING PRICE

IF RESERVED, FOR WHOM

SHAPE PATTERN No. 5073. COPPER LUSTRE & (HARVEST BODY)
FREE-HAND U/G.
SIZES MADE

DATE PRODUCED

LITHO NUMBER

OPEN/RESERVED

COLOURS USED

RED:- TERRA COTTA MAYER.
YELLOW:- 8484 BLYTHE
GREEN:- DRAKE NECK. MAYER.
BROWN:- 3607. BLYTHE.

ESTIMATE SHEET No.

SELLING PRICE

IF RESERVED, FOR WHOM

SHAPE (HARVEST BODY.) PATTERN No. 5074. COPPER LUSTRE &
UNDERGLAZE FREE-HAND
SIZES MADE

DATE PRODUCED

LITHO NUMBER

OPEN/RESERVED

COLOURS USED

COLOURS USED:-

RED:- TERRA COTTA MAYER. 1712A
GREEN:- DRAKE NECK · 4653
BROWN:- 5607. BLYTHE
17199.

ESTIMATE SHEET No.

SELLING PRICE

IF RESERVED, FOR WHOM

76

SHAPE

PATTERN No. 4899

SIZES MADE 4/6 AS 4884.

DATE PRODUCED FINISHED IN WASH-BANDS & LINES. 9/6.

LITHO NUMBER COLOURS USED { EN-GREEN -158 BLYTHE.

OPEN/RESERVED { EN-(CHOC)BROWN. 237. J.MATTHEY.

COLOURS USED

DASHED HANDLE

ESTIMATE SHEET No.

SELLING PRICE

IF RESERVED, FOR WHOM

SHAPE

PATTERN No. 4900

SIZES MADE 4/6. AS 4879.

DATE PRODUCED FINISHED 9/6. FREE-HAND & WASH-BANDS.

LITHO NUMBER COLOURS USED { EN-GREEN -158 -BLYTHE

OPEN/RESERVED { EN-(CHOC)BROWN - 237. I.MATTHEY}

COLOURS USED

L. BANDS.

DASHED HDLE

ADDED FREE-HAND

ESTIMATE SHEET No.

SELLING PRICE

IF RESERVED, FOR WHOM

SHAPE

PATTERN No. 4884 (CANE BODY)

SIZES MADE

4/6. FREE-HAND & COPPER LUSTRE FINISH.

DATE PRODUCED COLOURS USED { 4/6 RED 1351 HARR

LITHO NUMBER { 4/6 PURPLE 4211 BLYTHE

OPEN/RESERVED { 4/6 OLIVE GREEN 120 "

COLOURS USED { 4/6 AUT. BROWN 3607 "

{ 4/6 STRONG

COP. LUSTRED TO 1/4" INSIDE

NOTE. NO LINING ON THIS PART.

SOLID HDLE

ALL COVERS SOLID LUSTRE

ESTIMATE SHEET No.

SELLING PRICE

IF RESERVED, FOR WHOM

SHAPE

PATTERN No. 4882 (CANE-BODY)

SIZES MADE

4/6 FREE-HAND & COPPER LUSTRE FINISH.

DATE PRODUCED COLOURS USED { 4/6 RED No 1351 HARR.

LITHO NUMBER { 4/6 PURPLE 42H BLYTHE. 17200

OPEN/RESERVED { 4/6 OLIVE GREEN 120 " 17198

COLOURS USED { 4/6 STRONG ORANGE 8484 "

{ 4/6 AUTUMN BROWN 3607 " 17199.

COPPER LUSTRED TO 1/4" INSIDE

NOTE
THERE IS NO 4/6 LINING
IN THIS PATTERN.

SOLID HDLE

ALL COVERS SOLID LUSTRE

ESTIMATE SHEET No.

SELLING PRICE

IF RESERVED, FOR WHOM

77

SHAPE

SIZES MADE

DATE PRODUCED

LITHO NUMBER

OPEN/RESERVED

COLOURS USED

PATTERN No. C.L. 4811.

COPPER LUSTRE
CANE BODY.

ESTIMATE SHEET No.

SELLING PRICE

IF RESERVED, FOR WHOM

SHAPE

SIZES MADE

DATE PRODUCED

LITHO NUMBER

OPEN/RESERVED

COLOURS USED

PATTERN No. F.M. 4833

"CANE BODY"

ENAMEL. PLUN. No 61.M. JOHNSON·MATTHEY
    "   GREEN. = 158   BLYTHE
    "   EGG·YELLOW = 1821. BAINES.
    "   BLACK   = A.Y14   BLYTHE
    "   SILVER.GREY = 402. ROBT. EMERY

ESTIMATE SHEET No.

SELLING PRICE

IF RESERVED, FOR WHOM

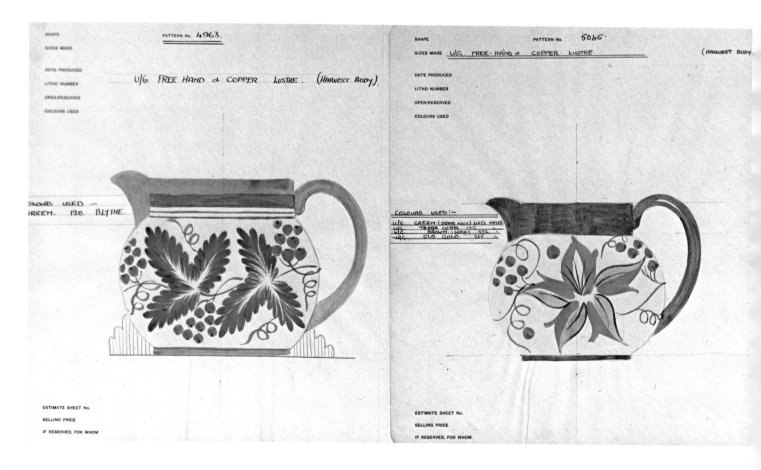

SHAPE

SIZES MADE

DATE PRODUCED

LITHO NUMBER

OPEN/RESERVED

COLOURS USED

PATTERN No. 4963.

U/G FREE HAND & COPPER LUSTRE. (HARVEST BODY).

COLOURS USED —
GREEN. 120. BLYTHE.

ESTIMATE SHEET No.

SELLING PRICE

IF RESERVED, FOR WHOM

SHAPE

SIZES MADE U/G. FREE-HAND & COPPER LUSTRE.   (HARVEST BODY

DATE PRODUCED

LITHO NUMBER

OPEN/RESERVED

COLOURS USED

PATTERN No. 5045.

COLOURS USED :—
U/G. GREEN·(DRAKE NECK) 4454 MAYER
U/G. TERRA COTTA 1712
U/G. BROWN·(SEMI) 272
U/G. OLD GOLD. 265

ESTIMATE SHEET No.

SELLING PRICE

IF RESERVED, FOR WHOM

78

SHAPE   PATTERN No. **4879**   (CANE BODY)

SIZES MADE

DATE PRODUCED

LITHO NUMBER

OPEN/RESERVED

COLOURS USED

4/6. FREE-HAND & COPPER LUSTRE FINISH.

COLOURS USED —
4/6 ORANGE 8484   BLYTHE.
4/6 RED No. 1351   HARR.
4/6 PURPLE - 4211   BLYTHE
4/6 GOLDEN BROWN 2008   "
4/6 OLIVE GREEN 120   "
4/6 LINED IN OLIVE GREEN 20 BLYTHE

COPPER LUSTRED TO 1/4 INSIDE

SAND HOLE

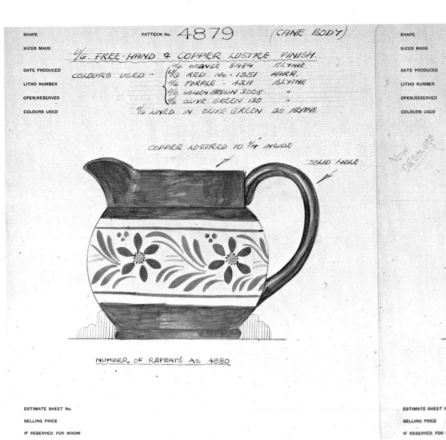

NUMBER OF REPEATS AS 4880

ESTIMATE SHEET No.

SELLING PRICE

IF RESERVED, FOR WHOM

SHAPE   PATTERN No. **4881.**   (CANE BODY)

SIZES MADE

DATE PRODUCED

LITHO NUMBER

OPEN/RESERVED

COLOURS USED

4/6 FREE-HAND & COPPER LUSTRE FINISH.

COLOURS USED
4/6 STRONG ORANGE 8484 BLYTHE
4/6 RED No. 1351. HARR.
4/6 GOLDEN BROWN 2008 BLYTHE
4/6 OLIVE GREEN 120 "
4/6 PURPLE 4211

4/6 LINED IN OLIVE GREEN 120 BLYTHE.
COP. LUSTRED TO 1/4" INSIDE

Now OBSOLETE

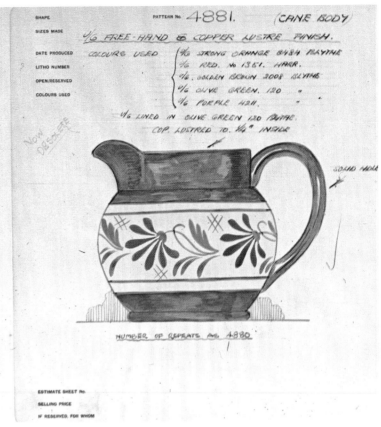

SAND HOLE

NUMBER OF REPEATS AS 4880

ESTIMATE SHEET No.

SELLING PRICE

IF RESERVED, FOR WHOM

SHAPE

SIZES MADE

DATE PRODUCED

LITHO NUMBER

OPEN/RESERVED

COLOURS USED

PATTERN No. **6111**

EN: FREE-HAND.

COLOURS :-
EN CORAL 1990.
- GREEN 1990.
- BROWN Z 237.
COPPER LUSTRE FINISH.

ESTIMATE SHEET No.

SELLING PRICE

IF RESERVED, FOR WHOM

SHAPE

SIZES MADE

DATE PRODUCED

LITHO NUMBER

OPEN/RESERVED

COLOURS USED

PATTERN No. **6193**

AERO IN U/G DELFT BLUE 1528
(G.H. HEATH.)

COPPER LUSTRE TRACED RAISED
ENAMEL COLOUR
COPPER LUSTRE FINISH.

COLOURS AS PATT. 6192.

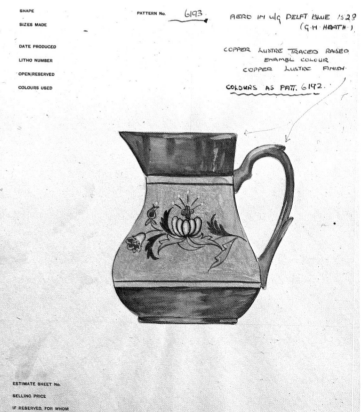

ESTIMATE SHEET No.

SELLING PRICE

IF RESERVED, FOR WHOM

79

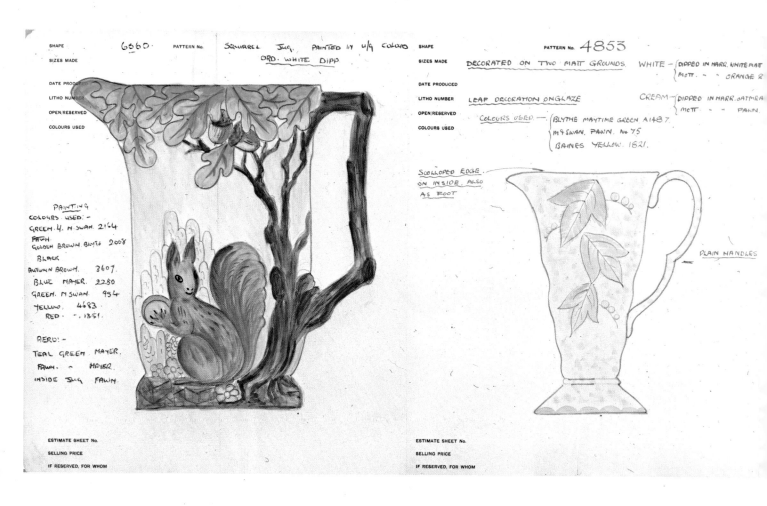

SHAPE   6660   PATTERN No.   SQUIRREL Jug. PAINTED IN 4/9 COLOURS
SIZES MADE   ORD. WHITE DIPP.

DATE PRODUCED
LITHO NUMBER
OPEN/RESERVED
COLOURS USED

PAINTING
COLOURS USED:-
GREEN.4. M.SWAN. 2164
FAWN.
GOLDEN BROWN BLYTH 2008
BLACK
AUTUMN BROWN. 3607.
BLUE MAYER. 2280
GREEN. M.SWAN. 954
YELLOW 4683.
RED . .1351.

AERO':-
TEAL GREEN. MAYER.
FAWN. - MAYER.
INSIDE JUG FAWN.

ESTIMATE SHEET No.
SELLING PRICE
IF RESERVED, FOR WHOM

SHAPE   PATTERN No. 4853
SIZES MADE   DECORATED ON TWO MATT GROUNDS   WHITE - { DIPPED IN MARR. WHITE MATT
                                                          { MOTT. - " ORANGE R
DATE PRODUCED
LITHO NUMBER LEAF DECORATION ONGLAZE   CREAM - { DIPPED IN MARR. OATMEAL
OPEN/RESERVED   { MOTT. - " FAWN.
COLOURS USED COLOURS USED:- { BLYTHE MAYTIME GREEN A1487.
                              { M & SWAN. FAWN. No 75
                              { BAINES YELLOW. 1621.

SCALLOPED EDGE
ON INSIDE. ALSO
AS FOOT

PLAIN HANDLES

ESTIMATE SHEET No.
SELLING PRICE
IF RESERVED, FOR WHOM

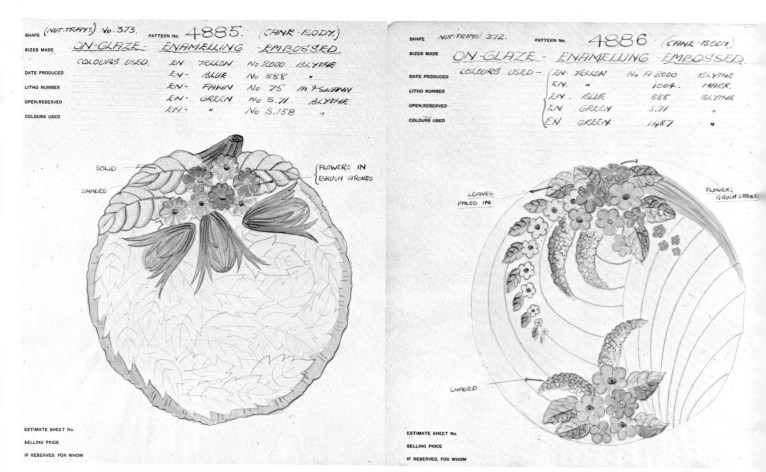

SHAPE (NUT-TRAYS) No.373. PATTERN No. 4885. (CANE-BODY.)
SIZES MADE   ON-GLAZE - ENAMELLING - EMBOSSED.
             COLOURS USED.   EN - YELLOW   No 2000 BLYTHE
DATE PRODUCED   EN - BLUE   No 888   "
LITHO NUMBER   EN - FAWN   No 75   M & SWANN
OPEN/RESERVED   EN - GREEN   No S.71   BLYTHE
COLOURS USED   EN - "   No S.158   "

SOLID
SHADED
FLOWERS IN
BRUSH STROKES

ESTIMATE SHEET No.
SELLING PRICE
IF RESERVED, FOR WHOM

SHAPE NUT-TRAYS 372.   PATTERN No. 4886 (CANE-BODY)
SIZES MADE   ON-GLAZE - ENAMELLING - EMBOSSED.
             COLOURS USED - EN - YELLOW   No A.2000   BLYTHE
DATE PRODUCED   EN. "   1004.   MARR.
LITHO NUMBER   EN. BLUE   888   BLYTHE
OPEN/RESERVED   EN GREEN   S.71   "
COLOURS USED   EN GREEN.   1487   "

LEAVES
PALED IN.

FLOWERS
BRUSH STROKES

SHADED

ESTIMATE SHEET No.
SELLING PRICE
IF RESERVED, FOR WHOM

SEA LION CORKSCREW *1960.*

The Sea Lion forms the base with the multi-colored ball forming the handle of the corkscrew. This model had a black & gold label marked "Genuine Wade Porcelain".

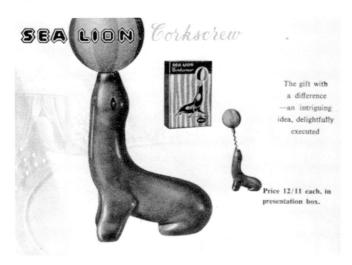

FIG. 31.

TV PET SERIES *1959-1965.*
(Copyright Cooper Features Ltd.)

A series of ten animal figurines, nine dogs and one cat, based on a popular T.V. children's program. All figurines have fine parallel molded ridges on the underside of the base and were originally issued with the black and gold paper labels marked "WADE GENUINE PORCELAIN MADE IN ENGLAND". Following is a list of the figurines in order of issue.

BENGO, SIMON, PEPI, FIFI, MITZI and CHEE-CHEE all issued in 1959.
BRUNO JNR. and DROOPY JNR. both issued in 1961.
PERCY and WHISKY both issued in 1965.

FIG. 32.

No. 65. DROOPY JNR.—measures 2¼" high by 1¾" across the base.
No. 66. PERCY—measures 1½" high by 1¼" across the base.
No. 67. PEPI—measures 2⅛" high by 1¼" across the base.
No. 68. FIFI—measures 2⅝" high by 1¼" across the base.

For illustrations of the complete series see FIG. 32.

ZOO LIGHTS *1959.*

The candlestick bases were decorated with animal models from the early "Whimsie" series in front of the actual holder for the candle. The holders were supplied in a variety of colors.

FIG. 33.

"TOM AND JERRY" *1973-1979.*

The long running and popular cartoon series featuring the two characters, Tom and Jerry, inspired Wade to produce two figurines, based upon these two characters, as an addition to their giftware line.

Both figurines have the typical fine parallel molded ridges on the underside of the base and both are mold marked "WADE ENGLAND © M.G.M." on the edge of the base.

No. 69. JERRY—measures 1⅞" high by 1⅛" across the base.
No. 70. TOM—measures 3⅝" high by 2⅛" across the base.

We would like to acknowledge the co-operation and ownership of copyright for the items illustrated.
© 1940 Loew's Incorporated
Ren. 1967 Metro-Goldwyn-Mayer Inc.
(formerly known as Loew's Incorporated)

SPIRIT CONTAINERS *CIRCA 1961.*

In the early 1960's, Henry Stratton & Co. Limited, a leading U.K. distiller, commissioned Wade to design and manufacture a set of five containers in which to package their product. Unfortunately, due to unforseen circumstances, the containers were never used for their original purpose and were eventually distributed by a major U.K. drugstore chain as ornamental items.

The set of five containers comprised of porcelain figurines in the shape of various birds which were a Cockatoo, Baby Chick and three different sizes of Penguins. All the containers were marked with the black and gold paper label.

No. 71. BABY CHICK—measures 3⅜″ high with a 2″ diameter base.

No. 72. COCKATOO—measures 5″ high with a 2½″ diameter base.

No. 73. PENGUIN (MIDDLE SIZE)—measures 4¼″ high with a 2¼″ diameter base. The two Penguin containers not shown are similar to the one illustrated with the large container measuring approx. 4¾″ high and the smaller container measuring approx. 3¾″ high.

"HAT BOX" SERIES *1956-1965.*

Walt Disney animated movies have proven to be a very popular source of inspiration for various attractions since their introduction in the 1930's. The large number of memorable and lovable characters featured in some of the animated movies became a very successful theme for a series of porcelain miniatures issued by George Wade & Son Ltd., starting in 1956, with additions to the line over the following years. The original line, which ran between the years 1956-1965, was known as the "The Hat Box" series and consisted of twenty six figurines from six of the most popular Disney movies.

The "Hat Box" series consisted of BABY PEGASUS from the movie "FANTASIA," DUMBO from the movie of the same name, BAMBI, THUMPER and FLOWER all from the movie "BAMBI," LADY, JOCK, SCAMP, DACHSIE, TRAMP, PEG, SI, AM, TRUSTY, BORIS and TOUGHY, all from "LADY AND THE TRAMP." Next came THE COLONEL, SGT. TIBBS, ROLLY and LUCKY from the movie "101 DALMATIONS" and finally, GIRL SQUIRREL, MERLIN (as a Hare), MERLIN (as a Turtle), MERLIN (as a Caterpillar), MADAM MIM and ARCHIMEDES from the movie, "SWORD IN THE STONE." For "SWORD IN THE STONE" figurines see FIG. 34.

The term "Hat Box" came from the colorful round container used to package the individual figurines. See FIG 35.

FIG. 35.

The "Hat Box" series was discontinued in 1965, and Wade did not manufacture any figurines based on Walt Disney animated characters until a new series was introduced in 1981, using some figurines from the "Hat Box" series and adding completely new figurines from later Walt Disney animated movies. This new series was named simply "Disneys."

DISNEY MONEY BOXES *1962.*

A set of five money boxes, with removable rubber plugs on the underside, finished in a bright color glaze and featuring one of five Walt Disney figurines from the "Hat Box" series: LADY, SCAMP, JOCK, ROLLY, and LUCKY.

The Six Latest Hat Box Characters

Taken from
WALT DISNEY'S film

"THE SWORD IN THE STONE"

The new characters are :-
MADAM MIM (Hen)
MERLIN AS TURTLE
ARCHIMEDES (Owl)
MERLIN AS HARE
THE GIRL SQUIRREL
MERLIN AS CATERPILLAR

Suggested Retail selling price **3/6** each

(Copyright MCMLXIII Walt Disney Productions)

FIG. 34.

(Copyright Walt Disney Productions)

copyright Walt Disney Productions Ltd.

FIG. 36.

"DISNEYS" *1981-1987.*

With the re-introduction of a number of the original "Hat Box" figurines and the addition of new figurines from later Walt Disney animated movies, the packaging was changed from the cardboard "Hat Box" container to a round, brown plastic box. (see FIG. 37.)

FIG. 37.

and was changed yet again in 1986 with the re-issue of "PEG" (from the "Hat Box" mold) and a re-designed "TRAMP" when the round plastic container was changed to a rectangular paper box colorfully decorated with pictures from the "Disneys" series. Wade ceased production of the "Disneys" in February, 1987.

The "Disneys" series consisted of LADY, SCAMP, JOCK, DACHSIE, BAMBI and THUMPER, all re-issues from the "Hat Box" series, with four new figurines added to the "Disneys" line, which were COPPER, BIG MAMA, CHIEF and TOD from the movie "THE FOX AND THE HOUND". In 1986, the figurine "PEG" and the re-designed "TRAMP" were added to the line. Most figurines, in both the "Hat Box" and "Disneys" series, unless noted otherwise, were marked with an oval gold paper label worded: "© Walt DISNEY PRODUCTIONS WADE ENGLAND".

No. 74. BIG MAMA (1981-1987)—measures 1¾" high by 1¾" overall.

No. 75. TOD (1981-1987)—measures 1¾" high by 1⅞" overall.

No. 76. COPPER (1981-1987)—measures 1⅝" high by 1½" overall.

No. 77. CHIEF (1981-1987)—measures 1⅞" high by 1" across the base.

No. 78. ROLLY (1960-1964)—measures 1⅝" high by 1⅜" overall.

No. 79. SGT. TIBBS (1960-1964)—measures 2" high by 1⅝" overall.

No. 80. THE COLONEL (1960-1964)—measures 2" high by 1½" overall.
LUCKY (not shown) a small Dalmation puppy was also issued in this time period.

No. 81. DUMBO (1958-1965)—measures 1⅜" high by 1⅝" overall.

No. 82. MERLIN AS A HARE (1965)—measures 2¼" high by 1⅜" across the base.
The following figurines were also issued in this time period but not illustrated.
MERLIN AS A TURTLE
MERLIN AS A CATERPILLAR
GIRL SQUIRREL
ARCHIMEDES (the owl)
MADAM MIM (the hen)

No. 83. JOCK (1956-1965 and 1981-1987)—measures 1¾" high by 1⅝" overall.

No. 84. LADY (1956-1965 and 1981-1987)—measures 1½" high by 1¾" overall.

No. 85. TRAMP (1956-1965)—measures 2⅛" high by 1⅞" overall and is transfer marked "WADE ENGLAND".

No. 86. TRAMP (1986-1987)—measures 1⅞" high by 1¼" overall.

No. 87. AM (1958-1965)—measures 1⅞" high by 1" overall.
SI (not shown) a Siamese cat was also issued in this time period. Similar in design to "Disney Blow-ups" No. 99 in the color section.

No. 88. DACHSIE (1958-1965 and 1981-1984)—measures 1¾" high by 1½" overall. During the earlier production run this figurine was referred to as "Dachie".

No. 89. THUMPER (1958-1965 and 1981-1987)—measures 1⅞" high by 1¼" across the base.

No. 90. BAMBI (1958-1965 and 1981-1987)—measures 1½" high by 1⅜" overall.

No. 91. FLOWER (1958-1965)—measures 1½" high by 1¾" overall.

No. 92. BABY PEGASUS (1958-1965)—measures 1¾" high by 1⅜" overall.

No. 93. TOUGHY (1960-1965)—measures 2" high by 1¼" overall.

No. 94. PEG (1957-1965 and 1986-1987)—measures 1½" high by 1⅝" overall.

No. 95. TRUSTY (1956-1965)—measures 2⅜" high by 1⅜" overall base.

No. 96. SCAMP (1957-1965 and 1981-1987)—measures 1½" high by 1½" overall.

No. 97. BORIS (1960-1965)—measures 2⅜" high by 1" diameter base.

DISNEY "BLOW-UPS" *1961-1965.*

Between 1961-1965, George Wade & Son Ltd. produced a set of ten large versions of the popular Disney "Hat Box" series. These large figurines which ranged up to 5½" tall were popularly known as "Blow-Ups" by Wade employees; however, they were officially marketed under the name "Disneys". The larger models were hand decorated in both under-glaze and on-glaze colors and individually gift-boxed. The ten figurines chosen for the large size models were LADY, TRAMP, SCAMP, JOCK, SI, AM, DACHIE and TRUSTY from the movie "LADY AND THE TRAMP" and BAMBI and THUMPER from the movie "BAMBI" and are illustrated in FIG'S. 38 and 39.

The figurines are found marked either "WADE POR-CELAIN COPYRIGHT WALT DISNEY PRODUCTIONS MADE IN ENGLAND" (Type "A") or "WADE PORCELAIN ENGLAND" (Type "B") both of which are transfer marks.

No. 98. SCAMP—measures 4⅛" high by 5" overall. Mark Type "A".

No. 99. SI—measures 5½" high by 5" overall. Mark Type "B".

"DISNEYS"

"LADY" "TRAMP" "BAMBI" "SCAMP"

Larger models of Walt Disney's most
loveable characters. Hand-decorated
in delightful under-glaze and on-glaze
colours.
(Copyright Walt Disney Productions)

FIG. 38.

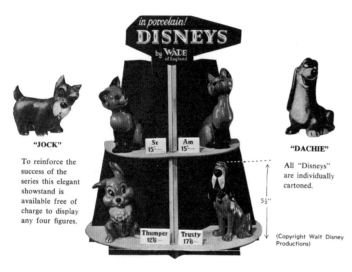

"JOCK" "DACHIE"

To reinforce the
success of the
series this elegant
showstand is
available free of
charge to display
any four figures.

All "Disneys"
are individually
cartoned.

(Copyright Walt Disney
Productions)

FIG. 39.

DOGS AND PUPPIES SERIES
1969-1982.

Starting in 1969, a retail line of miniature porcelain dogs
accompanied by two puppies of the same breed made its
appearance in the Wade range of giftware. The adult dogs
were packaged singly in boxes designed to appear as a small
book. The puppies were packaged in a similar style box with
both puppies in a single box. Three sides of the boxes were
white with black lines representing the pages of a book.
The third side represented the spine of the book with the
name of the breed only for the adult dog, and the word
"puppies" added to the breed name for the box containing
the puppies.

Five sets of adult dogs and puppies were issued in a total
of ten boxes. The first six boxes were colored blue with the
wording of "WHIMSIES" above the breed name. The
remaining four boxes were colored red but this time the
wording "Whimsies" was replaced by "DOG SERIES".

Unless noted otherwise, all figurines had the oval shaped
black and gold paper label with the wording "WADE MADE
IN ENGLAND" and all have the fine molded parallel ridges
on the underside of the base.

SET 1. Issued in 1969.
No. 100-1. ALSATIAN (Adult)—measures 2½" high
by 2⅜" overall.
No. 100-2. ALSATIAN (Puppy)—measures 1¼" high
by 2" overall.
No. 100-3. ALSATIAN (Puppy)—measures 1¾" high
by 1⅝" overall.

SET 2. Issued in 1979.
No. 101-1. CORGI (Adult)—measures 2¼" high
by 2¼" long and is mold marked "WADE
ENGLAND" on back face of base.
No. 101-2. CORGI (Puppy)—measures 1⅝" high
by 1⅜" overall and is mold marked "WADE"
on one side of tail and "ENGLAND" on the
other.
No. 101-3. CORGI (Puppy)—measures 1⅛" high
by 1⅝" overall and is mold marked "WADE
ENGLAND" on the back.

SET 3. Issued in 1973.
No. 102-1. RED SETTER (Adult)—measures
2¼" high by 2⅞" overall.
No. 102-2. RED SETTER (Puppy)—measures
1½" high by 1¾" overall.
No. 102-3. RED SETTER (Puppy)—measures
1½" high by 1¾" overall.

SET 4. Issued in 1969.
No. 103-1. CAIRN (Adult)—measures 2½" high
by 2¾" overall.
No. 103-2. CAIRN (Puppy)—measures 1½" high
by 1⅜" overall.
No. 103-3. CAIRN (Puppy)—measures 1⅜" high
by 2" overall.

SET 5. Issued in 1979.
No. 104-1. YORKSHIRE TERRIER (Adult)—measures
2⅛" high by 1⅝" overall and is mold marked
"WADE ENGLAND" on the back.
No. 104-2. YORKSHIRE TERRIER (Puppy)—measures
1⅜" high by 1½" overall.
No. 104-3. YORKSHIRE TERRIER (Puppy)—measures
1½" high by 1¼" overall.

The order of issue as it appears on the back of box No. 10
(Yorkshire Terrier Puppies) differs from the order as noted
above and is as follows: Set 1. ALSATIAN (German Shepherd),
Set 2. CAIRN, Set 3. RED SETTER (Irish Setter), Set 4.
CORGI and Set 5. YORKSHIRE TERRIER.

CAT AND PUPPY DISHES *1974-1981.*

During the run of the Dog and Puppy Sets, an addition
was made to this line of giftware by the manufacturer of
porcelain basket-shaped dishes into which the ten puppies
were mounted. These dishes were given the name "PUPPY
DISHES". During the same period, a porcelain figurine of a
cat, larger in size than the puppies, was also made and mounted

in a similar basket. This was known as the "CAT DISH". The cat measures 2⅜″ high by 1¾″ overall. For the size of puppies refer to the "Dogs and Puppies" sets.

The size and shape of the dishes is similar for all puppies and cat being oval shaped and measuring 2⅞″ long by 2½″ across. The side of the basket is ¾″ high at the front and 1″ high at the back. All basket dishes have smooth bases and are mold marked "WADE ENGLAND". All the puppy dishes are the same grey color but the cat dish is brown.

No. 105. CAT DISH.
No. 106. ALSATIAN PUPPY DISH.
No. 107. ALSATIAN PUPPY DISH.
No. 108. RED SETTER PUPPY DISH.
No. 109. RED SETTER PUPPY DISH.
No. 110. CAIRN PUPPY DISH.
No. 111. CAIRN PUPPY DISH.
No. 112. YORKSHIRE TERRIER PUPPY DISH.

The following models were also issued in this time period but are not illustrated. They were: YORKSHIRE TERRIER PUPPY DISH, CORGI PUPPY DISH, CORGI PUPPY DISH.

NURSERY FAVOURITES *1972-1981.*

This retail giftware line of handpainted underglaze porcelain Nursery Rhyme figurines was marketed at approximately the same time period as the miniature Nursery figurines used for the Red Rose Tea promotion. It is probable that this giftware line was introduced due to the popularity of the tea figurines.

A number of the Nursery Favourites, the name given to the larger retail nursery figurines, were similar in design to their smaller, premium counterparts, and others, although similar characters, were of a different design. Three of the twenty characters (Mary Lamb, Polly Kettle and Tommy Tucker) did not appear in the premium nursery series.

The Nursery Favourites were issued in four sets of five over a period of nine years, each set having a distinctive colored box containing the figurine. Set 1 was packaged in green boxes, Set 2 in blue boxes, Set 3 in yellow boxes and Set 4 in purple boxes.

There is a difference in the sequence of issue in the last set between "Flyer type" literature issued by Wade and the sequence of issue appearing on the boxes containing the last five figurines. Following is a list of the twenty figurines taken in the order as listed on the purple boxes of the last set.

SET 1. 1972.
No. 113-1. JACK—measures 2⅞″ high by 1⅛″ diameter base.
No. 113-2. JILL—measures 2⅞″ high by 1⅛″ diameter base.
No. 113-3. MISS MUFFET—measures 2⅝″ high by 1⅞″ across the base.
No. 113-4. JACK HORNER—measures 1⅞″ high by 1¼″ across the base.
No. 113-5. HUMPTY DUMPTY—measures 1⅜″ high by 1¾″ across the base.

SET 2. 1973.
No. 114-6. WILLIE WINKIE—measures 1¾″ high by 1½″ across the base.
No. 114-7. MARY LAMB—measures 2⅞″ high by 1⅜″ across the base.
No. 114-8. POLLY KETTLE—measures 2⅞″ high by 1¼″ across the base.
No. 114-9. KING COLE—measures 2½″ high by 1⅞″ across the base.
No. 114-10. TOM PIPER—measures 2¾″ high by 2″ across the base.

SET 3. 1974.
No. 115-11. BOY BLUE—measures 2⅞″ high by 1⅛″ diameter base.
No. 115-12. MARY MARY—measures 2⅞″ high by 1⅛″ diameter base.
No. 115-13. CAT & FIDDLE—measures 2⅞″ high by 1⅜″ across the base.
No. 115-14. QUEEN OF HEARTS—measures 2⅞″ high by 1⅞″ across the base.
No. 115-15. TOMMY TUCKER—measures 3″ high by 1⅛″ diameter base.

SET 4. 1976.
No. 116-16. PUSS-IN-BOOTS—measures 2⅞″ high by 1⅛″ diameter base.
No. 116-17. THREE BEARS—measures 2⅞″ high by 2¼″ across the base.
No. 116-18. GOOSEY GANDER—measures 2⅝″ high by 1⅛″ square base.
No. 116-19. BO-PEEP—measures 2⅞″ high by 1⅛″ diameter base.
No. 116-20. OLD WOMAN (Who Lived in a Shoe)— measures 2½″ high by 2⅛″ along the base.

All figurines are mold marked "WADE ENGLAND" at the back of the base and most have fine parallel molded ridges on the underside of the base, some more pronounced than others.

HAPPY FAMILIES *1962-1965.*

The "Happy Family" series was first issued starting in 1962. Each set featured a larger size parent figurine accompanied by two baby figurines. The miniature families were based on popular wild animals and, in the three year period, five sets of three figurines each were issued. These sets were HIPPO, TIGER, GIRAFFE, RABBIT, and MOUSE. The figurines in this first issue may or may not have been marked with the Wade black and gold paper label, which does not adhere well to the ribbed base so typical of the later Wade figurines. The series was discontinued in 1965.

HAPPY FAMILES *1978-1986.*

Due to the popularity of the first series of the Happy Families, the series was re-introduced starting in 1978. Of the five original families, four were re-used, the Tiger family not being included in the new set. Following is a listing of the current series:

No. 117-1. GIRAFFE (Baby)—measures ⅝" high by 1¼" along the base.

No. 117-2. GIRAFFE (Parent)—measures 2⁵⁄₁₆" high by 1½" along the base.

No. 117-3. GIRAFFE (Baby)—measures 1⁹⁄₁₆" high by 1" along the base.

No. 118-1. RABBIT (Baby)—measures 1⅛" high by ⅞" along the base.

No. 118-2. RABBIT (Parent)—measures 2" high by 1" across the base.

No. 118-3. RABBIT (Baby)—measures 1¼" high by 1" along the base.

No. 119-1. HIPPO (Baby)—measures ⅝" high by ¾" along the base.

No. 119-2. HIPPO (Parent)—1⅛" high by 1⅛" along the base.

No. 119-3. HIPPO (Baby)—measures 1" high by ⁶⁄₈" across the base.

No. 120-1. MOUSE (Baby)—measures 1" high by 1" along the base.

No. 120-2. MOUSE (Parent)—measures 2" high by 1" across the base.

No. 120-3. MOUSE (Baby)—measures 1¹⁄₁₆" high by 1¹⁄₁₆" along the base.

No. 121-1. Frog (Baby)—measures ⅝" high by 1⅜" across the base.

No. 121-2. FROG (Parent)—measures ⅞" high by 1⁹⁄₁₆" across the base.

No. 121-3. FROG (Baby)—measures 1" high by ⅞" across the base.

No. 122-1. PIG (Baby)—measures ⅝" high by ¾" along the base.

No. 122-2. PIG (Parent)—measures 1⅛" high by 1⅛" along the base.

No. 122-3. PIG (Baby)—measures ⁹⁄₁₆" high by 1⅝" along the base.

No. 123-1. ELEPHANT (Baby)—measures 1¾" high by ⅞" along the base.

No. 123-2. ELEPHANT (Parent)—measures 1¼" high by 1⅛" along the base.

No. 123-3. ELEPHANT (Baby)—measures 1" high by ⅞" along the base.

No. 124-1. OWL (Baby)—measures 1" high by ¾" across the base.

No. 124-2. OWL (Parent)—measures 1¾" high by ⅞" across the base.

No. 124-3. OWL (Baby)—measures ⅞" high by ⅝" along the base.

No. 125-1. CAT (Kitten)—measures 1¼" high by 1¼" along the base.

No. 125-2. CAT (Parent)—measures 1⅞" high by 1¼" diameter.

No. 125-3. CAT (Kitten)—measures 1⅜" high by ¾" across the base.

No. 126-1. DOG (Puppy)—measures 1¼" high by 1⅜" long.

No. 126-2. DOG (Parent)—measures 2" high by 1½" along the base.

No. 126-3. DOG (Puppy)—measures 1¼" high by 1⅛" along the base.

All the above figurines have the fine, molded ribbed base and most are found with the black "WADE MADE IN ENGLAND" transfer backstamp. The two puppies have been found unmarked, and, no doubt, other figurines will also turn up unmarked. Baby Pig (No. 122-1) has been found with the transfer backstamp in red. Other figurines will probably be found with red or other color backstamps.

From information gathered, the order of issue of the Dog Family and the Cat Family varies. The list on the back of the box containing the three figurines of each family lists them in the reverse order as illustrated in the color section.

During the two periods that the Happy Family series have been issued in the Wade giftware line, the packaging has gone through a number of changes from simple white boxes with multi-colored lettering to the current highly decorated multi-colored boxes with plain black lettering.

CHAMPIONSHIP DOGS *1975-1981.*

Due to animal figurines having proven to be popular sellers in the Wade giftware lines, it was decided to introduce a set of five mid-size, quality, underglaze colored figurines based on popular purebred dogs. The name chosen for this addition to the Wade line of products was "Championship Dogs".

Each dog was mounted on an oval shaped base measuring 3½" long by 2¼" wide by ¼" deep. Each base has the fine, molded parallel ridges and was originally sold with an oval orange-colored paper label marked "CHAMPIONSHIP SERIES" at the top of the label, "WADE ENGLAND" surrounded by a thin black oval line placed slightly above center with the name of the appropriate dog name below in large capital letters. The front face of the base is also mold marked "CHAMPIONSHIP SERIES" and "WADE ENGLAND" on the back face.

The sizes given for the following figurines are all from top of base to highest point of head or ear, and length is from nose to tip of tail

No. 127. ENGLISH SETTER—measures 2¾" high by 4⅛" long.

No. 128. AFGHAN HOUND—measures 3" high by 3⅜" long.

No. 129. OLD ENGLISH SHEEP DOG—measures 3¼" high by 3" long.

No. 130. COLLIE—measures 3¼" high by 4" long.

No. 131. COCKER SPANIEL—measures 2⅞" high by 3⅝" long.

DOG PIPE RESTS *1973-1981.*

With the declining popularity of the "Dogs and Puppies" series marketed between 1969-1982, it was a logical step for Wade to introduce a set of five pipe rests featuring the large dogs, from this series. In order to decorate a basic pipe rest and also use up surplus stock, the Dog Pipe Rest sets were introduced over a period of eight years.

The pipe rests had slightly "off" circular bases measuring 3¼" in diameter by ¾" deep. To hold the pipe, a rounded indent was incorporated into the depth of the base with an extended rest projecting 2¼" high from the bottom of the base. A slight indent on the top of the base serves as the site for the dog figurine to be attached. The shape of this indent was such that it would hold the various shaped bases of the dogs. Each pipe rest bears the wording "WADE ENGLAND" molded onto the underside of the base.

No. 132. CAIRN TERRIER.
No. 133. IRISH SETTER.
No. 134. CORGI.
No. 135. GERMAN SHEPHERD (ALSATIAN).

A YORKSHIRE TERRIER pipe rest (not shown) was also issued as part of this series.

For dimensions and illustration of the "Yorkshire Terrier", refer to the "Dogs and Puppies" in the color section and corresponding text.

WHOPPAS *1976-1981.*

Starting in 1976, Wade introduced a new line of porcelain animal figurines marketed under the name of "Whoppas". This new line, although not exact copies of the popular Whimsies, were simply larger animals in the same theme. The main reason for producing the "Whoppas" was to fill a price gap in Wade's product range between the Whimsies and the Nursery Favourites.

Three sets of five animals each were produced over a period of three years starting in 1976, and remained in production until 1981. The fifteen figurines are all marked "WADE ENGLAND" on the side of the base and all have the "tell-tale" fine molded parallel ridges on the underside of the base.

SET 1. 1976.
No. 136-1. POLAR BEAR—measures 1½" high by 2¼" overall.
No. 136-2. HIPPO—measures 1⅜" high by 2¼" overall.
No. 136-3. BROWN BEAR—measures 1½" high by 1¾" overall.
No. 136-4. TIGER—measures 1⅛" high by 2½" overall.
No. 136-5. ELEPHANT—measures 2⅛" high by 2" overall.

SET 2. 1977.
No. 137-6. BISON—measures 1¾" high by 2¼" overall.
No. 137-7. WOLF—measures 2¼" high by 1¾" overall.
No. 137-8. BOBCAT—measures 1½" high by 1⅞" overall.
No. 137-9. CHIPMUNK—measures 2⅛" high by 1" diameter base.
No. 137-10. RACOON—measures 1½" high by 2¼" overall.

SET 3. 1978.
No. 138-11. FOX—measures 1¼" high by 2½" overall.
No. 138-12. BADGER—measures 1½" high by 1⅞" overall.
No. 138-13. OTTER—measures 1¼" high by 2" overall.
No. 138-14. STOAT—measures 1½" high by 2⅛" overall base.
No. 138-15. HEDGEHOG—measures 1¼" high by 1⅞" overall.

When the "Whoppas" were discontinued as a retail line, surplus stock was used as a Red Rose Tea premium promotion in Canada. See Premiums and Promotional Items section.

HORSE SETS *1974-1981.*

In 1974, a set comprising of a farm cart horse along with two foals was added to the Wade line of giftware. None of the three figurines were mold marked but were issued with paper labels. A second set, again comprising of a cart horse with two foals was issued in 1978. This second set is mold-marked "WADE ENGLAND" around the base. Both sets have the typical fine, molded, parallel-ridged base. This is a good means of identifying the first set, if the paper labels are missing, which they usually are. The measurements given are from bottom of base to the highest point (usually top of ear) and overall nose to tail unless noted otherwise.

SET 1. 1974.
No. 139-1. FOAL—measures 1⅞" high by 2" overall.
No. 139-2. HORSE—measures 2¾" high by 3" overall.
No. 139-3. FOAL—measures 1⅜" high by 2" overall base.

SET 2. 1978.
No. 140-1. FOAL—measures 1½" high by 1⅝" overall base.
No. 140-2. HORSE—measures 2½" high by 2¾" overall.
No. 140-3. FOAL—measures 1¼" high by 1⅞" overall.

WHIMSIE—LAND SERIES
1984 TO DATE.

When the second set of the popular Wade "Whimsies" was withdrawn in early 1984, a gap was left in the Wade retail giftware line of small inexpensive figurines. Due to the enormous success of the "Whimsies" George Wade & Son Ltd. decided to introduce a new retail line to fill the gap.

After some consideration, it was decided that the new line should continue with sets of miniature porcelain animals and birds to be issued in sets of five with a certain theme for each set. The new sets of figurines were given the name of "Whimsie-Land" with the hand decorated, underglaze colored figurines being slightly larger and more detailed than the 1971-1984 "Whimsies".

The first five sets of five figurines each are as follows:

WHIMSIE-LAND PETS 1984.
No. 141-1.   RETRIEVER—1¼" high
           by 1⅝" along the base.
No. 141-2.   PUPPY—1⅜" high by 1⅜" along the base.
No. 141-3.   RABBIT—2" high by ⅞" diameter base.
No. 141-4.   KITTEN—1" high by 1⅝" along the base.
No. 141-5.   PONY—1½" high by 1½" along the base.

WHIMSIE-LAND WILDLIFE 1984.
No. 142-6.   LION—1¼" high by 1⅞" along the base.
No. 142-7.   TIGER—¾" high by 1¾" along the base.
No. 142-8.   ELEPHANT—1⅜" high
           by 1⅜" along the base.
No. 142-9.   PANDA—1⅜" high by ⅞" diameter base.
No. 142-10. GIRAFFE—2" high by 1¼" across the base.

WHIMSIE-LAND FARMYARD 1985.
No. 143-11. ROOSTER—2" high by 1⅛" along the base.
No. 143-12. DUCK—1⅝" high by 1" along the base.
No. 143-13. COW—1¼" high by 1¼" along the base.
No. 143-14. PIG—1⅛" high by 1¼" along the base.
No. 143-15. GOAT—1¼" high by 1⅛" along the base.

WHIMSIE-LAND HEDGEROW 1986.
No. 144-16. SQUIRREL—1½" high
           by ¾" along the base.

No. 144-17. FOX—1⅜" high by 1¼" along the base.
No. 144-18. HEDGEHOG—⅞" high
           by 1¼" along the base.
No. 144-19. BADGER—1" high by 1⅜" along the base.
No. 144-20. OWL—1½" high by ⅞" along the base.

WHIMSIE-LAND BRITISH WILDLIFE 1987.

FIG. 40.

FIG. 40-A. OTTER—1½" high by 1⅝" long.
      B. FIELD MOUSE—1¼" high by 1½" long.
      C. PARTRIDGE—1½" high by 1¾" long.
      D. GOLDEN EAGLE—1⅜" high by 1¾" long.
      E. PHEASANT—1¼" high by 2" long.

The order of the figurines in the Hedgerow set, shown in the color section differs from the numbering listed in Wade literature. The correct order of issue is: Fox (16), Owl (17) Hedgehog (18), Badger (19) and Squirrel (20).

At the time of photographing the British Wildlife set, the order of the figurines, as they would appear in the set, was not known. The correct order is: Pheasant (21), Field Mouse (22), Golden Eagle (23), Otter (24), and Partridge (25).

All figurines are mold-marked "WADE ENGLAND" around the base and all, except for the Pig in the Farmyard set, have the fine parallel-molded ridges on the underside of the base. The Pig has a rim around the edge of the underside of the base with the center part recessed.

Whimsies 1953-1959 and 1971-1984,

"The World of Survival"

and

"The Connoisseurs Collection"

by

George Wade & Son Ltd.

WHIMSIES *1953-1959.*

In the early 1950's, the Wade Group of Potteries were badly hit by the cancelling of several large government contracts for insulators, and the demand for industrial ceramics dropped considerably. The Royal Victoria Pottery (Wade Heath Co. Ltd.) was returning to the manufacture of tableware and certain ornamental lines so was fully occupied. However, the Manchester Pottery (George Wade and Son Ltd.) and the Portadown Pottery (Wade Ireland Ltd.) were experiencing a big drop in their industrial orders. To keep the potteries in production the idea of producing attractive, inexpensive porcelain miniatures was devised.

With Wade's pre-World War II experience in the design and production of miniature ceramic animal figurines, it was a natural step to try and re-create their pre-War success in this field. This new venture proved to be an outstanding success far surpassing Wade's expectations. It was decided to gift package these figurines in sets of five models, with the exception of Set 5. which had only four models, and, of course, a name had to be chosen for this new line. The name decided upon was "WHIMSIES", and thus was born a name that has become synonymous with many Wade products from that date to the present time.

Due to the necessity of keeping both the Manchester and Portadown potteries in production, the manufacture of the new Whimsies was divided between the two potteries with George Wade and Son Ltd. producing the odd numbered sets i.e. Sets 1, 3, 5, 7, 9 and Wade (Ireland) Ltd. producing the even numbered sets i.e. Sets 2, 4, 6, 8 and 10. From all reports, this decision to make the Whimsies in the two potteries caused quite some competition for more production and higher quality of workmanship. Only a limited edition of each set was produced with the first five sets being made in even lesser quantities than the last five sets.

SET 1. 1953.
- No. 145-1. LEAPING FAWN—measures 1⅞" high by 1½" overall and is mold marked "WADE" on the side of the base.
- No. 145-2. HORSE—measures 1½" high by 2⅛" overall and is mold marked "WADE" on the side of the base.
- No. 145-3. SPANIEL—measures 1" high by 1¾" long and is unmarked.
- No. 145-4. POODLE—measures 1½" high by 1¾" overall and is unmarked.
- No. 145-5. SQUIRREL—measures 1¼" high by 1⅞" overall and is unmarked.

SET 2. 1954.
- No. 146-6. BULL—measures 1¾" high by 2⅛" overall and is transfer stamped "WADE MADE IN ENGLAND" on the underside of the base.
- No. 146-7. LAMB—measures 1⅞" high by 1¼" overall and is transfer stamped "WADE MADE IN ENGLAND."
- No. 146-8. KITTEN—measures 1⅜" high by 1¾" overall and is unmarked.

- No. 146-9. HARE—measures 1⅛" high by 1¾" overall and transfer marked "WADE MADE IN ENGLAND"
- No. 146-10. DACHSHUND—measures 1⅛" high by 1½" overall and is unmarked.

SET 3. 1955.
- No. 147-11. BADGER—measures 1¼" high by 2" overall and is unmarked.
- No. 147-12. FOX CUB—measures 1⅜" high by 1⅝" overall and is unmarked.
- No. 147-13. STOAT—measures 1⅛" high by 1¾" overall and is unmarked.
- No. 147-14. SHETLAND PONY—measures 1⅜" high by 2" overall and is mold marked "MADE IN ENGLAND" on edge of base.
- No. 147-15. RETRIEVER—measures 1¼" high by 1⅞" overall and is mold marked "WADE" on one side of base and "MADE IN ENGLAND" on the other side.

SET 4. 1955.
- No. 148-16. LION—measures 1¼" high by 1⅝" overall and is unmarked.
- No. 148-17. CROCODILE—measures ¾" high by 1⅝" overall and is ink stamped "MADE IN ENGLAND" on the underside of base.
- No. 148-18. MONKEY—measures 1⅞" high by 1⅝" overall and is unmarked but has been found marked with an ink stamp on the underside of base.
- No. 148-19. RHINOCEROS—measures 1¾" high by 2⅜" overall and is transfer stamped "WADE MADE IN ENGLAND."
- No. 148-20. BABY ELEPHANT—measures 1¼" high by 1⅞" overall and is ink stamped "MADE IN ENGLAND" on the underside of front feet.

SET 5. 1956.
- No. 149-21. MARE—measures 1⅞" high by 2" overall and is mold marked "WADE" on the side of the base.
- No. 149-22. COLT—measures 1⁷⁄₁₆" high by 1⅝" overall and is mold marked "WADE" on the side of base.
- No. 149-23. BEAGLE—measures ¾" high by 1" overall and is unmarked.
- No. 149-24. FOAL—measures 1¼" high by 1¾" overall and is mold marked "WADE" on the side of base.

SET 6. 1956. (Polar Set).
- No. 150-25. KING PENGUIN—measures 1³⁄₁₆" high by ⅝" diameter base and is unmarked.
- No. 150-26. HUSKY—measures 1¼" high by 1⅛" overall and is unmarked.
- No. 150-27. POLAR BEAR—measures 1¾" high by 1¾" overall and is unmarked.
- No. 150-28. BABY SEAL—measures ⅞" high by 1⅛" overall and is unmarked.

No. 150-29. BABY POLAR BEAR—measures ⅞" high
by 1⅛" overall and is unmarked.

SET 7. 1957. (Pedegree Dogs).
No. 151-30. ALSATIAN—measures 1⅜" high by
1⅝" overall and is unmarked.
No. 151-31. WEST HIGHLAND TERRIER—measures
1" high by 1¼" overall and is unmarked.
No. 151-32. CORGI—measures 1" high by 1¼" overall
and is unmarked.
No. 151-33. BOXER—measures 1⅜" high by 1½" and is
unmarked.
No. 151-34. SAINT BERNARD—measures 1½" high by
1⅞" overall and is unmarked.

SET 8. 1958. (Zoo Set).
No. 152-35. LLAMA—measures 1¾" high by 1⅛" overall
and is unmarked.
No. 152-36. LION CUB—measures 1" high
by 1" overall and is unmarked.
No. 152-37. GIANT PANDA—measures 1½" high
by 1" across the base and is unmarked.
No. 152-38. BACTRIAN CAMEL—measures 1½" high
by 1⅝" overall and is unmarked.
No. 152-39. COCKATOO—measures 1⅛" high by
1¼" across the wings and is unmarked.

SET 9. 1958. (North American Animals).
No. 153-40. SNOWY OWL—measures 1⅛" high
by 1³⁄₁₆ across the wings and is unmarked.
No. 153-41. RACOON—measures 1⅛" high
by 1⅛" overall and is unmarked.
No. 153-42. GRIZZLY BEAR—measures 1⅞" high
on a ⅞" diameter base and is unmarked.
No. 153-43. BEAR CUB—measures 1⅛" high by
1⅛" overall and is unmarked.
No. 153-44. COUGAR—measures ¾" high by
1⅞" overall and is unmarked.

SET 10. 1959. (Farm Animals).
No. 154-45. PIGLET—measures ⅞" high by 1½" overall
and is unmarked.
No. 154-46. ITALIAN GOAT—measures 1⅜" high
by 1½" overall and is unmarked.
No. 154-47. FOXHOUND—measures 1" high
by 1¾" overall and is unmarked.
No. 154-48. SWAN—measures ⅞" high by 1½" overall
and is unmarked.

FIG. 41-49. SHIRE HORSE.

FIG. 41. SHIRE HORSE.

WHIMSIES *1971-1984.*

After the success of the ten sets of Whimsies issued between 1953 through 1959, and the renewed popularity of the miniature figurines used as premiums for party crackers and boxes of tea bags, George Wade and Son Ltd., decided to extend the line of miniature porcelain animals, into a full fledged retail line to be once again marketed under the name "WHIMSIES".

The new line of Whimsies was introduced as a retail line in 1971, with a first set of five figurines, boxed either individually or as packages containing the complete set of five but with each figurine in its own box. Over the next few years the range was extended, at various intervals, with the issue of further sets of five figurines until the complete range comprised of sixty porcelain miniatures. Each set of five figurines was issued in different colored boxes. Starting from the first set of five, the color of the boxes were dark blue, red, green, yellow, dark red, light blue, orange, magenta, medium blue, light green, brown and dark blue again.

This second retail line of "WHIMSIES" was a great success and was eventually withdrawn from the Wade giftware range in 1984, Wade having felt that after thirteen years the popularity of the Whimsies had run its course and should be replaced by a new line of miniature figurines, a form of which, at that time, had yet to be decided upon.

Obviously, due to the length and enormous amount of figurines manufactured during the run of the second set of Whimsies, many variations have appeared. These occurred either as a result of a worn mold with a new mold being slightly different or the retooling of an existing mold due to production problems. These variations are noted in the text, but there is always the possibility that further variations, not noted here, will surface.

All figurines, unless noted otherwise, are mold marked "WADE ENGLAND" around the base and have the fine molded parallel ridges on the underside of the base. Following is the list of the sixty figurines in order of issue.

SET 1. 1971.
No. 155-1. FAWN—measures 1⅜" high by 1¼" long.
No. 155-2. RABBIT—measures 1⅛" high by
1⅞" overall. The Rabbit is found in two
variations, one with its ears together and the
second with its ears apart. See FIG. 42. The
original Rabbit was produced with ears
together, but this created problems in the
"fettling" process (cleaning up the clay seam
lines with a blade) as ear tips were being
removed accidentally. A further tool was
produced for making a new Rabbit with ears
apart.

FIG. 42.

No. 155-3. MONGREL—measures 1⅜″ high by 1½″ overall.

No. 155-4. KITTEN—measures 1⅜″ high by 1⅜″ overall and is marked "ENGLAND" only.

No. 155-5. SPANIEL—measures 1⅜″ high by 1⅜″ overall. Marked "WADE" on the front and "ENGLAND" on the back.

SET 2. 1972.

No. 156-6. DUCK—measures 1¼″ high by 1½″ overall. Marked "WADE" on one side of base and "ENGLAND" on the other.

No. 156-7. CORGI—measures 1½″ high by 1½″ overall. Marked "WADE" on the front and "ENGLAND" on the back.

No. 156-8. BEAVER—measures 1¼″ high by 1¼″ overall. A variation in the mold mark occurs on this figurine. Along with the usual "WADE ENGLAND" mold mark around the base it is also found with "WADE ENGLAND" molded into a recess on the underside of the base. See FIG. 43 B.

A   B   C

FIG. 43.

No. 156-9. BUSHBABY—measures 1¼″ high by 1⅛″ overall.

No. 156-10. FOX—measures 1⅜″ high by 1½″ overall.

SET 3. 1972.

No. 157-11. BEARCUB—measures 1⅜″ high by ⅞″ across. A variation in the mold mark occurs on this figurine. The later models are marked "WADE" at the front between the feet and "ENGLAND" on the back to the left of the tail. The earlier models were marked "WADE ENGLAND" molded into a recess on the underside of the base. See FIG. 43 C.

No. 157-12. OTTER—measures 1¼″ high by 1½″ overall.

No. 157-13. SETTER—measures 1⅜″ high by 1⅞″ overall.

No. 157-14. OWL—measures 1½″ high by ⅞″ across the base. A variation in the mold mark occurs on this figurine. Along with the usual "WADE ENGLAND" mark around the base this figurine was also made, in an earlier version, with "WADE ENGLAND" molded into a recess on the underside of the base. See FIG. 43 A. Of the three figurines with this type of mark variation, the Owl is the most difficult to find, especially in mint condition, the Beaver the second hardest to find and the Bear Cub the easiest to find.

No. 157-15. TROUT—measures 1⅛″ high by 1⅜″ overall.

SET 4. 1973.

No. 158-16. LION—measures 1⅜″ high by 1¾″ overall.

No. 158-17. ELEPHANT—measures 1⅜″ high by 1¾″ overall.

No. 158-18. GIRAFFE—measures 1½″ high by 1½″ overall.

No. 158-19. CHIMP—measures 1½″ high by 1⅜″ across.

No. 158-20. HIPPO—measures 1¹/₁₆″ high by 1¾″ overall. A variation in size occurs with this figurine. A smaller version, made later, is also found measuring ⅞″ high by 1½″ overall.

SET 5. 1974.

No. 159-21. SQUIRREL—measures 1⅜″ high by 1⅜″ overall.

No. 159-22. HEDGEHOG—measures ⅞″ high by 1¾″ overall. Mold marked "WADE ENGLAND" in a recess on the underside of the base.

No. 159-23. PINEMARTEN—measures 1⅜″ high by 1½″ overall.

No. 159-24. FIELD MOUSE—measures 1½″ high by ¾″ across the base. Marked "WADE" on one side and "ENGLAND" on the other side of the base.

No. 159-25. ALSATIAN—measures 1¼″ high by 1⅞″ overall.

SET 6. 1975.

No. 160-26. COLLIE—measures 1¼″ high by 1⅜″ overall.

No. 160-27. COW—measures 1¼″ high by 1½″ overall.

No. 160-28. PIG—measures ¹⁵/₁₆″ high by 1½″ overall. A variation in size occurs with this figurine. A later, smaller version was manufactured.

No. 160-29. HORSE—measures 1⅝″ high by 1⅜″ overall.

No. 160-30. LAMB—measures 1⅜″ high by 1⅛″ overall.

SET 7. 1976.

No. 161-31. RHINO—measures ⅞″ high by 1⅝″ overall.

No. 161-32. LEOPARD—measures ⅞″ high by 1⅞″ overall.

No. 161-33. GORILLA—measures 1½″ high by 1¼″ overall.

No. 161-34. CAMEL—measures 1⅜″ high by 1⅝″ overall.

No. 161-35. ZEBRA—measures 1⅝″ high by 1½″ overall.

SET 8. 1977.

No. 162-36. DONKEY—measures 1¼″ high by 1⅝″ overall.

No. 162-37. OWL—measures 1½″ high by 1″ across the base.

No. 162-38. CAT—measures 1½″ high by ⅞″ diameter base.

No. 162-39. MOUSE—measures 1½″ high by
    1″ diameter base.

No. 162-40. RAM—measures 1³/₁₆″ high by 1⅜″ overall.

SET 9. 1978.

No. 163-41. DOLPHIN—measures 1⅛″ high
    by 1¾″ overall.

No. 163-42. PELICAN—measures 1¾″ high by
    1⅜″ overall.

No. 163-43. ANGEL FISH—measures 1⅜″ high by 1¼″
    overall.

No. 163-44. TURTLE—measures ⁹/₁₆″ high by 2″ overall
    and is mold marked "WADE ENGLAND" in
    a recess on the underside of the base.

No. 163-45. SEAHORSE—measures 2″ high by
    ¾″ diameter base.

SET 10. 1979.

No. 164-46. KANGAROO—measures 1⅝″ high
    by 1⅛″ along the base.

No. 164-47. ORANGUTAN—measures 1¼″ high
    by 1¼″ across.

No. 164-48. TIGER—measures 1½″ high
    by 1⅛″ overall.

No. 164-49. KOALA BEAR—measures 1⅜″ high by
    1⅛″ overall.

No. 164-50. LANGUR—measures 1⅜″ high
    by 1½″ overall.

SET 11. 1979.

No. 165-51. BISON—measures 1⅜″ high by 1¾″ overall.
    A variation in size occurs with this figurine.
    A later, smaller version was made measuring
    1⅛″ high by 1⅜″ overall.

No. 165-52. BLUEBIRD—measures ⅝″ high by 1½″
    across the wings. Marked "WADE
    ENGLAND" in a recess on the underside of
    the base.

No. 165-53. BULLFROG—measures ⅞″ high by 1″
    across the base. Marked "WADE
    ENGLAND" in a recess on the underside of
    the base.

No. 165-54. WILD BOAR—measures 1⅛″ high by 1⅝″
    overall.

No. 165-55. RACCOON—measures 1″ high by
    1½″ overall.

SET 12. 1980.

No. 166-56. PENGUIN—measures 1⅝″ high by ¾″
    diameter base. Marked "WADE" at the front
    and "ENGLAND" at the back.

No. 166-57. SEAL PUP—measures 1″ high by
    1½″ overall.

No. 166-58. HUSKY—measures 1⁷/₁₆″ high
    by 1⅛″ overall.

No. 166-59. WALRUS—measures 1¼″ high by
    1¼″ overall.

No. 166-60. POLAR BEAR—measures 1⅛″ high by
    1⅝″ overall.

Various figurines from this series have been used as premiums at different times. In some cases, the colors have remained the same. However, after the series was discontinued as a retail line, the figurines used as premiums were given a single color glaze to avoid the cost of hand painting. For details of these premium figurines, refer to the "Premium and Promotional Items" section.

"THE WORLD OF SURVIVAL" SERIES *1978-1982.*

This range of twelve high quality slip-cast figurines of wild animals, issued in two sets of six, were hand decorated in matt enamels to give them a realistic texture and appearance. The figurines were manufactured under license to Survival Anglia Limited based on their award-winning television series "World of Survival", a documentary featuring many of the world's endangered species.

Each figurine bears a transfer type mark "WORLD of SURVIVAL SERIES by WADE OF ENGLAND COPYRIGHT SURVIVAL ANGLIA LIMITED, 1976 ALL RIGHTS RESERVED" and was individually packaged in a presentation carton along with information leaflets illustrating and describing the series. Due to the cost of forming the complicated molds and the hand decorating process these figurines proved to be an expensive venture and had a short production run. Following is the listing of both series in order of issue.

SERIES 1. 1978.

  1. African Elephant . . . . .10″ long by 6″ high
  2. Tiger . . . . .8″ long by 3½″ high
  3. Black Rhinoceros . . . . .9½″ long by 4½″ high
  4. African Lion . . . . .8″ long by 4½″ high
  5. Polar Bear . . . . .8½″ long by 4½″ high
  6. American Bison . . . . . . .8″ long by 4½″ high

SERIES 2. 1980.

  7. Gorilla . . . . .5¾″ long by 5½″ high
  8. American Cougar (Puma) .9″ long by 4″ high
  9. Hippopotamus . . . . .10″ long by 4½″ high
10. African (Cape) Buffalo . . .9¼″ long by 5″ high
11. American Brown Bear . . .5½″ long by 4″ high
12. Harp Seal & Pup . . . . . . .9″ long by 3¾″ high

No. 167. AFRICAN ELEPHANT.

No. 168. BLACK RHINOCEROS.

No. 169. AFRICAN LION.

No. 170. POLAR BEAR.

No. 171. AMERICAN BISON.

No. 172. HIPPOPOTAMUS.

No. 173. AMERICAN BROWN BEAR.

No. 174. TIGER.

No. 175. GORILLA.

No. 176. AMERICAN COUGAR (PUMA).

No. 177. AFRICAN BUFFALO (CAPE BUFFALO).

No. 178. HARP SEAL & PUP.

(Photographs courtesy of SURVIVAL ANGLIA LIMITED).

THE CONNOISSEUR'S COLLECTION *1978-1982.*

A series of twelve slip-cast reproductions of life-size British birds, issued in two sets of six. Each bird is modeled in its authentic setting and hand decorated in matt enamels giving a realistic finish. As with "The World of Survival" series, the bird figurines were packaged in presentation cartons along with information leaflets. This series of birds had a limited run due to high production costs. Each figurine is marked with a transfer type mark "The Connoisseur's Collection by WADE OF ENGLAND" followed by the name of the bird with its numerical position in the series. Following is the listing of both sets in order of issue.

SERIES 1. 1978.

1. Coaltit . . . . 5¾″ high
2. Wren . . . . 4½″ high
3. Goldcrest . . . . 5¼″ high
4. Robin . . . . 5″ high
5. Nuthatch . . . . 5½″ high
6. Bullfinch . . . . 7¼″ high

SERIES 2. 1980.

7. Bearded Tit . . . . 6½″ high
8. Kingfisher . . . . 7″ high
9. Redstart . . . . 7″ high
10. Yellow Wagtail . . . . 4½″ high
11. Woodpecker . . . . 6½″ high
12. Dipper . . . . 5½″ high

No. 179. NUTHATCH.
No. 180. COALTIT.
No. 181. KING FISHER.
No. 182. YELLOW WAGTAIL.
No. 183. WOODPECKER.
No. 184. DIPPER.
No. 185. BULLFINCH.
No. 186. ROBIN.
No. 187. WREN.
No. 188. GOLDCREST.

Premiums

and

Promotional Items

by

George Wade & Son Ltd.

PREMIUMS AND PROMOTIONAL ITEMS.

For many years, it has been proven by manufacturers of products as diverse as cigarettes, party crackers and packaged foods that the inclusion of a "give away item" or "premium" was a great incentive for the public to purchase that product. Needless to say, the manufacturing of the actual premiums has become, over the years, a very profitable sideline to industries specializing in plastic, paper, metal and porcelain products.

In the mid 1960's, George Wade & Son Ltd. decided to enter the manufacturing side of the premium business by producing a series of miniature porcelain animals at a low enough cost that they could compete in the premium market. The entire production of these miniature figurines was done by Wade. The process started by pressing damp clay dust into steel dies which were also manufactured by Wade. After drying, came the "fettling" process, the cleaning and cutting away of any unwanted mark or piece of clay sticking to the figurine after removal from the mold. The figurine was then ready for decoration. First underglaze colors were hand applied directly onto each figurine. Next the figurines were sprayed with a transparent glaze as they moved down a conveyor belt. Finally the miniatures were fired at 1250 degrees Celsius, cooled, packaged, and distributed.

At first, approximately 20 different figurines were made but by 1968, this number had increased to over 40 models, although Wade literature, at that time, only illustrated 40 figurines. It was from this range that Brooke Bond Foods Ltd. of Canada selected their first series of premiums to be included in their boxes of Red Rose Tea bags to be sold on the Canadian market. It is probable that the Red Rose Tea premiums were the major items to make the name of George Wade & Son Ltd. so well known on the North American continent, even though, over the past decades, the company along with its affiliate Wade Heath Ltd., had been supplying tableware, giftware and decorative pottery to their North American distributors.

The first Canadian promotion of 32 miniature porcelain animals proved to be such a success that Wade went on to develop the Red Rose Tea premiums into a full retail line of 60 miniature animals marketed under their trade name of "WHIMSIES" (See "Whimsies" 1971-1984 in the color section). Of the 32 premiums 7 were never included in the retail line. These are noted in the Red Rose Tea Promotion 1967-1973.

various areas of North America but should be considered hard to find. In 1977, the Zebra was included in the Whimsie retail line but with a color change from black to brown/tan, black being felt unsuitable for the retail market. The Zebra is 1⅝" high by 1⅜" overall and has a molded "Wade England" mark on the side of the base.

No. 190. BROWN BEAR—the approximate date of issue was the mid 1960's. There is no record of this figurine ever having been used as a premium; however, it was produced for this purpose and was not included in any retail line. The Bear has a dark brown body with lighter brown face, front and base. The figurine measures 1⅝" high by 1" across the base and is unmarked. Although similar to the bear in the 1950's set of Whimsies (No. 153-42) when set side by side, the differences are easily seen. It is suggested that collectors study both pictures of these figurines to avoid confusion.

No. 191. RHINO—this caricature figurine of a rhinoceros is one of a set of four comic figurines made as premiums for party crackers. Rhino, along with the other three of this set of prehistoric type figurines, was issued in the mid 1960's. Rhino is 1" high by 1⅝" long and is unmarked.

No. 192. BRONTI—the second of the comic prehistoric set of premiums is based on the brontosaurus. The figurine is two tone brown with blue ears and has dark brown spots on it's back. It measures 1" high by 1½" long and is unmarked.

No. 193. TIGER—this caricature version of the prehistoric animal set is based on a saber-toothed tiger. The figurine is tan colored with a series of black, horizontal stripes on the back of the head and body. It measures 1½" high by 1" diameter base and is unmarked.

No. 194. DINO—a comical version of a dinosaur, Dino is colored two-tone brown and like Bronti has dark brown spots on its back and has blue eyes and base. It measures 1⅜" high by 1⅜" long and is unmarked.

Although the above six premiums were made primarily for the U.K. market, they are found in North America but should be considered scarce, especially in mint condition.

MISCELLANEOUS PREMIUMS
MID 1960's.

No. 189. BLACK ZEBRA—this Zebra, basically colored all-over black but lightened by dark grey stripes, was issued as a premium in Great Britain around the mid 1960's. Although primarily found in the U.K., it has surfaced in

CANADIAN RED ROSE TEA PROMOTION *1967-1973.*

In 1967 Brooke Bond Foods Ltd. started to include miniature porcelain figurines in their boxes of Red Rose Tea bags sold in Canada. This first Canadian Red Rose Tea promotion consisted of 32 figurines chosen from the stock range of Wade premium models. The small porcelain animals proved to be an instant success with the public. From 1967 to 1973 when the animal series was discontinued, Wade supplied many millions of the figurines to Brooke Bond.

For illustrations of the first 25 figurines used in this promotion, the reader should refer to the 1971-1984 retail "Whimsies" in the color section. Note that the numbers preceding the name of the figurine denote the order of issue. Bracketed numbers after the figurine name correspond to those used for the retail "Whimsies" line for easier identification and also to avoid duplication of numbers for similar figurines.

1. FAWN . . . . (155-1)
2. RABBIT . . . . (155-2)
3. MONGREL . . . . (155-3)
4. KITTEN . . . . (155-4)
5. SPANIEL . . . . (155-5)
6. DUCK . . . . (156-6)
7. CORGI . . . . (156-7)
8. BEAVER . . . . (156-8)
9. BUSH BABY . . . . (156-9)
10. FOX . . . . (156-10)
11. BEAR CUB . . . . (157-11)
12. OTTER . . . . (157-12)
13. SETTER . . . . (157-13)
14. OWL . . . . (157-14)
15. TROUT . . . . (157-15)
16. LION . . . . (158-16)
17. GIRAFFE . . . . (158-18)
18. CHIMP . . . . (158-19)
19. HIPPO . . . . (158-20)
20. SQUIRREL . . . . (159-21)
21. HEDGEHOG . . . . (159-22)
22. ALSATIAN . . . . (159-25)
23. BISON . . . . (165-51)
24. BLUE BIRD . . . . (165-52)
25. WILD BOAR . . . . (165-54)

No. 195-26. FROG—same mold as the retail "Whimsie" bull frog but colored green/ yellow for the premium promotion. Marked "WADE ENGLAND" in relief in recess under base. Not a retail item in this color. The frog measures ⅞" high by 1⅛" across the base.

No. 196-27. BUTTERFLY—multi-colored butterfly molded in full flight. Marked "WADE ENGLAND" in relief in recess under base. The figurine measures ½" high by 1¾" across wing span.

No. 197-28. POODLE—white standard poodle figurine marked "WADE ENGLAND" molded around edge of the base. The poodle measures 1⅝" high by 1⅝" long. This miniature is becoming hard to find in mint condition.

No. 198-29. SEAL—tan colored seal on blue base marked "WADE ENGLAND" molded around edge of the base and measures 1½" high by 1¼" along the base.

No. 199-30. ANGEL FISH—this green fish on a blue base would appear to be more like a fantail goldfish but is referred to as "angel fish" in Wade literature. The figurine measures 1¼" high by 1⅜" long and is mold marked "WADE ENGLAND" on edge of the base. Wade appearing on one side and England on the other.

No. 200-31. TERRAPIN—this beautifully molded little figurine (sometimes referred to as a turtle) measures only ⅜" high at the head by 1⅝" long from head to tip of tail. It is mold marked "WADE ENGLAND" on underside of base.

No. 201-32. ALLIGATOR—the all over-green figurine measures ½" high at the head by 1½" long from tip of snout to the point where the tail curves. There are two variations of the "WADE ENGLAND" mark which appears on the underside of the base. One is in relief and the other, less easily found, is recessed.

The last seven figurines described above were never issued as retail items.

A number of variations can be found in some of these premium figurines. Most notable are the 2 sizes of the hippo and bison. The large hippo measures 1¹/₁₆" high from base to tip of ear by 1¾" long from tip of nose to tail. The corresponding measurements of the smaller hippo are ⅞" high by 1½" long. The large bison measures 1⅜" high at the shoulder by 1¾" long. The smaller bison is 1⅛" high by 1⅜" long. The change in size occurred when the molds were remade with the bison and hippo reduced in size to be more in scale with the figurines in the Whimsie series.

Other variations occur with the owl, bear cub and beaver. These three figurines were made with two types of "WADE ENGLAND" molded marks. The early models had the molded mark in a recess on the underside of the figurines as illustrated in FIG. 43. A, B, and C. When new molds were made for these figurines the regular "WADE ENGLAND" mark was cast around the bottom edge of the base of the figurine as are most marks in the Whimsie line. It has been observed that the owl with the mark on the underside of the base is the most difficult to find with the beaver second hardest and the bear cub most easily found.

It should be noted that in certain lists of this set of premiums three of the figurines have been referred to by different names.

FAWN sometimes referred to as Bambi.
CHIMP sometimes referred to as Monkey.
BISON sometimes referred to as Buffalo.

CANADIAN RED ROSE TEA PROMOTION *1971-1979.*

FIG. 44.

As public interest in the successful promotion of porcelain animal figurines began to wane, Brooke Bond Foods Ltd. approached George Wade & Sons Ltd. with a request to develop a new range of premiums for their Canadian sold tea bags.

Various ideas were submitted to Brooke Bond and by mutual agreement a new line of 24 miniature porcelain nursery rhyme and fairy tale figurines was introduced.

The new line of premiums was first used in various parts of Canada in 1971, and became nationally distributed by 1973. Wade supplied approximately 100 million pieces of these atrractive figurines to Brooke Bond by the time this second series of premiums was discontinued in 1979.

There is a discrepancy in the dates of these first two Red Rose Tea series of premiums. The years used are those from information supplied by Brooke Bond Foods Ltd. which are earlier than the dates given by George Wade & Son Ltd. Following is the listing of this promotion:

No. 202-1. OLD KING COLE—1½″ high by 1¼″ across the base.
No. 203-2. LITTLE JACK HORNER—1⅜″ high by 1″ across the base.
No. 204-3. HUMPTY DUMPTY—1½″ high by ⅞″ "T" shaped base.
No. 205-4. JACK—1¼″ high by 1¼″ across the base.
No. 206-5. JILL—1⅛″ high by 1¼″ across the base.
No. 207-6. TOM THE PIPER'S SON—1⅝″ high by 1⅜″ across the base.
No. 208-7. LITTLE BOY BLUE—1⅝″ high by 1″ across the base.
No. 209-8. LITTLE MISS MUFFET—1½″ high by 1⅜″ across the base.
No. 210-9. THE PIED PIPER—1¾″ high by 1⅛″ across the base.
No. 211-10. DOCTOR FOSTER—1¾″ high by ⅞″ diameter base.
No. 212-11. MOTHER GOOSE—1⅝″ high by 1¼″ across the base.
No. 213-12. OLD WOMAN WHO LIVED IN A SHOE—1⅜″ high by 1⅝″ across the base.
No. 214-13. GOOSEY GANDER—1⅜″ high by 1″ across the base.
No. 215-14. WEE WILLIE WINKIE—1¾″ high by 1″ across the base.
No. 216-15. LITTLE BO-PEEP—1¾″ high by ¾″ diameter base.
No. 217-16. THREE BEARS—1⅜″ high by 1½″ across the base.
No. 218-17. PUSS IN BOOTS—1¾″ high by ¾″ diameter base.
No. 219-18. THE HOUSE THAT JACK BUILT—1¼″ high by 1¼″ across the base.
No. 220-19. LITTLE RED RIDING HOOD—1¾″ high by ⅞″ across the base.
No. 221-20. QUEEN OF HEARTS—1¾″ high by 1″ across the base.
No. 222-21. BAA BAA BLACK SHEEP—⅞″ high by 1⅛″ long.
No. 223-22. HICKORY DICKORY DOCK—1¾″ high by ¾″ square base.
No. 224-23. GINGER BREAD MAN—1⅝″ high by 1¹⁄₁₆″ across the base.
No. 225-24. CAT AND THE FIDDLE—1⅞″ high by 1″ across the base.

It is interesting to note that the Mother Goose and Gingerbread Man have become very hard to find even though the number of these figurines issued was huge.

All the above figurines are mold marked "WADE ENGLAND" around the base with the exception of:

HUMPTY DUMPTY—marked "WADE ENGLAND" vertically on the back.

HICKORY DICKORY DOCK—marked "WADE" on the front of the base and "ENGLAND" on the back of the base and CAT AND THE FIDDLE—only marked "ENGLAND".

As with most Wade miniatures made after 1960, the underside of the base of these figurines is molded with a series of small parallel ridges, a helpful means of identifying Wade figurines that do not bear a mold mark.

The nursery figurines were not issued as a retail line by Wade although an attempt was made to produce a boxed set of five under the name of "NURSERIES" in 1979. The figurines chosen for this giftware line were Little Jack Horner, Woman in the Shoe, Old King Cole, Little Bo Peep and Cat and the Fiddle.

FIG. 45.

These figurines did not prove too popular with the public and were soon withdrawn from the market. No attempt was made to retail any other figurines from this series.

Because of the enormous number of figurines issued during the six years of this promotion, some variations have surfaced. These occurred when molds were remade due to wear or breakage. The major variation is found in the Queen of Hearts figurine. There are three variations of the heart design on her dress. See FIG. 46.

FIG. 46.

Types "A" and "B" appear to be easily found with type "C" being very scarce. Another but unexplained variation is the appearance of a large, 2½" high Bo Peep figurine. It is mold marked "WADE ENGLAND" around the base. See FIG. 47.

FIG. 47.

Reports of Hickory Dickory Dock missing the mouse have been noted but cannot be confirmed.

CANADIAN RED ROSE TEA PROMOTION *1981.*

FIG. 48. ADVERTISEMENT FROM "TO-DAY" MAGAZINE

After a hiatus of just over a year, when the nursery figurine promotion was discontinued, Brooke Bond Foods Ltd. introduced, in 1981, a third series of Wade figurines to promote the sale of their boxes of Red Rose Tea bags. Unlike the previous two promotions this third set of premiums was of a short duration, from early 1981, to the late Fall of the same year.

For this promotion the complete set (15) of the Wade retail line of "WHOPPAS" was used as the tea premium. The Whoppas had been a retail line since 1976, and discontinued as such in 1981, so presumably, this series of premiums was an ideal solution to clearing the stock of these figurines.

With the previous Red Rose Tea premiums the figurines were enclosed without charge. However, this series was a "mail-in offer" meaning collectors had to send in a premium tab, cut from the box, along with $1.00 to claim their figurine.

For illustrations of the individual figurines in the Whoppas series see the color section. For the measurements refer to the corresponding section in the text.

CANADIAN RED ROSE TEA PROMOTION *1982-1984.*

FIG. 49.

In the Fall of 1982, Brooke Bond Foods Ltd. began marketing their fourth series of Wade miniature porcelain premium figurines. This series consisted of 23 miniature animals selected from the Wade "Whimsies" line.

Of the 23 animals in the promotion six of them, rabbit, corgi, beaver, bush baby, fox, and giraffe had also been used in the 1967-1973 promotion, and two, turtle and angel fish, although similar in names, are from different molds.

FIG. 50. Illustrates the two types of TURTLES. Type "A"
is the Whimsie turtle used in this promotion
and also as a retail item. Type "B" is the
terrapin, sometimes referred to as a turtle,
from the 1967-1973 promotion and never used
in a retail line.

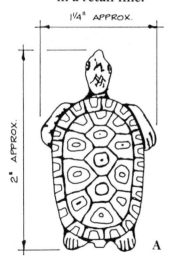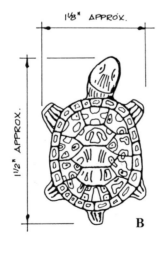

FIG. 50.

FIG. 51. Illustrates the two different types of ANGEL
FISH. Type "A" is the Whimsie angel fish from
the retail line and also used in this promotion.
Type "B" is the angel fish (fantail goldfish) used
in the 1967-1973 promotion and never used in
a retail line.

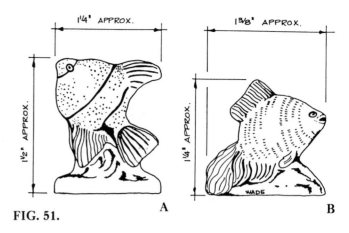

FIG. 51.

For illustrations of the 23 figurines, refer to the 1971-1984 retail "Whimsies" in the color section. Note that the numbers preceding the name of the figurine denote the order of issue. Bracketed numbers after the figurine name correspond to those used for retail "Whimsies" line to avoid duplication of numbers for similar figurines.

Following is the listing of the 1982-1984 figurines:

1. RABBIT . . . . (155-2)
2. CORGI . . . . (156-7)
3. BEAVER . . . . (156-8)
4. BUSH BABY . . . . (156-9)
5. FOX . . . . (156-10)
6. GIRAFFE . . . . (158-18)
7. PINE MARTEN . . . . (159-23)
8. COLLIE . . . . (160-26)
9. COW . . . . (160-27)
10. PIG . . . . (160-28)
11. HORSE . . . . (160-29)
12. LAMB . . . . (160-30)
13. RHINO . . . . (161-31)
14. LEOPARD . . . . (161-32)
15. GORILLA . . . . (161-33)
16. CAMEL . . . . (161-34)
17. ZEBRA . . . . (161-35)
18. PELICAN . . . . (163-42)
19. ANGEL FISH . . . . (163-43)
20. TURTLE . . . . (163-44)
21. SEA HORSE . . . . (163-45)
22. ORANGUTAN . . . . (164-47)
23. LANGUR. . . . . (164-50)

CANADIAN SALADA* TEA PROMOTION 1984.

*Registered Trade Mark of Kellogg Salada Canada Inc.

FIG. 52.

FIG. 53.

Between September through December of 1984, Kellogg Salada Canada Inc. offered a "mail-in" premium offer in their boxes of Salada tea bags sold on the Canadian market.

For this promotion six items from the Wade retail line of the "Whimsey-on-Why" village sets were chosen. Also available with this offer was a special issue of the full size Tea Caddy from the Wade retail line of "Village Stores" storage jars.

The six miniature houses were identical to those in the retail line with no special marking. For illustrations of these refer to the "Whimsy-on-Why" village sets in the color section. The letters preceding the model name denote the order in which the models were issued for this promotion. The bracketed numbers after the model name correspond to those used for the retail line.

A. TOBACCONIST'S SHOP from Set One . . . . . (268-4)
B. WHIMSEY STATION from Set Three . . . . . (270-18)
C. ANTIQUE STORE from Set Two . . . . (269-10)
D. POST OFFICE from Set Two . . . . (269-12)
E. PUMP COTTAGE from Set One . . . . (268-1)
F. GREENGROCER'S SHOP from Set Two . . . . (269-9)

The large Tea Caddy was a variation based on the retail line of storage jars, the difference being a change in the decal above the door. In the retail version the decal reads "Ye Olde Tearoom." For the tea promotion the decal was changed both to advertise the brand of tea and also was written in French and English to satisfy the bi-lingual requirements of the Canadian Government. This decal spreads right across the front of the caddy with the word "Salada" in the center with "Salon de thé" on the left and "Ye Olde Tearoom" on the right, above the door. See FIG. 53. for illustration.

This being a "mail-in" offer, the premiums were not included in the boxes of tea bags. Collectors were required to send in an order form, cut from the box, along with $3.50 plus one U.P.C. symbol (bar code) for each small house and $13.00 plus two U.P.C. symbols for the large tea caddy.

U.S.A. RED ROSE TEA PROMOTION 1983-1985.

FIG. 54.

After the successful completion of market testing in two areas of the U.S. (Pittsburgh and Pacific North West), Red Rose Tea was ready to launch their first major distribution of Wade miniature animal figurines as premiums to be offered in boxes of Red Rose Tea sold on the U.S. market.

Of this first series of fifteen figurines, thirteen were similar designs used for the Wade retail line of "Whimsies," the only difference being the coloring of the glazed finish. The remaining two figurines (rabbit and squirrel) were never used in a retail line or any previous tea promotions. For this promotion the figurines were not hand painted as were the figurines in the retail line. For economic reasons, only single glaze colors were used.

Following is the list of the figurines used in this promotion:

No. 226-1. CHIMP—sometimes referred to as Monkey and measures 1½" high by 1" across the base.
No. 227-2. LION—measures 1⁵⁄₁₆" high by 1½" along the base.
No. 228-3. BISON—measures 1³⁄₁₆" high by 1⅝" long.
No. 229-4. BUSH BABY—measures 1¼" high by 1" along the base.
No. 230-5. OWL—measures 1½" high by ¾" diameter base.
No. 231-6. BEAR CUB—measures 1⅜" high by ⅞" across the base.
No. 232-7. RABBIT—sometimes referred to as Hare and measures 1¾" high by ⅞" along the base.
No. 233-8. SQUIRREL—measures 1½" high by ¾" diameter base.
No. 234-9. BIRD—measures ⅝" high by 1⁷⁄₁₆" across the wing span.
No. 235-10. OTTER—measures 1¼" high by 1½" long.
No. 236-11. HIPPO—sometimes referred to as Baby Hippo measures ⅞" high by 1½" from nose to tail.
No. 237-12. SEAL—1½" high by 1¼" along the base.
No. 238-13. TURTLE—measures ⁹⁄₁₆" high by 1⅞" long.
No. 239-14. WILD BOAR—measures 1⅛" high by 1" along the base.
No. 240-15. ELEPHANT—measures 1⅞" high by 1⅛" along the base.

All figurines are mold marked "WADE ENGLAND" around the base except for the bird and turtle which are marked in relief in a recess on the underside of the base.

U.S.A. RED ROSE TEA PROMOTION *1985.*

With the success of the 1983-1985 U.S.A. Red Rose Tea promotion, a new series of figurines was introduced in mid-1985. Once again this set of premiums consisted of fifteen miniature figurines taken from the "Whimsies" retail line, the only difference being the single glaze color, consistent with the first U.S.A. series.

Following is a listing of these figurines:

FIG. 55.

No. 241-1. KOALA BEAR—measures 1⅜" high by ¾" diameter base.
No. 242-2. GIRAFFE—measures 1½" high by 1½" along the base.
No. 243-3. PINE MARTEN—measures 1⅜" high by 1¼" along the base.
No. 244-4. LANGUR—measures 1⅜" high by 1⅛" along the base.
No. 245-5. GORILLA—measures 1½" high by ⅞" along the base.
No. 246-6. CAMEL—measures 1⅜" high by 1⅛" along the base.
No. 247-7. KANGAROO—measures 1⅝" high by 1" along the base.
No. 248-8. TIGER—measures 1⁷⁄₁₆" high by 1" along the base.
No. 249-9. ZEBRA—measures 1⅝" high by 1⅛" along the base.
No. 250-10. POLAR BEAR—measures 1⅛" high by 1" along the base.
No. 251-11. ORANGUTAN—measures 1¼" high by 1" across the base.
No. 252-12. RACCOON—measures 1" high by 1⅜" along the base.
No. 253-13. RHINO—measures ⅞" high by 1¼" along the base.
No. 254-14. BEAVER—measures 1¼" high by 1⅛" along the base.
No. 255-15. LEOPARD—measures ¹³⁄₁₆" high by 1⅞" along the base.

All figurines are mold marked "WADE ENGLAND" around the base. The figurines of the two U.S.A. series of premiums have the typical Wade series of parallel molded ridges on the underside of the base except for the Turtle and Bird of the 1983-1985 promotion. The cooperation of "REDCO FOODS, Inc." for their help with the U.S. Red Rose Tea premium series is appreciated.

CANADIAN RED ROSE TEA PROMOTION *1985-1986.*

FIG. 56.

In June 1985, Brooke Bond Inc. was taken over by Thomas J. Lipton Inc. who, therefore, became the new Canadian distributor of Red Rose Tea. As did the previous distributor of Red Rose Tea, the new owners decided to follow their lead and introduce a set of Wade porcelain figurines to be included in their boxes of tea bags. For this promotion the premiums were offered only in the boxes of Red Rose "Premium Blend" tea bags.

The fifteen figurines used in this promotion are similar to the fifteen animals offered in the 1985 U.S.A. Red Rose Tea promotion. For a list and sizes of these figurines refer to the above U.S.A. promotion.

The cooperation of "Thomas J. Lipton Inc." for their help with all the Canadian Red Rose Tea premium series is appreciated.

K.P. FOODS LIMITED—
POTATO CHIP PROMOTION 1983.

This promotion comprised of a set of six miniature "FRIARS" and was limited to the United Kingdon only. However, many of the figurines from this promotion are found in North America. The first figurine of the set was free but the remaining five could only be obtained by submitting proof of purchase of a certain number of potato chip packages plus a service charge. This is most probably one of the reasons that the first figurine (Father Abbot) is the most easily found.

The figurines in order of issue were:

No. 256. FATHER ABBOT—the "Founder of the Famous KP Friary" who measures 1¾″ high by ⅝″ square base.

No. 257. BROTHER PETER—who "Tends the KP Friary Potato Patch" and measures 1⅝″ high by ¾″ square base.

No. 258. BROTHER BENJAMIN—who "Bags the Best Foods in the Land" and measures 1⅝″ high by ¾″ square base.

No. 259. BROTHER CRISPIN—who "Makes Sure KP are the Crispiest Crisps ever Created" and measures 1⅝″ high by ¾″ square base.

No. 260. BROTHER ANGELO—"Keeper of the Good Book of Delicious KP Recipes" measures 1⅞″ high by ¾″ square base.

No. 261. BROTHER FRANCIS—who "Delivers KP Fast and Fresh from the Friary" and measures 1⅝″ high by ¾″ square base.

All figurines have the name of the character portrayed on the front of the base, and all are mold marked "WADE" on the back of the base. As with so many of the Wade premiums, this series also has the typical small parallel ridges molded on the underside of the base. The cooperation of "KP FOODS, Heathgate House, 57 Colne Rd., Twickenham, Middlesex" is appreciated.

ST. BRUNO PIPE TOBACCO PROMOTION *1986.*

In 1986 Imperial Tobacco Limited, makers of St. Bruno pipe tobacco, commissioned Wade to produce an appropriate porcelain figurine as a premium to help promote their brand of St. Bruno tobacco.

The premium agreed upon was a miniature porcelain figurine of a St. Bernard dog to be used as a key chain with the chain portion attached at the back of the head. The gold-colored collar painted around the neck of the dog holds a yellow box at the front with the lettering "St. Bruno."

The cooperation of "Imperial Tobacco Limited, makers of St. Bruno pipe tobacco" is appreciated.

No. 262. ST. BERNARD DOG—measures 1¼″ high by ⅞″ along the base, is unmarked but has the ridged molded base.

TOM SMITH & CO. LTD. PARTY CRACKERS *1967-1985.*

For a number of years George Wade & Son Ltd. have been supplying porcelain miniature figurines to be enclosed, along with party hats, snaps and mottos, to Tom Smith & Co. Ltd., manufacturers of quality Christmas Party Crackers. It has been the custom for the sets of figurines to be used for a period of two years with each set having a theme which was characterized by the type of miniatures used. In some cases figurines from the "Whimsie" retail line were chosen, but in most cases special figurines were molded exclusively for Tom Smith & Co. Ltd.

The cooperation of "TOM SMITH & CO. LTD. NORWICH" is appreciated.

SAFARI SET *1976-1977.*

No. 263-1. LION—1⅛" high by 1¾" along the base.
No. 263-2. TIGER—1⅜" high by 1" along the base (similar to Whimsie retail model).
No. 263-3. LEMUR—1⅜" high by 1⅛" across the base (similar to Whimsie retail model).
No. 263-4. WALRUS—1¼" high by 1¼" along the base (similar to Whimsies retail model).
No. 263-5. KOALA BEAR—1¼" high by ¾" diameter base (similar to Whimsie retail model but different color).
No. 263-6. RACCOON—1" high by 1⅜" along the base (similar to Whimsie retail model).
No. 263-7. POLAR BEAR—1⅛" high by 1¼" along the base (similar to Whimsie retail model).
No. 263-8. MUSK OX—1" high by 1" along the base.
No. 263-9. KANGAROO—1⅝" high by 1" along the base (similar to Whimsie retail model).
No. 263-10. ORANGUTAN—1¼" high by ¾" across the base (similar to Whimsie retail model but different color).

Figurines No. 263-2, 3, 4, 5, 6, 7, 9 and 10 were originally exclusive to Tom Smith & Co. Ltd. for two years and subsequently included in the 1971-1984 range of Whimsies. All figurines are mold marked "WADE ENGLAND" around the base and have the typical fine parallel molded ridges on the underside of the base.

CIRCUS ANIMAL SET *1978-1979.*

No. 264-1. MALE MONKEY (MACAQUE)—1⅝" high by ¾" diameter base.
No. 264-2. POODLE—1¾" high by ⅝" diameter base.
No. 264-3. SEAL—1⅝" high by 1⅛" along the base.
No. 264-4. FEMALE MONKEY (MACAQUE)—1½" high by ¾" diameter base.
No. 264-5. HORSE—1¾" high by 13/16" along the base.
No. 264-6. BEAR—1 3/16" high by 1" along the base.
No. 264-7. TIGER—1⅝" high by ¾" diameter base.
No. 264-8. ELEPHANT—1¼" high by 1" along the base.
No. 264-9. LION—1 9/16" high by ⅞" along the base.
No. 264-10. ELEPHANT—1 3/16" high by ⅞" along the base.

All figurines sit on or are incorporated onto a drum type base which is mold marked "WADE ENGLAND". The underside of the base has the molded ridged effect.

WILDLIFE SET *1980-1981.*

No. 265-1. FIELDMOUSE—1 1/16" high by 1⅛" along the base.
No. 265-2. PARTRIDGE—1⅛" high by 1⅛" along the base.
No. 265-3. WEASEL—1⅜" high by 1½" along the base.

No. 265-4. MOLE—⅞" high by 1 9/16" along the base.
No. 265-5. HARE—1¾" high by ⅞" along the base.
No. 265-6. SQUIRREL—1½" high by ¾" diameter base.
No. 265-7. BADGER—1 1/16" high by 1¼" along the base.
No. 265-8. FOX—1⅜" high by 1⅜" along the base.

Each figurine in this set is mold marked "WADE ENGLAND" around the base and, as usual, has the ridged effect on the underside of the base. The hare and squirrel are similar to the rabbit (hare) and squirrel in the 1983-1985 U.S.A. Red Rose Tea promotion but with different color glazes.

FARMYARD SET *1982-1983.*

No. 266-1. PIG—⅞" high by 1" along the base.
No. 266-2. GOOSE—1⅜" high by 1" along the base.
No. 266-3. DUCK—15/16" high by 1¼" along the base.
No. 266-4. GOAT—1½" high by 1⅛" along the base.
No. 266-5. HORSE—1½" high by 1¼" along the base.
No. 266-6. COW—1⅛" high by 1⅛" along the base.
No. 266-7. DOG—1" high by 1¾" along the base.
No. 266-8. BULL—1⅛" high by 1¼" along the base.

The pig figurine is similar to the "Whimsie" retail model but in a different color. The goose figurine is from the same mold as "Goosey Gander" from the 1971-1979 Canadian Red Rose Tea promotion. The duck has been found in an all-over blue color and the dog has been found in an all-over light brown color. All the figurines are mold marked "WADE ENGLAND" around the base along with the ridged effect on the underside of the base.

SURVIVAL SET *1984-1985.*

No. 267-1. NORTH AMERICAN BISON—1 3/16" high by 1⅛" along the base.
No. 267-2. GORILLA—1½" high by 1⅜" across the base.
No. 267-3. BLUE WHALE—⅞" high by 1¼" along the base.
No. 267-4. GREEN TURTLE—1¼" high by 1¼" along the base.
No. 267-5. ARMADILLO—1" high by 1⅜" along the base.
No. 267-6. POLAR BEAR—1" high by 1¼" along the base.
No. 267-7. GOLDEN EAGLE—1¾" high by ⅞" across the base.
No. 267-8. HARP SEAL—1½" high by 1¼" along the base.

The North American bison (sometimes called buffalo) is similar to the "Whimsie" retail model but a different color. The harp seal is similar to the seal in the 1967-1973 Canadian Red Rose Tea promotion but in a different color. All figurines are mold marked "WADE ENGLAND" around the base, and, as with the other figurines in this series, the fine molded ridges occur on the underside of the base.

Whimsey-on-Why Village Sets
by
George Wade & Son Ltd.
and
Miscellaneous Items
by
George Wade & Son Ltd.
and
Wade Heath & Company Ltd.

WHIMSEY-ON-WHY VILLAGE SETS *1980 TO PRESENT.*

Whimsey-on-Why is the name given to a mythical English village made up of a series of miniature porcelain houses and buildings so often found in a typical British village.

The sets, the first of which was issued in 1980, have been issued with eight models comprising each set. Along with the miniature porcelain houses, Wade has also published four issues of the "Whimsey-on-Why CHRONICLE". This was a "spoof" newspaper as Wade felt that a true village should have its own paper. As well as introducing the latest "Whimsey-on-Why" village set, the "Chronicle" also announced a number of other additions to the Wade giftware line. The four papers so far issued are dated: No. 1. Feb. 1980, No. 2. Feb. 1981, No. 3. Feb. 1982 and No. 4. Feb. 1984.

All models are decorated with intricate and colorful fired-on transfers and each model bears its number in the series, enclosed in a circle, usually located at either the rear or on the corner of the miniature house. The transfer is applied to the walls of the houses with the colored roofs being attached separately. All models are mold marked on the base or in a recess on the base "WADE ENGLAND." The exceptions to this are No. 16, the Windmill and No. 32, the Market Hall which are not marked.

SET 1. 1980.

No. 268-1. PUMP COTTAGE—measures 1⅛″ high by 1¼″ long by ¾″ deep.

No. 268-2. MORGAN'S THE CHEMIST—measures 1¾″ high by 1½″ long by ¾″ deep.

No. 268-3. DOCTOR HEALER'S HOUSE—measures 1¾″ high by 1½″ long by ¾″ deep.

No. 268-4. TOBACCONIST'S SHOP—measures 1½″ high by 1½″ long by ¾″ deep.

No. 268-5. WHY KNOTT INN—measures 1⅜″ high by 1½″ long by ¾″ deep.

No. 268-6. BLOODSHOTT HALL—measures 2″ high by 3⅛″ long by 1¼″ deep.

No. 268-7. ST. SEBASTIAN'S CHURCH—measures 2⅛″ high by 3″ long by 1⅛″ deep.

No. 268-8. THE BARLEY MOW—measures 1½″ high by 3″ long with 1″ deep "L" shaped base.

SET 2. 1981.

No. 269-9. GREENGROCER'S SHOP—measures 1½″ high by ¾″ deep, corner shaped base.

No. 269-10. ANTIQUE SHOP—measures 1½″ high by ¾″ deep, corner shaped base.

No. 269-11. WHIMSEY SERVICE STATION—measures 1½″ high by 1½″ long by ⅞″ deep.

No. 269-12. POST OFFICE—measures 1½″ high by 1½″ long by ⅞″ deep.

No. 269-13. WHIMSEY SCHOOL—measures 1⅝″ high by 1⅞″ long with "L" shaped base, long leg ⅞″ deep and short leg ⅝″ deep.

No. 269-14. WATER MILL—measures 1¾″ high by 2½″ long by 1″ deep at the widest point.

No. 269-15. THE STAG HOTEL—measures 1⅞″ high by 2½″ long by 1″ deep at widest point.

No. 269-16. WINDMILL—measures 2¼″ high by 1³⁄₁₆″ diameter base.

SET 3. 1982.

No. 270-17. TINKER'S NOOK—measures 1⅜″ high by 1″ long by ¾″ deep.

No. 270-18. WHIMSEY STATION—measures 1½″ high by 1½″ long by ¹³⁄₁₆″ deep base.

No. 270-19. MERRYWEATHER FARM—measures 1⅞″ high by 1⅞″ "L" shaped base by 1″ deep.

No. 270-20. THE VICARAGE—measures 1⅝″ high by 2″ long with "L" shaped base, long leg ⅞″ deep and short leg ⅝″ deep.

No. 270-21. BROOMYSHAW COTTAGE—measures 1⅝″ high by 1½″ long by ¾″ deep.

No. 270-22. THE SWEET SHOP—measures 1⅝″ high by 1½″ long by ¾″ deep.

No. 270-23. BRIAR ROW—measures 1⅜″ high by 3″ long by ¾″ deep.

No. 270-24. THE MANOR—measures 1⅞″ high by 2½″ long by 1″ deep at widest point.

SET 4. 1984.

No. 271-25. DISTRICT BANK—measures 1⅞″ high by 1½″ long by ⅞″ deep.

No. 271-26. OLD SMITHY—measures 1″ high by 1¾″ long by ¾″ deep.

No. 271-27. PICTURE PALACE—measures 2⅛″ high at peak by 2½″ long by 1½″ deep.

SET 4. 1985.

No. 271-28. BUTCHER SHOP—measures 1⅝″ high by 1″ square.

No. 271-29. THE BARBER SHOP—measures 1⅝″ high by 1″ square.

No. 271-30. MISS PRUNES HOUSE—measures 1½″ high by 1½″ long by ⅞″ deep.

No. 271-31. FIRE STATION—measures 1⅝″ high by 1¾″ long by 1⅜″ wide.

No. 271-32. MARKET HALL—measures 1⅞″ high by 2″ square.

Four new models were added to The Whimsey-on-Why Series in 1987. See FIG. 158 in Miscellaneous Items by The Wade Group of Companies.

"PAINTED LADIES"—

SAN FRANCISCO MINI MANSIONS 1984-1986.

The beautifully decorated but short-lived "San Francisco Mini Mansions" set is similar in theme to the Whimsey-on-Why village sets but on a slightly larger scale. Unlike the Whimsey-on-Why models, the roofs of the Mini Mansions were not a separate, added feature. This caused some problems in tooling the molds. A companion piece to the Mini Mansions was a miniature Cable Car so typical of San Francisco. All models, including the Cable Car are marked "WADE Porcelain England SF/1 through SF/6". This mark is located on the side wall of the Mini Mansions and on the back end of the Cable Car.

No. 272-1. PINK-LADY—measures 2¼" high by 1" wide by 1¼" deep.

No. 272-2. WHITE LADY—measures 2¼" high by 1" wide by 1¼" deep.

No. 272-3. BROWN LADY—measures 2½" high by 1¼" square.

No. 272-4. YELLOW LADY—measures 2½" high by 1¼" square.

No. 272-5. BLUE LADY—measures 2⅞" high by 1½" square.

No. 272-6. CABLE CAR—measures ⅞" high by 1½" long by ¾" wide.

MISCELLANEOUS ITEMS

After the years of World War II, when George Wade & Son Ltd. had devoted their resources to aiding the war effort, the pottery continued with the production of industrial ceramics for a number of years. In the early 1950's, when demand for industrial items began to decrease, the pottery started to get back into the ornamental and giftware lines.

Unlike the highly decorative, ornamental ware produced prior to the war, the pottery started off its new lines in a rather limited and subdued manner. Much of this was due to restrictions for economic reasons by the British Government and by taxes imposed on non-functional ceramic ware.

Items produced during this period up until the mid 1950's, were usually made in single glaze colors, green or brown,

and occasionally white, e.g. the Log Posy Bowls, etc. Within a few years the products produced at the Manchester Pottery became more elaborate and the variety of pieces increased in number.

No. 273. BRIDGE POSY HOLDER 1954-1958.
This bowl was produced with an all over green glaze as well as the beige version illustrated. Wade informs us that this bowl was also produced in a similar design but with a flat parapet rather than the curved shape as illustrated. The bowl is mold marked "WADE ENGLAND" under one arch and marked "REGD. IN GT. BRITAIN No. 871653" under the other arch. It measures 1⅜" high at the center by 6" long by 2" wide at each end where the molded ducks occur as part of the design.

No. 274. STRAIGHT POSY LOG WITH SQUIRREL 1954-1959.
As with most of the inexpensive bowls and vases produced by Wade during the 1950's, this posy bowl was made in both green and beige glazes. This log bowl was also made with a rabbit in place of the squirrel. The straight Posy Log bowl was also made without the addition of either squirrel or the rabbit and was also produced between 1954 through 1959. The log measures 1¼" high by 4¾" long by 1½" wide. It is mold marked "WADE ENGLAND" on the underside of the base.

FIG. 57. PORCELAIN NOVELTIES 1954.
Six attractive high fired porcelain novelty items, decorated in a variety of color glazes.

Barbecue Tankard S.25/22
(Half pint)

Egg Cup S.25/21

Redskin Dish S.25/37

Novelty Egg Cup S.25/30
(Santa Claus).

FIG. 57. A. HALF PINT BARBECUE TANKARD.
        B. REDSKIN DISH (3½" diameter).
        C. EGG CUP.
        D. SANTA CLAUS EGG CUP.

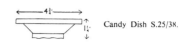
Candy Dish S.25/38.

Fluted Honey Jar S.25/35

FIG. 58.

FIG. 58. A. CANDY DISH (4¾″ diameter by 1¼″ high).
B. FLUTED HONEY JAR (3¼″ diameter
by 2⅜″ high).

No. 275. "C" SHAPED POSY LOG 1954-1959.
This Posy Log bowl was also made in the beige glaze. It measures 1⅜″ high by 6″ across the front by 1¼″ wide and is mold marked "WADE ENGLAND" on the underside of the base.

No. 276. "S" SHAPED POSY LOG 1954-1959.
As usual this posy bowl was made in the beige glaze as well as the green glazed bowl illustrated. The bowl measures 1½″ high by 6½″ from point to point of the "S" shape and sits on a ¾″ wide base. It is mold marked "WADE ENGLAND" on the underside of the base.

No. 277. "S" SHAPED POSY LOG WITH RABBIT 1954-1959.
As with the bowl above, this bowl was produced in similar color and size but with the addition of a small post to serve as a base for the rabbit figurine. The bowl was also decorated with a squirrel figurine similar to the squirrel on the Straight Posy Log.

No. 278. RABBIT BUTTER DISH 1955-1959.
Although this dish resembles an ashtray or pintray, it is officially described by Wade as a "Butter Dish" so that it would come under the classification of "Tableware." As well as the green glazed dish illustrated, the dish was also made in the beige color. Along with the rabbit decoration as shown, this butter dish was made with the squirrel figurine (see Fig. 141. in Miscellaneous Items by The Wade Group of Companies) and the Disney figurine, Jock, from the movie "Lady and the Tramp." The bowl of the dish measures ⅞″ high by 3¼″ diameter and is mold marked "WADE ENGLAND" on the underside of the dish.

No. 279. LARGE TRADITIONAL POSY BOWL 1955-1959.
This two handled posy bowl was made in three colors: beige, as illustrated, and green or white. The bowl measures 3″ high from base to top of handle by 6¼″ overall handle by 2¼″ wide at the widest point. The recessed base is mold marked "WADE ENGLAND".

No. 280. SMALL TRADITIONAL POSY BOWL 1955-1959.
The small bowl was made in the same colors as its larger counterpart. The bowl measures 2″ high from base to top of handle by 4⅛″ overall handles by 1⅝″ wide at its widest point. The mold mark is the same as that of the larger bowl.

No. 281. CHEVALINE POSY BOWL 1955-1959.
A decorative posy bowl with a similar design of three horses and leaves on both sides. The bowl was made in the green glaze as well as the beige illustrated. It measures 2¾″ high at the handles by 6″ long overall by 2″ wide and is mold marked "WADE ENGLAND" in the recessed base.

No. 282. SMALL MERMAID POSY BOWL 1955-1959.
Another highly decorative posy bowl with mermaids forming the handles. This bowl was made in both beige and white as well as the green illustrated. The bowl stands 2¼″ high at each end by 4″ overall by 1¼″ wide and is mold marked "WADE ENGLAND" in the recessed base.

No. 283. LARGE MERMAID POSY BOWL 1955-1959.
A larger version of the bowl described above and made in similar colors. It measures 3¼″ high at each end by 5⅞″ overall by 2″ wide and is mold marked "WADE ENGLAND."

No. 284. SCALLOPED DISHES 1954-1962 (1971-1984).
These dishes were issued in a variety of solid colors and given the name "Scalloped Dishes". In 1962, for a short time, they were made in a variety of marbelized colors and given the name "CRACKLE DISHES." After a number of years the dishes were re-issued in 1971 again with the name "CRACKLE DISHES" but reverting back to a variety of solid colors. The dishes measure 1⅜″ high by 3¼″ diameter. The recessed base is mold marked "WADE ENGLAND."

No. 285. DOG DISH CIRCA 1957.
This was a very short run of a pintray/ashtray decorated by the addition of a porcelain figurine of a Terrier as illustrated. A second dish was also produced with a Spaniel used as decoration. The tray measures ¾″ deep by 4″ overall by 3″ at its widest point. The recessed base bears the impressed mark "WADE MADE IN ENGLAND." This dish is also found in green glaze.

No. 286. SOUVENIR DISH CIRCA 1957.
Due to the short run of the Dog Dishes, it is most probable that Wade was left with a stock of dishes, and, as had been the custom in certain other cases of left over stock, these dishes were supplied to giftware manufacturers who added their own decoration. The dish illustrated bears a metal model of Tower Bridge, one of the most famous bridges crossing the Thames River in London. Sizes and marking are similar to the Dog Dishes.

No. 287. SOUVENIR DISH CIRCA 1957.
Other than the applied decoration, a miniature metal model of Buckingham Palace, this Souvenir Dish is similar to the one described above. The paper label "Souvenir of London" is often missing.

No. 288. BARGE POSY BOWL 1954.
A posy bowl made in both green and beige glazes. It measures 2½″ high at the highest point and 1¼″ high at the bowl portion by 8″ from bow to stern by 1⅜″ wide. The recessed base has the mold mark "WADE ENGLAND" and below that "REG. IN GT. BRITAIN No. 871886."

FIG. 59. "HARLEQUINS" 1957-1958.

FIG. 59.

A set of four, boxed, multi-colored dishes marked "WADE PORCELAIN MADE IN ENGLAND."

FIG. 60. PEGASUS POSY BOWL 1958-1959.

FIG. 60.

Although this attractive bowl was produced in the late 1950's, its design has a strong resemblance to the Art Deco designs of the 1920's. The bowl has an off-white glaze finish with the mane, tail, eyes, hoofs and the wavy lines below the belly highlighted in pale blue. The bowl measures 4⅜″ high by 5⅝″ overall by 2¼″ wide at its widest point. It is mold marked with Mark Type 24 on the underside of the curved arch.

No. 289. LEAF DISH 1957-1959.

Pin dish in the shape of a "Horse Chestnut" leaf, also produced in beige glaze. The leaf measures 3¼" long by 2¾" wide by ⅝" deep. This dish was sold in boxed sets of two and was made in both England and Ireland. The beige color of the Irish-made leaves was considerably lighter than the English-made leaves. They were also packaged in boxes of different design and size.

FIG. 61.

The English-made Leaf is impressed with the mark "WADE MADE IN ENGLAND" in a circular recess on the underside of the base. The Irish made leaf is mold marked with the Irish mark "Type 41." The Horse Chestnut leaf dish was re-issued in the early 1970's through 1984.

FIG. 62.

No. 290. LEAF DISH 1957-1958.

This second leaf-shaped dish was made in the shape of an "Oak Leaf" and was also available in beige color. As with the previous leaf dish it was marketed in boxed sets of two. The leaf measures 4" long by 2½" wide by ¾" high and is mold marked with Mark Type 25 in the recessed base.

No. 291. LEAF DISH 1958-1959.

The third leaf was designed to resemble an "Ash" leaf. As with the other leaf dishes it was also made with a green glaze finish and sold in pairs. It measures 7½" long by 1⅜" wide at its widest point by ½" high and is mold marked "WADE Porcelain Made in England" (similar to Mark Type 24).

No. 292. CHERUB BOWL 1957-1959.

This posy bowl measures 3¾" high with the bowl measuring 2" high by 4" diameter at the rim and 1⅜" diameter at the base. It is mold marked with Mark Type 25 on the underside of the base.

A similar bowl to the "Cherub" bowl but without the Swan, Cherub and center post was made between 1957-1959 and named, by Wade, the "PRIMROSE BOWL."

BALLET *CIRCA LATE 1950's.*

A set of ornamental vases and trays, produced by Wade Heath, with decorations depicting ballet dancers in various poses. The dancers are in silhouette on a white background. Items produced in this series were:

Bud Vase (shape No. 478)	12" high
Vase (shape No. 460)	7" high
Mini Bud Vase (shape No. 483)	4½" high
Mini Vase (shape No. 467)	4" high
Mini Bud Vase (shape No. 484)	4½" high
Vase (shape No. 458)	7" high
Vase (shape No. 468)	9" high
Bud Vase (shape No. 477)	9" high

Trays boxed singly, in fours, and combinations of a tray and two mini bud vases were available as gift sets.

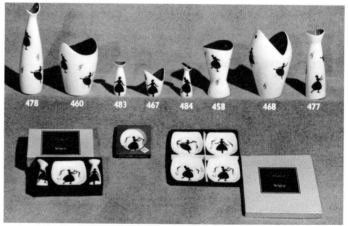

FIG. 63. BALLET VASES AND TRAYS

ZAMBA *1957.*

A set of ten various contemporary shaped ornamental trays, bowls, and vases with a decoration of jet black figures drawn on a pure white glaze produced by Wade Heath.

No. 293. ZAMBA WARE ASHTRAY—the ashtray illustrated is part of the set of Zamba ware items. The ashtray measures 1¼" square by ⅞" high at the corners and bears a red transfer mark "WADE ENGLAND." See Mark Type 19.

No. 294. ZAMBA WARE BUD VASE—the bud vase
measures 4¾″ high on a 1½″ diameter base
and bears a red transfer Mark Type 19.

No. 295. ZAMBA WARE ASHTRAY—for details see
description of No. 288. above. All "Zamba"
ware although marked "WADE ENGLAND" was
produced by WADE HEATH & CO. LTD. For
additional shapes produced in the "Zamba"
pattern see FIG. 64.

FIG. 65.

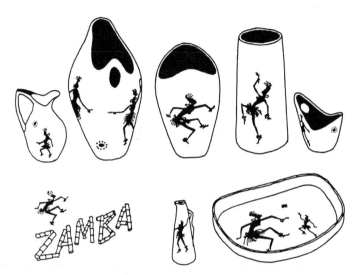

FIG. 64.

No. 296. BLUE BIRD TREE TRUNK POSY VASE
1957-1959.
A variation to the popular log-shaped Posy
Vases of the mid 1950's. The shape of the later
Posy Bowls was changed to a vertical format
as illustrated by the Tree Trunk shaped vase.
As well as the green glaze finish, this posy bowl
was also made with a white glaze finish. Both
color vases had similar colored "Blue Birds"
attached to the molded branch. The vase
measures 4″ from base to tip of bird wing
with a 2¾″ diameter base and is mold marked
with Mark Type 25.

No. 297. KOALA BEAR TREE TRUNK POSY VASE
1957-1959.
A Posy Vase on a similar theme as the Blue
Bird Posy Vase but with a much shorter trunk.
The vase measures 2¼″ from base to top of the
bear's head by 3¼″ overall and is mold marked
with Mark Type 25 in a recess in the base.

No. 298. AQUA DISHES SET 1. 1958-1960.
"Angel Fish" shaped pintray/ashtray sold in
pairs as illustrated. The dish measures 4″
across the fins by 3⅛″ from nose to tail by
⅝″ high and is mold marked "WADE
PORCELAIN MADE IN ENGLAND." See Mark
Type 25. This dish was re-issued in 1973-1984
and mold marked "WADE MADE IN
ENGLAND." See Mark Type 27. The Angel Fish
tray was also made in Ireland with an Irish
molded mark.

No. 299. BLUE BIRD DISH 1958-1959.
This oval shaped dish is decorated with a
similar porcelain blue bird figurine as was
used for the Tree Trunk Posy Vase. The dish
measures 5¾″ long by 2⅜″ wide by 1½″ high
from base to top of the bird's wing. The bowl
itself measures ⅞″ high and is mold marked
"WADE PORCELAIN MADE IN ENGLAND."
See Mark Type 24.

FIG. 65A.

No. 300. AQUA DISHES SET 2. 1960.
This flat "Herring" type pintray/ashtray dish
was also sold in boxed sets of two. It was in
production for a very limited period, no doubt
not being too popular with the public due to
its unusual shape. The dish measures 4″ long
by 2⅞″ wide by ⅞″ high and is mold marked
"WADE PORCELAIN MADE IN ENGLAND."
See Mark Type 25.

111

FIG. 66. T.T. TRAY 1959-1960.

Produced in a combination of bright and subdued colors with the dish in a subtle grey glaze. This Ashtray commemorates the Tourist Trophy motorcycle races held on the Isle of Man.

FIG. 66.

No. 301. **PET-FACE DISHES SET 1. 1959-1960.**

This dish, in the shape of a face of a "Siamese Cat," was designed to be used as a wall hung ornament. It measures 3¼" from ear to chin by 3⅛" across by ¾" high and has an impressed mold mark "WADE PORCELAIN MADE IN ENGLAND." See Mark Type 25.

No. 302. **PET-FACE DISHES SET 2. 1960.**

Similar to Pet-Face Dish Set 1, this dish, in the shape of the face of a "Pekingese Dog," was also designed to be a wall hung ornament. Both dishes from Set 1 and Set 2 were sold in boxed sets of two. This dish measures 3" from top to bottom of head by 3¾" wide by ¾" high and has an impressed mold mark similar to "Pet-Face Dishes Set 1."

No. 303. **CHIMPANZEE POSY VASE 1959-1960.**

The bowl section of this Posy Vase is somewhat similar to the Koala Bear Vase, but this time the animal figurine stands beside the tree trunk. The vase measures 3⅛" high at the chimp by 3⅝" overall and is mold marked "WADE PORCELAIN MADE IN ENGLAND." See Mark Type 25.

No. 304. **STARFISH TRAY 1959-1960.**

After a short production run when this dish was made in England and marked with an impressed mold mark "WADE MADE IN ENGLAND" (See Mark Type 26.), it was re-introduced between 1973-1984. The re-issue was made in Ireland and bears the mold Mark Type 41. The "Starfish" dish measures 4½" overall by ⅞" deep.

FIG. 67. FAMOUS AIRCRAFT TRAYS 1959.

A set of three individually boxed porcelain trays featuring historically famous aircraft. Records indicate this is Set 1 of a series but there is no evidence that this series was continued further.

FIG. 67.

No. 305. **COVERED SHORE CRAB DISH 1960.**

This dish, in the shape of a "Shore Crab," has a removable lid giving the dish various uses as a container for small items. It measures 3¾" wide by 3" deep by ¾" high and is mold marked on the underside of the base "WADE PORCELAIN MADE IN ENGLAND." See Mark Type 25.

No. 306. **VIKING SHIP POSY VASE 1959-1965.**

This Posy Bowl is found in a variety of shades of brown and blue glazed finishes, a result of the hand applied underglaze color which would, of course, vary due to the many different color applicators and different batches of glazes used over the years. The "Viking Posy Vase" measures 7⅜" overall by 1⅞" wide by 3½" high at the bow and is mold marked "WADE PORCELAIN MADE IN ENGLAND." See Mark Type 25. The bowl was re-issued in 1976-1982.

FIG. 68.

112

FIG. 68. "WILDFOWL" 1960.
A set of four duck wall decorations by Wade Heath & Co. Ltd. The ducks in the set are: Shoveller Drake, Pintail, Mallard Drake, and Shoveller.

No. 307. COVERED HEDGEHOG DISH 1961.
The "Hedgehog Dish," like the Crab dish, has a removable lid formed by the back of the Hedgehog, leaving a shallow dish with the head still attached. The covered dish measures 4″ overall by 2⅜″ wide by 2¼″ high. The dish without the lid measures ⅞″ high around the edge by 1⅝″ at the head and is mold marked "WADE PORCELAIN MADE IN ENGLAND" on the underside of the base. See Mark Type 25.

No. 308. TREASURE CHEST COVERED DISH 1961.
The lid of this dish is completely removable forming a small container for "knickknacks." The dish measures 3⅝″ overall by 2⅝″ wide overall the projecting latch and hinges by 1½″ high. The depth of the dish without the lid is 1¼″. The dish is mold marked "WADE PORCELAIN MADE IN ENGLAND" on the underside of the base. See Mark Type 25.

FIG. 69. SILHOUETTE SERIES 1962.
The silhouette decoration is carried out in a two-tone effect. The Giraffe decoration appears on both faces of the vase.

FIG. 70. CAMEO DISHES 1965.
A set of six small dishes of various shapes with the design of animals, birds and flowers embossed on the flat, inside face of the dish. The dishes were made in both green and beige colors.

THE CAMEO DISHES

This range, decorated in a combination of coloured translucent glazes, with six subjects on three shapes of dish, all individually boxed, should prove to be a really good seller.

Suggested Retail selling price **5/11d.** each

FIG. 70.

No. 309. PET DISH—CAIRN TERRIER 1979-1982.
This re-issue of the earlier Cameo Dish of similar design measures 4⅜″ across by ⅞″ deep and is mold marked "WADE ENGLAND" on the underside of the base. Also issued with a green glaze finish.

No. 310. PET DISH—FAWN 1979-1982.
A re-issue of the Cameo Fawn Dish. This dish measures 4⅜″ long by 3⅞″ wide by ⅞″ deep and is mold marked "WADE ENGLAND." Also issued with a beige glaze finish.

No. 311. FAWN DISH CIRCA MID 1960'S.
For this pintray/ashtray dish, Wade reverted to the log type design frequently used in the 1950's, using the shape of a hollowed out log to form the dish. The dish measures 4½″ from back to front by 4″ across by 2¼″ high at the Fawn with the rim of the tray only 1″ high. The mold mark, "WADE PORCELAIN MADE IN ENGLAND" appears on the underside of the base. See Mark Type 25.

HERE ARE THE LATEST ADDITIONS TO OUR

Silhouette Series

Viking Ship Tray
A delightfully detailed tray in a charming two-tone effect. See it in the shops to appreciate its full appeal.

4/6 each

in attractive presentation carton

Giraffe Vase
This attractive vase is beautifully proportioned for flower arrangements. The Silhouette decoration is carried out on *both* faces.

FIG. 69.

113

VILLAGE STORES *1982-1986.*

With the popularity shown by Wade collectors of the miniature "Whimsey-on-Why" village sets, an obvious development of the mini houses was to go to an interesting, but larger size line of kitchen containers using a similar theme. A set was then developed that certainly added interest to the kitchen of a Wade collector's home.

The original set comprised of ten models: four storage jars, covered butter dish, covered cheese dish and two size sets of salt and pepper shakers, a larger, range top size and a smaller size for use at the table. The smaller set of shakers was dropped from the line a year of two before the complete range was discontinued in 1986.

The roof of the storage jars forms a removable lid of the containers and each is lined with a plastic seal on the inside to help preserve the contents.

For illustrations of the complete set of the Village Stores refer to the color section.

No. 312-1. "YE OLDE TEA ROOM"—Tea Caddy.
No. 313-2. "THE COFFEE HOUSE"—Coffee Storage Jar.
No. 314-3. "B. LOAF, BAKER & CAKES"—Flour Storage Jar.
No. 315-4. "MRS. SMITH, ICE CREAM & SWEETS"—Sugar Storage Jar.
 All storage jars measure 7½" from base to top of chimney and are 3⅝" square. All four containers are marked "Village Stores by WADE Staffordshire ENGLAND."
No. 316-5. "THE CHALK AND CHEESE"—The Covered Cheese Dish. The white base is 7¼" long by 5¼" wide and 11/16" deep. The base is unmarked. The house, in the design of an English Pub, is 5" high by 6¼" long by 4⅜" wide and is marked on the inside face of the back wall "Village Stores by WADE Staffordshire ENGLAND."
No. 317-6. "THE VILLAGE STORE POST OFFICE"—The Covered Butter Dish. The base and lid combined measures 5" high, the roof being the removable lid. The base measures 5¼" long by 3¾" wide and is marked on the underside "Village Stores by WADE Stafforshire ENGLAND."
No. 318-7. "POST OFFICE"—Salt Shaker (small size).
No. 319-8. "POST OFFICE, ROYAL MAIL"—Pepper Shaker (small size).
 Both shakers are from the same mold but with a different design even though both depict a Post Office. The houses measure 2⅛" high by 1¼" long by 1" wide. Both are marked "WADE ENGLAND" on the face of the back wall.
No. 320-9. "A. SALT, GREENGROCER"—Salt Shaker (large size).
No. 321-10. "B. PEPPER, FAMILY BUTCHER"—Pepper Shaker (large size).
 As with the small shakers, the two larger, range top shakers are from the same mold. The name of each model describes the theme of the design used to decorate the two shakers. They measure 2¾" high by 2⅛" long by 1⅜" deep and are marked on the underside of the base "Village Stores by WADE Staffordshire ENGLAND." Both sets of shakers have removable plastic plugs on the underside of the base.

WHIMTRAYS *1958-1965.*

With the withdrawal of the early series of "Whimsies" in the late 1950's, Wade was left with a large quantity of some of the figurines remaining in stock. As there were not enough figurines available to form complete sets, a decision had to be made as to the best way of clearing these left over figurines. The idea of producing small round "pintrays" with a small ledge incorporated into the dish was decided upon to create a new giftware item and also use up the spare Whimsie figurines. The figurines were mounted onto the flat ledge. With the addition of the Whimsie figurines to the trays the obvious name for the tray was "WHIMTRAY."

The early Whimtrays, 3" in diameter and ⅝" high, were produced in a variety of colors, yellow, green, black, blue/green (dark turquoise) and pink. The first trays were made in the Stoke-on-Trent potteries and had a ledge resembling the segment of an intersecting circle measuring 2⅛" across by ¾" at its widest point. See FIG. 71 Whimtray Type "A".

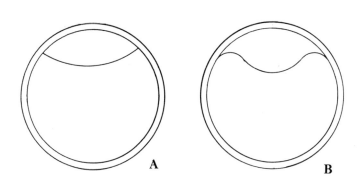

A   B

FIG. 71. WHIMTRAY TYPES.

These trays were all mold marked on the underside of the base "WHIMTRAYS" WADE PORCELAIN MADE IN ENGLAND. At sometime during the period of production the manufacturing of the Whimtrays was transferred to WADE (Ireland) Ltd. in Portadown. With the change in location of manufacture also came a change in the shape of the ledge supporting the figurines. The ledge on the Irish made trays is in the shape of a half circle with the edges curved back to blend in with the upturned edge of the tray. See FIG. 71. Whimtray Type "B". The mold mark on the underside of the base was changed to the Irish pottery Mark Type 41.

No. 322. LION CUB—from Set 8 of the 1953-1959 Whimsies. This tray has the "Made in England" mold mark.

No. 323. LLAMA—from Set 8 of the 1953-1959 Whimsies. This tray has the "Made in England" mold mark.

No. 324. POLAR BEAR CUB—from Set 6 of the 1953-1959 Whimsies. This tray has the "Made in Ireland" mold mark.

No. 325. CAMEL—from Set 8 of the 1953-1959 Whimsies. This tray has the "Made in England" mold mark.

No. 326. PENGUIN—from Set 6 of the 1953-1959 Whimsies. This tray has the "Made in Ireland" mold mark.

No. 327. HUSKY—from Set 6 of the 1953-1959 Whimsies. This tray has the "Made in Ireland" mold mark.

No. 328. PANDA—from Set 8 of the 1953-1959 Whimsies. This tray has the "Made in England" mold mark.

WHIMTRAYS *1971-1987.*

After a lapse of a few years, "WHIMTRAYS" were re-introduced but this time the figurines were from the 1971-1984 series of Whimsies. Only three figurines are used on black, green and blue trays giving nine possible combinations. Of these current Whimtrays, all that we have seen bear the "Made in Ireland" mold mark, except for one interesting tray we found in a small giftshop during our research trip to England. This tray, which is green and bears the Trout figurine is shape Type "B" but the molded mark on the underside of the base is marked simply "WADE MADE IN ENGLAND." To date this is the only Whimtray we have seen so marked.

The shape of the ledge on which the figurines are mounted is similar to the earlier Irish made Whimtrays, there is a slight variation with the addition of a raised rim around the curved ledge. This implies a new mold must have been made for the 1971 re-issue.

No. 329. FAWN—Model No. 1. of the 1971-1984 Whimsies.

No. 330. DUCK—Model No. 6 of the 1971-1984 Whimsies.

No. 331. TROUT—Model No. 15 of the 1971-1984 Whimsies.

A new range of Whimtrays was issued in 1987. See FIG. 157 in Miscellaneous Items by The Wade Group of Companies.

"BOULDRAY" TRAY
CIRCA LATE 1960'S TO EARLY 1970'S.

The "BOULDRAY" trays were a reserved (special contract) line supplied by Wade as a special order for a client. They were never used as a retail line. Wade supplied only the tray and porcelain decoration (if any) with the client adding the additional metal portion of the decoration. The Whimtray mold was used as the basic shape for the tray; however, the mold was retooled to add the client's name to the tray in place of the ususal name, Whimtray.

No. 332. BLUE BIRD "BOULDRAY" TRAY—the Blue Bird is mounted on a metal stand surrounded by a metal ring. The tray is similar to Whimtray shape Type "A" and is mold marked on the underside of base "BOULDRAY" WADE PORCELAIN 2 MADE IN ENGLAND. The number 2 most probably is a reference, for record keeping, of the client's order.

No. 333. ELF "BOULDRAY" TRAY—the elf decoration is metal and was not supplied by Wade. As with the metal mounting for the Blue Bird described above, the metal Elf is held by a single screw fixed on the underside through a hole incorporated into the mold. The molded marking on the underside of the base is similar to the tray described above.

"PEERAGE" TRAY
CIRCA LATE 1960'S TO EARLY 1970'S.

The "Peerage" tray was also a reserved line and, as with the "Bouldray" tray, was based on the Whimtray. Once again Wade supplied only the porcelain portion of the tray with the metal decoration supplied and affixed by the client.

No. 334. PEKINGESE "PEERAGE" TRAY—this metal figurine of a small dog, with the word "Pekingese" below, is mounted on a stand fixed to the tray as previously described. The molded mark on the underside of the base reads: "Peerage" WADE PORCELAIN MADE IN ENGLAND. The shape of the tray is similar to the Whimtray shape Type "B."

Numerous other designs are to be found in both the "Bouldray" and "Peerage" trays.

ADDIS SHAVING MUGS
MID 1960'S TO PRESENT.

For a number of years right up to the present time, Wade Heath has been producing a line of shaving mugs, working to an ADDIS design, for ADDIS Ltd., a leading British brush, health and beauty product manufacturer, established in 1780. The shaving mugs were and still are supplied to ADDIS Ltd. as part of their shaving gift set range. The gift set, along with the mug, also consisted of a round, flat-topped cake of soap and a shaving brush. Many of these gift sets have found their way to North America and the shaving mugs are often found in both the U.S. and Canada.

The mugs are decorated by hand-applied transfers which are fired-on along with the glaze finish as is the transfer mark, "WADE ENGLAND." See Mark Type 19. All mugs in the color section measure 3⅝" high by 7⅝" from spout to back of handle.

We would like to thank Addis Limited for their co-operation and acknowledge their copyright ownership of the items illustrated.

No. 335. "STEAM COACH" BY GURNEY 1827.
No. 336. "LA MANCELLE" BY BOLLEE 1878.
No. 337. "STEAM ROLLER" BY AVELING 1893.
No. 338. 1920'S CONVERTIBLE.
No. 339. SINGLE ENGINED BI-PLANE.
FIG. 72. ADMIRAL LORD HORATIO NELSON—born 1758 and died 21st October 1805. The transfer is black and white and unlike the other Shaving Mugs, which have four holes in the dish shaped top, this mug has only one hole. The mug is transfer marked "WADE ENGLAND" on the underside of the base and measures 3¼" high by 7¼" from spout to back of handle.

FIG. 72.

WESTMINISTER PIGGY BANK FAMILY *1983 TO PRESENT.*

In December 1983, the National Westminister Bank devised the novel idea of producing a set of piggy banks which would be given, as gifts, to children as a means of encouraging them to increase their awareness for saving money.

A set of five piggy banks were designed to be given to young depositors at various intervals of their Piggy account balance levels. All five Piggies are mold marked "WADE ENGLAND" on the underside of the base along with a removable, black rubber plug marked "NatWest."

We would like to acknowledge National Westminister Bank's ownership and copyright of the Piggy Bank designs.

No. 340-1. WOODY—received upon opening an account. Woody is 5" tall.
No. 341-2. ANNABEL—received after the first statement with a balance of 25 pounds sterling or more. Annabel is 6⅜" tall from base to tip of ear.
No. 342-3. MAXWELL—received after the second statement with a balance of 50 pounds sterling or more. Maxwell is 6¾" tall.
No. 343-4. LADY HILLARY—received after the third statement with a balance of 75 pounds sterling or more. Lady Hillary measures 7" from base to tip of ear.
No. 344-5. SIR NATHANIEL—received after the fourth statement with a balance of 100 pounds sterling or more. This last Piggy in the set measures 7¼" high.

ROMANCE RANGE *1983-1985.*

This series of porcelain giftware items given the name "Romance Range" consisted of two rectangular and one heart shaped picture frames, a rectangular trinket box with lid, an egg-shaped trinket box with lid and a pomander. All are modeled in high relief and decorated in soft translucent colors. These items were available in contrasting color treatments of either grey/white glazed background or a cream glazed background with the raised decoration highlighted in blues, yellows and white and packaged in attractive handled gift boxes. All items in the Romance Range are mold marked with Mark Type 26.

No. 345. RECTANGULAR PICTURE FRAME—measures 5½" by 4⅝" and has the mold mark on the back of the frame. A similar, larger version measuring 6¾" by 5½" was also made.
No. 346. RECTANGULAR TRINKET BOX—measures 2⅝" long by 2¼" wide by 1⅞" high.
FIG. 73. HEART SHAPE PICTURE FRAME—measures 5½" high by 5½" at it's widest point.

FIG. 73.

FIG. 74. POMANDER—measures 2¾″ diameter by 2″ high.

FIG. 74.

FIG. 75. EGG SHAPE TRINKET BOX—measures 2¾″ long by 1¾″ high.

FIG. 75.

MAN IN BOAT *1978-1984.*

No. 347. MAN IN BOAT, a giftware item based on an earlier mold of the boat with a sea-gull decoration. Other than the addition of the reclining man, the only change to the mold was the removal of a small circular base on which the sea-gull perched. The boat measures 6″ from bow to stern by 1⅝″ high at the bow and is mold marked "WADE PORCELAIN MADE IN ENGLAND" on the base. See Mark Type 25.

SEA-GULL BOAT *1961.*

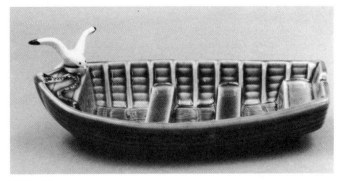

FIG. 76.

FIG. 76. SEA-GULL BOAT, the original mold on which the Man in Boat was based but with a much darker all-over brown glaze finish. The sea-gull is white with a yellow beak, black eyes and black tips to the wings. The back of the bird is highlighted with grey/blue. The size and mold mark is similar to the Man in Boat.

CANDLEHOLDERS *1965-1982.*

The candleholders illustrated were produced as a contract line for Price's Patent Candle Company Limited. A company was formed in 1847, under the name of "E. Price and Company." However, there never was a "Mr. Price." the company was actually formed by two businessmen, William Wilson and Benjamin Lancaster. The name Price was the family name of an aunt of Lancaster's although this lady never had anything to do with the business. None of the candles illustrated bear a Wade mark; however, many are marked with a set of figures referring to the number of the contract. The following information was supplied by "Price's Patent Candle Company Limited, London."

No. 348. MAYFAIR HOLDER S2/15—measures 3⅛″ long by 2¾″ wide by 1¼″ at the highest point. This shape was produced between 1965-1973 (104,000 were made).

No. 349. VENETIAN HOLDER S2/12—measures 2½″ in diameter by 1½″ high and is mold marked "MADE IN ENGLAND" in a circular recess on the underside of the base. This shape was produced between 1973-1979 (25,000 were made).

No. 350. MINI-HOLDER S2/11—measures 1¾″ in diameter by ⅞″ high and is mold marked "MADE IN ENGLAND" in a circular recess on the underside of the base. This shape was produced between 1965-1973 (334,000 were made).

No. 351. FLOWERLIGHT ROUND HOLDER— measures 4″ in diameter by 1″ high. This shape was produced between 1963-1979 (427,000 were made).

FIG. 77. VENETIAN SCATTER CANDLESTICK produced between 1970-1982 (109,000 were made in this shape).

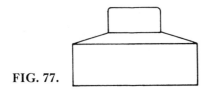

FIG. 77.

FIG. 78. FLOWER LIGHT LEAF HOLDER produced between 1963-1973 (224,000 were made in this shape).

FIG. 78.

LESNEY TRAY *CIRCA 1968-1975.*

These trays were a special reserved line manufactured for Lesney Industries Ltd., the producers of the famous "Matchbox" toy cars, etc. A number of different sized ceramic trays were produced on which some of their more expensive veteran cars were mounted. The Lesney trays were never issued as a retail line.

No. 352. "BUS" LESNEY TRAY—the tray measures 6″ overall by 3½″ across the actual tray measuring ⅞″ high. The tray only was manufactured by Wade with the metal model of the "double decker" bus supplied and mounted onto the tray by Lesney Industries Ltd. In a recess on the underside of the base the tray is mold marked **"AN R.K. PRODUCT BY WADE OF ENGLAND."**

THOMAS THE TANK ENGINE AND FRIENDS *1985-1987.*

In late 1985, George Wade and Son Ltd. introduced four new models to their giftware line based on the extremely popular children's T.V. series "Thomas the Tank Engine and Friends."

The T.V. series is based upon two books, titled *Three Railway Engines,* first published in 1945, and *Thomas the Tank Engine* first published in 1946, both authored by the Reverend W. Awdry. To date, two television series of "Thomas the Tank Engine and Friends" have been filmed. Both were narrated by Ringo Starr. The first T.V. series was screened for the first time in the U.K. in the fall of 1984, and the second series in the Fall of 1986.

As of this time, neither of the two T.V. series have been shown in the U.S. but are currently shown on a Canadian children's T.V. program. Even though "Thomas the Tank Engine and Friends" has yet to be seen on the T.V. screens in the United States, it is interesting to note that the program won a Bronze Award in the 1984 International Film and T.V. Festival held in New York City.

No. 353. "PERCY" MONEY BANK—measures 7″ long by 3½″ wide by 4½″ high and is unmarked. Later issues were marked WADE ENGLAND along with a copyright mark.

No. 354. "PERCY" MINIATURE—A slip cast miniature version of the money bank measuring 1½″ long by ⅞″ wide by 1⅛″ high and is transfer marked "WADE MADE IN ENGLAND".

No. 355. "THOMAS" MONEY BANK—measures 6½″ long by 3⅝″ wide by 4¾″ high and is unmarked. Later issues were marked WADE ENGLAND along with a copyright mark.

No. 356. "THOMAS" MINIATURE. A slip cast miniature version of the money bank measuring 1⅝″ long by ⅞″ wide by 1¼″ high at the smoke stack and is transfer marked "WADE MADE IN ENGLAND".

We would like to acknowledge the co-operation and ownership of copyright for the items illustrated.
© Kaye & Ward Limited 1984
© Britt Allcroft Limited 1984

WAGON TRAIN DISHES *1960.*

Due to the popularity of the T.V. series "Wagon Train," Wade produced two shallow dishes using the two major characters from the series as decoration. The two characters used in the design of the dishes were Seth Adams portrayed by actor Ward Bond and Flint McCullough portrayed by Robert Horton. Both dishes have impressed marks on the underside of the base "WADE PORCELAIN MADE IN ENGLAND".
© 1960 by REVUE STUDIOS. Both oval shaped dishes measure 5½″ long by 5″ wide by 1¼″ high at the rim.

No. 357. WAGON TRAIN—SETH ADAMS.
No. 358. WAGON TRAIN—FLINT McCULLOUGH.

We would like to acknowledge the co-operation and copyright ownership of the items illustrated:
© 1959 Universal City Studios, Inc.

Decorative Pitchers

by

Wade Heath & Company Ltd.

PITCHERS BY WADE HEATH & COMPANY LTD.
CIRCA 1934-1955.

Since the early years of the twentieth century, Wade & Co. had been involved primarily with the production of tableware and decorative pitchers or jugs as they are usually called in the United Kingdom.

By 1933, Wade & Co. had changed its name to Wade Heath & Co. Ltd. Along with A.J. Wade Ltd., it came under the control of G.A. Wade, son of the original George Wade. With both companies now under the same management, Wade Heath & Co. Ltd. proceeded to concentrate on the production of decorative ware leaving A.J. Wade Ltd. to continue with the manufacture of tiles and fireplace surrounds.

The 1930's, saw a long and interesting line of decorative pitchers produced by Wade Heath. Many had a strong Art Deco influence in their shape and design. The shape of the pitchers varied from the simple, clean lines popular in the 1930's, to the highly decorated molded shapes featuring birds, animals, etc. A popular form of decoration applied to the more simply-shaped pitchers was a mottled/spatter type of decoration. This style of finish was reintroduced after the war but was more in the form of an overall color rather than the pre-war mottled effect. For a number of years the pitchers were backstamped with the name "WADEHEATH" but in the mid-1930's, the word "FLAXMAN" or "FLAXMAN-WARE" was added to the backstamp. For further information, see the section on Mark Types and Backstamps.

In 1938, Wade Heath expanded its production of tableware by taking over the Royal Victoria Pottery in Burslem. In the early years of WW II, Wade Heath stopped production of all decorative ware to concentrate on the war effort. It is believed, however, that a small amount of plain, undecorated tableware was produced by the pottery during the war years.

The "Glost Warehouse" Circa 1951.
(The warehouse housing wares in the "Fired Glaze State". Items awaiting either gilding, enamelling or both
& then fired again in the enamel kiln after which items are sent to the "Finished Warehouse".)

At the end of the war, Wade Heath gradually began to reintroduce some of the decorative pitchers so popular in the pre-war years. Due to government restrictions on the use of certain materials, most of the shapes reintroduced were made in plain, all-over colors. Complete records of the 1930 molds brought back into use are not available, but it is known the number of shapes reused was greatly reduced. A number of the molds were amended to omit some of the more complicated ornamental parts such as the pitcher shape No. 169 where the bird was omitted from the top of the handle.

By the mid 1950's, very few decorative pitchers were made. However, those still in production were made with the original full color decoration such as shape No. 143. Production of the Wade Heath pitchers ceased in the late 1950's. Shortly after this, Wade Heath halted production of all tableware, leaving the Royal Victoria Pottery to produce advertising ware and contract lines.

Identifying the pitchers is often done by referring to a "shape No." This is the mold number sometimes found impressed into the base of the pitcher or, in some cases, located in company literature. A number of pitchers were made in two or three sizes, miniature, medium and large. This is sometimes apparent in the shape number where the number will be followed by either Min. or M (miniature) or MS (medium size). Full size pitchers were marked with the mold number only.

Dating the pitchers is not an easy task. Production dates were not recorded and the only means of dating the various pitchers is by the backstamp. As the use of many of the backstamps overlapped for a few years, it is only possible to give approximate years of production. For these dates, reference should be made to the section illustrating and describing the various Wade Mark Types. For the following examples of typical Wade Heath decorative pitchers, refer to the color section.

No. 359. PITCHER—decoration No. 3302 with Mark Type 2. The pitcher measures 7¾″ high.

No. 360. PITCHER—shape No. 131 with Mark Type 2. The pitcher measures 8½″ high.

No. 361. PITCHER—shape No. 106 with decoration No. 1580 and Mark Type 4. This shape of pitcher was made in three sizes, miniature, medium and large. The one illustrated is 9″ high (large size).

No. 362. PITCHER—shape No. 106 with decoration No. 3708 and Mark Type 2. This pitcher measures 9″ high (large size).

FIG. 79. PITCHER—shape No. 106 with decoration No. 1624 and Mark Type 4. The pitcher illustrated has an overall "leaf" type design in blue, gold and rust colors. The spout, handle and wide band around the top part of the pitcher are blue. The pitcher measures 7¼″ high and is the medium size of shape No. 106.

FIG. 79.

No. 363. PITCHER—shape No. 92 with "spatter" decoration and Mark Type 5. This pitcher measures 8¼″ high.

No. 364. PITCHER—shape No. 113M with "spatter" decoration and Mark Type 2. This shape pitcher was made in three different sizes, miniature, medium and large. The one illustrated measures 5¼″ high. (miniature size).

No. 365. PITCHER—shape No. 106M with Mark Type 5. This pitcher measures 5½″ high (miniature size of shape No. 106).

No. 366. PITCHER—shape No. 106M with "spatter" decoration and Mark Type 5. The pitcher measures 5½″ high (miniature size of shape No. 106).

FIG. 80. PITCHER—shape No. 14 with decoration No. 1514 and Mark Type 2. The pitcher illustrated has a yellow background with green and orange/red molded birds perched on brown branches with green leaves. The handle is in the form of a brown branch. The pitcher is 6¾″ high.

FIG. 80.

121

No. 367. PITCHER—variation of shape No. 13 with decoration No. 1590 and Mark Type 2. The Pitcher is 7″ high.

No. 368. PITCHER—shape No. 106M with Mark Type 5. The pitcher measures 5½″ high (miniature size of shape No. 106).

No. 369. PITCHER—shape No. 133MIN with "spatter" decoration and Mark Type 4. This shape pitcher was made in three different sizes, miniature, medium and large. The one illustrated is 5¼″ high (miniature size).

No. 370. PITCHER—shape No. 88 with decoration No. 138 and Mark Type 4. This shape pitcher was made in three different sizes, miniature, medium and large. The one illustrated is 8¼″ high (large size).

No. 371. VASE—decoration No. 138 with Mark Type 4. The vase measures 5″ high.

No. 372. PITCHER—shape No. 88M with Mark Type 5. The pitcher measures 5½″ high (miniature size of shape No. 88).

No. 373. PITCHER—shape No. 121A with "spatter" decoration and Mark Type 4. The pitcher measures 10″ high.

No. 374. PITCHER—shape No. 155 with Mark Type 6. The pitcher measures 9″ high. This shape was reintroduced between the mid 1940's and early 1950's as part of the "Gothic" line.

No. 375. PITCHER—shape No. 120 with "spatter" decoration and Mark Type 4. The pitcher measures 8½″ high and is not known to have been reproduced after WW II.

No. 376. PITCHER—shape No. 301 with "spatter" type decoration and Mark Type 6. The pitcher is 9″ high. This shape was used for a short time after WW II.

No. 377. PITCHER—shape No. 127 with "spatter" type decoration and Mark Type 4. The pitcher is 7½″ high. This shape was not produced after WW II.

No. 378. PITCHER—shape No. 124 with "spatter" type decoration and Mark Type 4. This pitcher is 3″ high and is a companion piece to shape No. 120 in a "squashed" version.

No. 379. PITCHER—shape No. 147MS with Mark Type 6. The pitcher measures 7½″ high. This shape was made in three sizes, miniature, medium and large. The pitcher illustrated is the medium size.

No. 380. BIRDHOUSE PITCHER—shape No. 168 with Mark Type 7. The pitcher is 8¾″ high and was made with a green and blue background as well as the yellow background on the pitcher illustrated.

No. 381. RABBIT JUG—"mottled" type decoration with Mark Type 6. The jug measures 4″ high and is not known to have been reproduced after WW II.

No. 382. PITCHER—shape No. 148Min with "mottled" type decoration and Mark Type 6. The pitcher measures 5¾″ high, the smallest of the three sizes made in this shape and design.

No. 383. PITCHER—shape No. 148M/S with "mottled" type decoration and Mark Type 6. The pitcher measures 7¾″ high, the medium size of the three sizes of pitchers made in this shape and design.

No. 384. PITCHER—shape No. 149Min with "mottled" type decoration and Mark Type 6. The pitcher measures 5½″ high, the miniature size of the three sizes of pitchers made in this shape and design.

No. 385. PITCHER—shape No. 149M/S with "mottled" type decoration and Mark Type 6. The pitcher measures 7½″ high, the medium size of the three sizes of pitchers made in this shape and design.

No. 386. RABBIT PITCHER—shape No. 169 with Mark Type 7. The pitcher is 7¾″ high and was made with birds in a variety of colors, the rabbits remaining a brown color. The production of this shape and design was limited.

No. 387. PITCHER—shape No. S302 with "mottled" type decoration and Mark Type 8. The pitcher measures 9″ high and was in production prior to and after WW II. A variation of this shape was issued after the war with the band of diagonal ribs omitted under the description of shape No. 335.

No. 388. SQUIRREL PITCHER—shape No. 154 with Mark Type 10. The pitcher is 8¼″ high and was produced with a fawn background with the squirrel and handle in brown along with green leaves around the rim. The colored version was given the pattern No. 6060.

No. 389. PITCHER—shape No. 371 with Mark Type 10. The pitcher is 9″ high and was produced in "mottled" colors prior to WW II.

No. 390. RABBIT PITCHER—shape No. 169 with the bird on the handle omitted. The pitcher bears Mark Type 10 and is 7½″ high.

No. 391. BIRDBATH PITCHER—shape No. 143 with Mark Type 4 and measures 6¼″ high from base to rim.

No. 392. BIRDBATH PITCHER—similar to above but with Mark Type 8.

No. 393. BIRDBATH PITCHER—similar to above but with Mark Type 7. The "Birdbath" pitchers were produced both prior to and after WW II. Pattern No. 6059 was given to the post war items. There are no records of pattern numbers for the pre war pitchers. The "Birdbath" pitcher was also made in a larger size, 8¼″ high from base to rim. Both sizes of this pitcher were made with a single, all over glaze. The single glaze pitchers have Mark Type 10 on the base.

No. 394. PITCHER—shape No. 88M with "mottled" type decoration and Mark Type 4. The pitcher measures 5½″ high.

FIG. 81. FLAXMAN WARE.

No. 395. PITCHER—shape No. 405 with decoration No. 6088 and Mark Type 10. The pitcher measures 5¼″ high from base to tip of spout.

No. 396. THE McCALLUM—character jug with Mark Type 14. This jug, which was produced in three sizes, was both hand painted in multicolored versions and in the single overall glaze as illustrated. The medium size (illustrated) is 4½″ high, the smallest size is 2¾″ high, and the largest size 7″ high measured from base to the highest point at the rim.

No. 397. GOLFBAG JUG—is 3½″ high with a transfer Mark Type 15.

For additional shapes of pitchers, vases, baskets, and wall pockets in assorted mottled colors with a matt finish see FIG. 81 and FIG. 81A. From available information it is known that shapes: 301, 159, 335, 247, 146, and 244 were first issued in the mid 1930's. It is most probable that all shapes illustrated were in production in the 1930's and were re-introduced, for a short time, after WW II.

Illustration No.		Shape No.	Approx. Height
1.	Jug	371	9″
2.	Vase	333	9″
3.	Vase	313	9″
4.	Vase	362	9″
5.	Vase	332	9″
6.	Vase	314	9″
7.	Jug	334	9″
8.	Jug	301	9″
9.	Jug	145	9″
10.	Wall Pocket	159	
11.	Jug	144	9″
12.	Jug	335	9″
13.	Flower Holder	343	5″
14.	Basket	247	2½″
15.	Basket	246	2½″
16.	Basket	248	2½″
17.	Flower Holder	244	5″

FIG. 81A. FLAXMAN WARE

Illustration No.		Shape No.	Approx. Height
1.	Jug	135	9″
2.	Vase	214	
3.	Jug	132	9″
4.	Jug	134	9″
5.	Vase	216	
6.	Jug	133	9″
7.	Jug	131	8½″
8.	Wall Pocket	224	8½″
9.	Jug	120	8½″

Tableware

by

Wade Heath & Company Ltd.

WADEHEATH STANDARD TABLEWARE SHAPES.

DANDY JUGS

42s	36s	30s	24s
4½″ high	5¼″ high	5¾″ high	6¼″ high

DANDY CREAMS & SUGARS

Vase 1

S/s
1¾″ high

S/s
3″ high

L/s
2″ high

L/s
3½″ high

Vase 2

Vase 3

Cigarette Box
5″L x 3¾″W x 2″H

Finger Bowl
4″ dia.

Powder Bowl

Ash Tray
4″L x 3″W x ¾″H

Candy Box
6¾″L x 5″W x 3½″H

Beer Mug
5″ high

Trinket Box

NELSON TEAPOTS

42s	36s	30s	24s
4½″ high	5″ high	5½″ high	5¾″ high

DUTCH JUGS

42s	36s	30s	24s
4″ high	4½″ high	5″ high	5¼″ high

FIG. 82.

Note: Heights are approximate.

126

TABLEWARE *CIRCA LATE 1930'S-1960.*

Some items listed in this section have not been given production dates due to lack of records. In some cases, both ex-employees and present employees of Wade Heath have been able to assist with an estimate of production dates. These dates are noted as "circa" followed by the approximate date of production. In other cases, where memories failed to recall a certain item or pattern, the type of backstamp (Mark Type) is noted. The reader should refer to the backstamp section at the front of this book where approximate dates are given for the period the backstamp was in use.

Shape No. refers to the mold shape of a certain item. Certain shapes were used for one decoration (Decoration No.) and then retired. At a later date, a number of retired mold shapes were sometimes brought back into use but with a different Decoration No. However, the Shape No. would remain the same.

Wade Heath also had a standard line of tableware shapes (see FIG. 82) which were used for numerous decorations both hand-applied and later transfer-type decorations. A number of Wade Heath pieces bear the word "Harvest ware" on the backstamp. Harvest ware refers to the cream colored "body" of the ware to which the decoration is applied. Although not appearing alongside the backstamp, the term "cane" body is frequently used and has the same meaning as Harvest ware.

The sizing of teapots, jugs etc. came about through a system of payment to the maker for work done. For example the potter would have to make twelve teapots before he was paid, thus the size 12s. The next size down, 24s, he would make 24 before being paid the equivalent price of the 12 larger items. In other words the numbers 24s, 36s, and 42s refer to the "potters dozen." This system was in effect many years before Wade was even established.

PEONY *(Decoration No. 4871).*

This small line of tableware, with free-hand underglaze decoration, was marketed between approx. 1947 to mid 1950's. The shapes of the items used were of pre WW II. origin, reintroduced with a new decoration and given the name, Peony, designed by Georgina Lawton.

The Peony line consisted of the following items (see FIG. 83):

Vase	Shape No. 342	11″ high
Vase	Shape No. 394	9″ high
Plaque	Shape No. 398	12½″ diameter
Vase	Shape No. 333	9″ high
Jug	Shape No. 93	11″ high
Vase	Shape No. 362	9″ high
Vase	Shape No. 332	9″ high
Vase	Shape No. 313	9″ high
Vase	Shape No. 343	9″ high
Basket	Shape No. 248	2½″ high
Fruit Bowl	Shape No. 369	14½″ long
Vase	Shape No. 69	8″ high

FIG. 83. PEONY SHAPES.

No. 398. PEONY FRUIT BOWL—shape No. 369 with Mark Type 13.

No. 399. PEONY PLAQUE—shape No. 398 with Mark Type 13.

Jug	Shape No. 157	11½″ high
Jug	Shape No. 155	9″ high
Vase	Shape No. 360	8½″ high
Bowl		9″ diameter

GOTHIC

This line of decorative vases and pitchers was first introduced in the late 1930's with a limited number of items. The pre WW II. pieces were produced in both solid colors and two tone pastel shades. The line was reintroduced between the late 1940's and the mid 1950's with new underglaze colors along with the addition of some new shapes. Photographs taken at the 1954 British Industries Fair show the Jug (Shape No. 157) converted into a table lamp.

Known items in the pre WW II. line were the following:

Vase	Shape No. 359	6½″ high
Wall Pocket	Shape No. 159	6½″ high
Vase	Shape No. 366	9″ high

After WW II., the line was extended with the addition of a basket, Shape No. 413 in large, medium and small sizes. The full line of gothic shapes (with the possible exception of the 9″ dia. bowl) was produced in decoration No. 4851, an "oatmeal" colored background highlighted in pink and green and decoration No. 4854 which had a cane body relieved by underglaze colors of green, yellow and mauve and traced with gold lustre.

No. 400. BOWL—9″ dia. with overall glaze finish and Mark Type 9.

No. 401. BASKET—shape No. 413, decoration No. 4854 with Mark Type 11. The basket measures 7″ from base to top of handle.

No. 402. VASE—shape No. 359, decoration No. 4854 with Mark Type 9.

FIG. 84. GOTHIC LUSTRE WARE SHAPES

MISCELLANEOUS ITEMS.

No. 403. COTTAGE STYLE BUTTER DISH—decoration No. 4023, was an individual line of tableware produced circa the mid 1930's. The butter dish measures 7" square at the base by 4½" high and has an ink backstamp Mark Type 2.

FIG. 85. BUTTER DISH—from a set of tableware based on characters from the popular 1938 animated Walt Disney movie, Snow White and the Seven Dwarfs. The butter dish, which measures 7" dia. by 4½" high at the top of the finial, is in the shape of a tree trunk decorated with yellow/brown rabbits and blue birds and the figure of "Dopey" forming the finial sitting on the lid of green leaves. Items in this line have an ink backstamp "WADEHEATH BY PERMISSION WALT DISNEY, ENGLAND".

(Copyright Walt Disney Productions)

FIG. 85.

No. 404. SWEET TRAY—one of a set of trays featuring scenes from Walt Disney's animated movie, Lady and the Tramp. The 4¼" dia. tray was issued circa 1956 and has a transfer backstamp incorporating the name of the movie and "by WADE of ENGLAND COPYRIGHT WALT DISNEY PRODUCTIONS".

No. 405. CEREAL BOWL—part of a set of children's dishes, produced in the late 1930's, featuring scenes from the movie Snow White and the Seven Dwarfs. The bowl measures 6" square by 1½" high and has an ink backstamp, "WADEHEATH BY PERMISSION WALT DISNEY, ENGLAND".

No. 406. CUP & SAUCER—part of a set of children's dishes as described in No. 405 above. The saucer measures 4" in dia. and the cup is 1¾" high. Both cup and saucer are marked with a similar backstamp to the cereal bowl.

No. 407. ROSE WALL POCKET—shape No. 281 in "Rose" decoration with Mark Type 7. The wall pocket measures 8½" high.

HONEY POTS *CIRCA 1939 and 1946.*

A variety of Honey pots were produced by Wade Heath shortly before and for a brief time after WW II., three of which are illustrated.

No. 408. BEEHIVE HONEY POT—measures 3" dia. by 4" high with Mark Type 7 on the base.

No. 409. FLOWER HONEY POT—measures 2½" dia. at the base by 4" high with Mark Type 7 on the base.

No. 410. BUTTERFLY HONEY POT—measures 3" dia. at the base by 4" high with Mark Type 7 on the base.

No. 411. FLOWER HOLDER—shape No. 244 with "Mottled" type decoration and Mark Type 6. The flower holder is 5" high with a removable frog and is not known to have been reproduced after WW II.

CRANKY TANKARDS
1947-EARLY 1950'S.

The standard Wade Heath 4½" high Beer Mug (actual measured height is close to 5") was the mold used for this set of six tankards. Each tankard was decorated with a cartoon character and a rhyme, written in a humorous style, describing the cartoon. The transfer type decoration was applied to a "Harvest" colored body. Mark Type 13 appears on tankards No. 1, 2 and 5 and Mark Type 14 appears on tankards No. 3, 4 and 6. These marks could vary from other tankards found as they were both used during the same time period.

No. 412-1. THE MIASMA.
> The lesser known Miasma, though
> a somewhat ugly creature
> has got a heart of gold and that's
> a most important feature.
> He gives away his breakfasts and
> his dinners to the needy
> and as he hates the sight of beer,
> he's always looking seedy.

No. 413-2. THE HANGOVAH.
> Bring in the ice-packs and
> don't make a noise
> walk very softly—the
> Hangovah's here.
> Oh what a night he had
> out with the boys!
> Oh what a shame they mixed
> gin with his beer!

129

No. 414-3. THE DRUMBLETUM.

The Drumbletum's capacity is
really quite abnormal
he'll drink ten quarts of bitter
in a manner most informal;
Such recklessness has made him
very liverish and spotted—
his doctor says his blood stream
is most definitely clotted.

No. 415-4. THE FLOPPITY.

The vacant-minded Floppity
will often cause a titter
by going to a milk bar and
then ordering a bitter.
Refusal doesn't daunt him
for he slowly ambles out
and seeks the haven of a pub
where he consumes milk stout.

No. 416-5. THE HYPERFLOOGIE.

The hirsute Hyperfloogie's looks will
shock the least fastidious
and he himself devoutly wishes he
weren't quite so hideous;
he has no ears and so he never knows
when people greet him,
and—what's far sadder—never hears
them should they want to treat him.

No. 417-6. THE SNOOZLE.

Will someone please
produce a cloth
to wipe away the
cloud of froth
that's settled on
the Snoozle's snout—
he simply dotes on
foaming stout?

NUT TRAYS *CIRCA 1939 AND 1946.*

Two styles of very popular nut-trays were made by Wade Heath before and just after WW II. Both of these embossed shapes were produced in two color variations of underglaze enamel on a "cane" colored body.

No. 418. NUT-TRAY—shape No. 373 with decoration No. 4878 and Mark Type 7. This shape was also produced in decoration No. 4885 with the major difference being a color change of the flowers to blue and yellow and the nuts to brown. The tray measures 7″ in diameter.

No. 419. NUT-TRAY—shape No. 372 with decoration No. 4877 and Mark Type 7. This shape was also produced in decoration No. 4886 with the major difference being the color change of the flowers to blue and yellow. The tray measures 7″ in diameter.

No. 420. ASHTRAY—decoration No. 5024 of copper lustre tracing on a white body applied to the standard shape Wade Heath ashtray. The ashtray measures 4″ by 3″ by ¾″ high and has a transfer Mark Type 15.

No. 421. BASKET—shape No. 247 with "Mottled" type decoration and Mark Type 6. This shape is not known to have been reintroduced after WW II. The basket is 5½″ long by 5″ high from base to top of handle.

FIG. 86. BASKET—shape No. 246 with "Mottled" blue/green/beige type decoration and Mark Type 6. The oval-shaped basket measures 6″ long by 5¼″ from base to top of handle and is not known to have been reintroduced after WW II.

FIG. 86.

No. 422. CUP & SAUCER—decoration No. 4880 with Mark Type 7. This underglaze, free-hand decoration was in production prior to WW II. and was applied to the full range of the standard Wade Heath tableware shapes (See FIG. 82). This decoration was also produced in free-hand underglaze color and copper lustre combination; however, the decoration number remained the same.

No. 423. PLANTER—with "Mottled" type decoration and Mark Type 4, measuring 10″ long by 5″ wide by 4½″ high. This planter is not known to have be reintroduced after WW II.

No. 424. ASHTRAY—with decoration No. 4884 and Mark Type 13. This underglaze free-hand decoration was applied to the standard shaped ashtray and also to the full range of standard tableware shapes (See FIG 82.).

No. 425. FINGER BOWL—with decoration No. 4883 and Mark Type 7. This 4″ dia. bowl shows the red flower from the two flower design of decoration No. 4883.

No. 426. TEA POT STAND—with decoration No. 4883 and Mark Type 13. This 6¼" dia. stand was introduced to the standard line of tableware shapes in the early 1950's.

No. 427. FINGER BOWL—with decoration No. 4883 and Mark Type 13. This 4" dia. bowl shows the blue flower from decoration No. 4883. Decoration No. 4883 was applied to the full range of standard tableware shapes (see FIG 82.).

No. 428. CIGARETTE BOX—shape No. 242 (standard shape) with decoration No. 4811 and Mark Type 7 on the base. The box measures 5" long by 3½" wide by 1¾" high. This decoration was applied to the full range of standard tableware shapes.

BASKET WARE
(Decoration U.4804) CIRCA 1946.

Decoration No. U.4804 is believed to be one of the first, if not the first, line of tableware produced by Wade Heath after WW II and marketed circa 1946. This decoration, of colored flowers and green leaves, was applied to a yellow background. At least two variations of this design of tableware were made. One had colored flowers and green leaves, highlighted with copper lustre above the flowers on a white background. The other variation was in a simple mottled finish.

No records are available to give absolute proof of the extent of this line but the following list indicates items known to have been made.

    Sugar
    Creamer
    Dish 9¼"
    Covered Cheese Dish
    Covered Butter Dish
    Covered Honey Pot
    Cruet Set
    (Covered Mustard, Salt, Pepper and Tray)

No. 429. "BASKET WARE" DISH—with decoration No. U.4804 and Mark Type 7. The dish measures 9¼" in diameter.

No. 432. "BASKET WARE" DISH—with mottled finish and Mark Type 7. The dish measures 9¼" in diameter.

No. 439. "BASKET WARE" HONEY POT—with decoration No. U.4804 and Mark Type 7. The pot is 3¼" in dia. by 5" high to top of finial.

No. 440. "BASKET WARE" BUTTER DISH—with decoration No. U.4804 and Mark Type 7. The dish measures 4½" in dia. at the rim by 3½" high to top of finial.

No. 441. "BASKET WARE" CREAMER—with white background and copper lustre highlighted decoration and Mark Type 7. The creamer is 3¼" high.

No. 442. "BASKET WARE" SUGAR—with decoration and Mark Type as the creamer above. The sugar is 3" in dia. at the rim by 2" high.

No. 443. "BASKET WARE" COVERED MUSTARD—with decoration No. U.4804 and is unmarked. The mustard measures 2¾" high to top of finial.

No. 444. "BASKET WARE" PEPPER SHAKER—with decoration No. U.4804 and is unmarked. The shaker measures 2¾" high.

No. 445. "BASKET WARE" SALT SHAKER—with similar decoration and measurement as the pepper shaker above. This shaker is also unmarked.

FIG. 87. "BASKET WARE" CRUET SET WITH TRAY—the yellow tray is undecorated other than the molded lattice design. The tray measures 5½" in dia. by ½" to top of raised lip and has Mark Type 7 on the underside of the base.

FIG. 87.

No. 446. "BASKET WARE" SUGAR—with decoration No. U.4804 and Mark Type 7. The sugar measures 3" in dia. by 2" high.

No. 447. "BASKET WARE" CREAMER—with decoration No. U.4804 and Mark type 7. The creamer measures 3¼" high.

No. 448. "BASKET WARE" CHEESE DISH—with decoration No. U.4804 and Mark Type 7 on the base only. The butter dish measures 6" long by 4¾" wide by 4¼" to top of finial.

EMPRESS (Decoration No. 5082)
CIRCA LATE 1940'S—LATE 1950'S.

A range of ornamental pieces in classical shapes, (see FIG. 88), decorated in Regency style with rich underglaze colors of blue, maroon, and green highlighted with burnished gold finish. The Empress line was also available in undecorated Satin white glaze finish. Items produced in this line were:

131

Vase	Shape No. 400	4″ wide x 8½″ high
Jug	Shape No. 401	4½″ wide x 8½″ high
Vase	Shape No. 402	5½″ wide x 8½″ high
Bowl	Shape No. 403	11″ wide x 6¾″ high
Vase	Shape No. 404	10″ wide x 11″ high
Bowl	Shape No. 408	15½″ wide x 6½″ high
	(Satin white glaze only)	

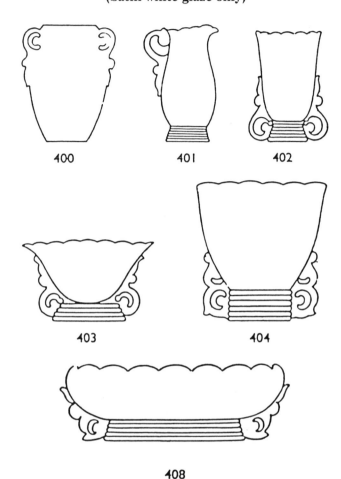

FIG. 88. EMPRESS SHAPES.

"GRAPE" DECORATION TABLEWARE *CIRCA 1953.*

This full line of tableware in elegant shapes is rich in color with embossed texture and hand gilded/painted vine design. It was produced in a variety of color combinations for a number of years after its introduction in the early 1950's. Not each color variation was given a name but each was given a decoration number. Two of these were located in an old Wade Heath catalog: decoration No. 6113 (Rubytone) and decoration No. 6143 (Regal Green). The items in this line are marked with a transfer type decoration with or without the pattern name.

Items produced in this line of tableware were:

Cup and Saucer	Tray
Plate 5″	Covered Butter Dish
Plate 7″	Honey Pot
Sauce Boat and Stand	Jug

Teapot (large size)	Salad Bowl
Teapot (medium size)	Salad Servers
Teapot (small size)	Cheese Dish
Open and Covered Sugar	Fruit Dish 7″
Creamer	Fruit Dish 5″
Cruet Set (covered mustard, salt and pepper shakers and tray)	
Salt and Pepper Shakers	

No. 430. PLATE—measures 7″ in diameter, unmarked. This plate was from a trial run made prior to the line going into production. We are grateful to Mrs. Georgina Lawton, designer of this table ware line, who gave us this plate as a gift, the only prototype piece she had.

No. 431. "GRAPE" DESIGN CUP AND SAUCER—this green/white decoration was the final color combination used for the above mentioned prototype when the line went into production. The saucer is 5½″ in diameter and the cup is 2½″ high with a 3½″ diameter rim. Both pieces have a transfer Mark Type 17 on the base.

No. 433. "REGAL GREEN" CREAMER—with decoration No. 6143 and Mark Type 16. The creamer measures 6″ overall by 3½″ high at the handle.

No. 434. "GRAPE" DESIGN TEAPOT—with gold decoration on white background. The tea pot measures 11″ overall by 6½″ high to top of finial and has Mark Type 16 on the base.

No. 435. "GRAPE" DESIGN SUGAR—with gold decoration on white background and Mark Type 16. The bowl measures 5″ overall by 3½″ to tip of finial.

No. 436. "GRAPE" DESIGN CREAMER—with gold decoration on white background and Mark Type 16. The creamer measures 6″ overall by 3½″ high at the handle.

No. 437. "RUBYTONE" SALAD BOWL—with decoration No. 6113 and Mark Type 16. The bowl measures 11″ long by 3″ high at the handles.

No. 438. "RUBYTONE" SALAD SERVERS—with decoration No. 6113. Both the 8½″ long spoon and fork are unmarked.

Rubytone

FIG. 89. "RUBYTONE" SAUCE BOAT AND STAND—with decoration No. 6113 and Mark Type 16 on both pieces. The sauce boat measures 6″ long by 3″ high at the handle and the stand measures 6½″ long by 1¼″ high at the handle. It should be noted that the shape of the sauce boat and creamer are very similar but can be differentiated by the size of the base and height. The sauce boat base is 3″ long and the creamer base is 2¾″ long.

FIG. 89.

DECORATIVE PLATES
CIRCA 1951-1960.

The establishment of the silk-screen printing department in the early 1950's resulted in the introduction of more detailed and elaborate designs, these would have not been possible with the earlier, handpainted, underglaze decorations. Amongst the first articles produced, using the silk-screen process, was a line of "wall plates" given the name of "Romance." This range was comprised of a variety of decorative scenes from flowers to eighteenth century "courting couple" designs, placed in the center of the plate and surrounded by wide bands of either maroon, dark blue or dark green. The term "Romance" referred to the plates with the wide, colored bands rather than the decoration in the center. Close examination of photographs taken of the Wade Heath exhibit at the 1954 British Industrial Fair, reveals three 18th century scenes and two flower designs giving a total, in combination with the three different colored bands, of fifteen variations.

No. 449. ROMANCE WALL PLATE—measuring 10½″ in dia. with transfer Mark Type 17.
No. 450. CRETONNE WALL PLATE—measuring 10½″ in dia. with Mark type 10. Plates in the Cretonne pattern can be found with a plain rim as well as the style illustrated.
No. 451. ROMANCE WALL PLATE—measuring 10½″ in dia. with Mark Type 10.

BUDDIES *CIRCA 1960.*

No. 452. "CLARA" BUD VASE—measuring 4½″ high with "WADE ENGLAND" transfer mark. A companion bud vase, "CLARENCE" was issued at the same time. See FIG. 90.

BUDDIES

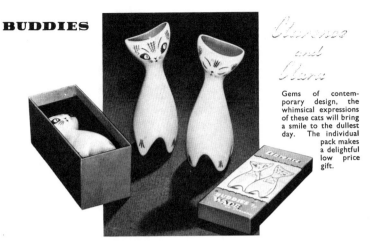

Clarence and Clara

Gems of contemporary design, the whimsical expressions of these cats will bring a smile to the dullest day. The individual pack makes a delightful low price gift.

FIG. 90.

"MEADOW" DECORATION TABLEWARE *CIRCA 1951-1960.*

This silk screen type decoration was used for a variety of tableware items first introduced as early as 1951. Due to lack of records, actual issue dates are not available. The basic color in the "Meadow" pattern was blue but variations of the basic pattern were issued highlighted with other colors.

No. 453. MEADOW PLATTER—with the basic single blue color. The platter measures 11¾″ long by 9″ wide and is marked "WADE MEADOW ENGLAND."
No. 454. MEADOW PLATE—with multicolored pattern applied to a 10″ dia. dinner plate. The backstamp is similar to that described above.

In addition to the two items illustrated the line also included the following: Dessert plate, Bread & Butter plate, Cup & Saucer, Creamer & Covered Sugar, Teapot, and Covered Serving Bowl.

TEA AND DINNER WARE ORB SHAPE *CIRCA EARLY 1950'S.*

These tea and dinnerware sets consisted of eighteen different sets with transfer type decoration. Where bands are used in the decoration, they were available in blue, yellow, green, or fawn. See FIG. 91.

FIG. 91. ORB SHAPES.

No.	Decoration No.	Type of Decoration
1.	4931	Transfers Giving Hand-painted Effect
2.	4942	Transfers Giving Hand-painted Effect
3.	4939	Cup & Saucer, Transfers Giving Hand-painted Effect
3A.	4953	Plate, Transfers Giving Hand-painted Effect
4.	4950	Lytho and Colored Bands
5.	4940	Transfers Giving Hand-painted Effect
6.	4953	Cup & Saucer, Transfers Giving Hand-painted Effect
6A.	4939	Plate, Transfers Giving Hand-painted Effect
7.	4891	Bands & Lines
8.	4868	Bands & Silver Lines
9.	4943	Bands
10.	4932	Lytho
11.	4809	Lytho Poppy Pattern
12.	4806	Lytho Apple Blossom Pattern
13.	4959	Lytho Filled in with Enamel
14.	4808	Lytho Lavender Lady Pattern
15.	4941	Transfer Bands and Lines
16.	4964	Lytho Gold Bands and Lines
17.	4895	Chintz Thistle Pattern, Green & Purple
18.	4937	Chintz, Floral

EVERLASTING CANDLES
1953-1954.

These porcelain candles were made in two pieces: a scalloped base and a hollow candle. They were intended to be used as a table centre-piece decoration, but due to slow sales they were withdrawn fairly speedily from the Wade range. The candles were marketed in boxes divided into sections with the two bases in the centre and a candle at each side. The candle had a small wick which was fueled by parafin or kerosene contained by a rubber plug at the base. The Everlasting Candles were made in a variety of background colors and decorated with a number of different flower decals, each of which was given a separate decoration name. These candles were made by George Wade and Son Ltd. at the Manchester Pottery.

No. 455. EVERLASTING CANDLES—with "Flower Spray" decoration. The base measures 4″ in dia. and combined with the candle is 8½″ high. The base, as well as the candle, has a transfer Mark Type 19.

MODE SHAPE
CIRCA 1953-EARLY 1960'S.

This line of tableware was first introduced in the early 1950's with handpainted, underglaze decorations. Later, when the silk screen department was added to the Manchester Pottery, it was made with transfer type decorations.

RITA *(Decoration No. 6056) 1953.*

This handpainted, underglaze decorated dinner/tea service was produced in the early 1950's. The items in this line were ink backstamped with Mark Type 17. Each item was also marked "Rita" below the backstamp.

No. 456. "RITA" COVERED SUGAR—measures 3¾" from base to top of finial by 6" across the handles.

No. 457. "RITA" CUP & SAUCER—the saucer is 5¾" in dia. and the cup is 2½" high by 3½" dia. at the rim.

CAPRI *(Decoration No. 6057) 1953.*

This handpainted, underglaze decorated dinner/tea service was produced in 1953.

No. 458. "CAPRI" BREAD & BUTTER PLATE—measures 6" in dia. with an ink backstamp Mark Type 15.

MODE WARE *(Decoration No. 6105) 1953.*

This handpainted, underglaze decorated dinner/tea service was produced in the early 1950's. The items in the line were ink backstamped with Mark Type 17. Another decoration, similar to the "MODE WARE" line, was also produced at this time with decoration No. 6106. This pattern had two large flowers (one red and one purple) along with large green and small brown and blue leaves.

No. 459. "MODE WARE" SNACK SET—made up of a 9½" tab handled plate with cup ring and matching cup. The cup is similar in size and shape to the cup in "Rita" pattern.

MODE *CIRCA LATE 1950'S EARLY 1960'S.*

Four distinctive transfer type patterns were applied to the standard range of the "Mode Shape" line of tableware. See FIG. 92.

MODE

FIG. 92.

OVENWARE *CIRCA 1939.*

A range of cooking ware items that was to be produced by George Wade & Son Ltd. in 1939. With the outbreak of WW II. this line never went into production beyond the "sampling" stage. The only color this line was sampled in was green mottled light brown.

Sample items made were:

Shallow Baking dish in three sizes
(L/S, M/S and S/S.)
Covered Casserole in three sizes
(2 pt, 1½ pt, and 1 pt.)
Deep Pie Dish (uncovered) in three sizes
(2 pt, 1½ pt, and 1 pt.)
Tea Pot and Hot Water Jug.

No. 460. "OVENPROOF" DISH—measures 7" square by 1½" high with an ink backstamp Mark Type 23.

QUACK QUACKS
CIRCA 1936-1939 AND
CIRCA 1953-LATE 1950'S.

A seven piece set of Nursery Ware was produced with the export market in mind. This attractive set of children's dishes was designed by Robert Barlow and shows a family of humorous ducks in different attitudes and occupations. Items in the set were:

1. Heavy Baby Plate
2. Oatmeal Bowl
3. Jug ½ pint
4. Cup and Saucer
5. Mug
6. Plate 4½" (actual size 6")
7. Plate 6" (actual size 8")

FIG. 93. QUACK QUACKS NURSERY WARE

This set of dishes was advertised with free standing models of a mother and father duck which were also available as retail items. The silk screen decoration and backstamp were similar for both the pre and post-war lines. The pre-war decorations were produced by a firm other than George Wade & Son Ltd. as this was well in advance of Wades producing their own printing method.

This group of nursery ware features a very attractive family of humorous ducks in different attitudes and occupations. The lines produced are cups and saucers, mugs, oatmeals, 4½-in. plates, and heavy, deep, baby plates. It is proving a very popular line, and delivery can be effected about six weeks from receipt of order.

WADE, HEATH & CO., LTD.
ROYAL VICTORIA POTTERY,
BURSLEM.

FIG. 94.

HARMONY TABLEWARE
CIRCA 1957-EARLY 1960'S.

A line of decorative tableware items designed in a modernistic style, so popular in the 1950's, this line was comprised of both regular and miniature sized items.

Bowl	Shape No. 438		**Miniatures.**	
Bowl	Shape No. 439			
Bowl	Shape No. 440		Bowl	Shape No. 449
Jug	Shape No. 433		Bowl	Shape No. 450
Jug	Shape No. 435		Vase	Shape No. 452
Jug	Shape No. 436		Jug	Shape No. 453
Vase	Shape No. 434			
Vase	Shape No. 458			
Tray	Shape No. 455			

These shapes were produced under the names of "SHOOTING STAR" (regular and miniature sizes), "FERN" (regular and miniature sizes), "PARASOL" and "CARNIVAL" (regular sizes only) and "HARMONY." The "HARMONY" pattern was produced in two-tone color glazes (green/peach and grey/pink), satin white (regular and miniature sizes) and in single color glazes of black, yellow and teal (miniature sizes only).

136

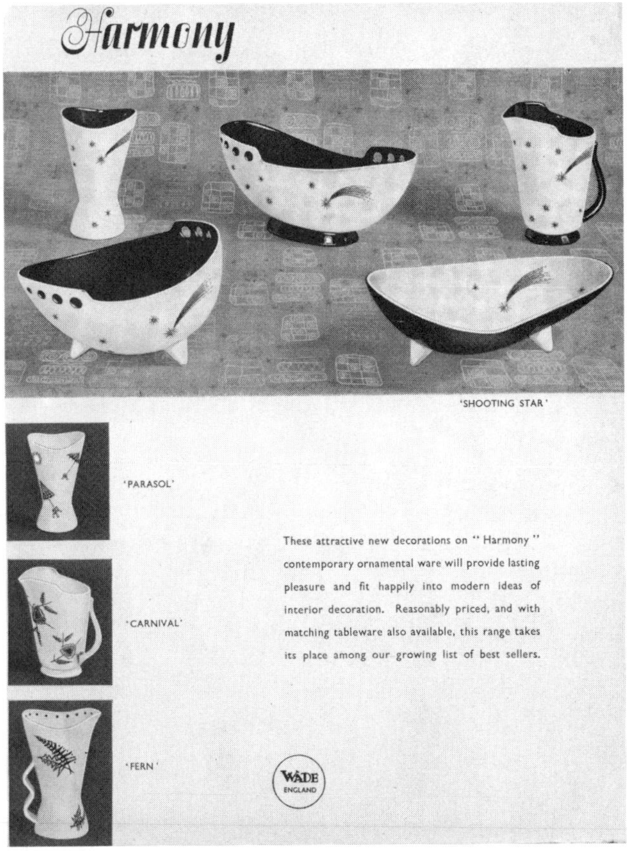

FIG. 95.

FIG. 96.

No. 461. "SHOOTING STAR"—miniature bowl shape
No. 450. The bowl is 5⅛" long by 2½" at the
highest point.

No. 462. CIGARETTE BOX—measures 5" long by 3¾"
wide by 2" high and is marked, on the underside
of the lid only with a transfer Mark Type 19.

BASKET WARE "2" *CIRCA MID 1950'S.*

This decoration was produced circa the mid 1950's, using molds from an earlier "Basket ware" design (decoration No. U.4804) which is known to have been in production in 1946. The molded design is quite apparent on the 1946 issue of this pattern. It is a lot less noticeable on the 1950's re-issue due to the busy, all over, goldcolored leaf and flower decoration. The decoration of this later issue of the "Basket ware" is a combination of an all-over applied silk screen design of gold leaves, etc. with hand-painted flowers and leaves formed by the mold, all on a white background. The other major difference is the use of metal lids with acrylic finials on the covered items of the later issue.

Following is a list of items produced in Basket ware "2":

> Sugar Covered and Uncovered
> Creamer
> Covered Cheese Dish
> Covered Butter Dish
> Covered Honey Pot
> Cruet Set (Mustard, Salt, Pepper and Tray)
> Salad Bowl and Servers
> Teapot
> Biscuit Barrel
> Flat Fruit Bowl

No. 463. BASKET WARE "2" BUTTER DISH—with
Mark Type 16. The dish measures 4½" in dia.
at the rim by 3¼" high from base to top of
finial.

No. 464. BASKET WARE "2" HONEY POT—with Mark
Type 16. The pot is 3¼" in dia. by 4¾" high to
top of finial.

LATTICE WARE
(Decoration No. 6191) *CIRCA LATE 1950'S.*

This was a complete line of salad ware and a number of individual pieces with a celadon green glaze finish. Items in this line were:

> Teapot (large size)
> Teapot (small size)
> Sugar
> Cream
> Jug
> Dish 5"
> Dish 6"
> Covered Cheese Dish
> Covered Butter Dish
> Honey Pot
> Biscuit Barrel with handle
> Sauce Boat
> Sauce Boat Stand
> Triple Tray
> Salad Bowl
> Salad Servers
> Oval Dish
> Cruet Set (Mustard, Salt, Pepper, and Tray)

For illustration of a number of these items see FIG. 97.

FIG. 97.

FLAIR TABLEWARE
CIRCA EARLY 1960'S.

Flair was the name given to a shape of tableware with numerous transfer type decorations designed by Georgina Lawton and Robert Barlow. Decorations produced in the Flair line were "GALAXY," "PLANTAIN," "RED POLKA," "COCKEREL" (see FIG. 98.)

FIG. 98.

For preliminary designs of the "COCKEREL" line by Robert Barlow, see FIG. 99.

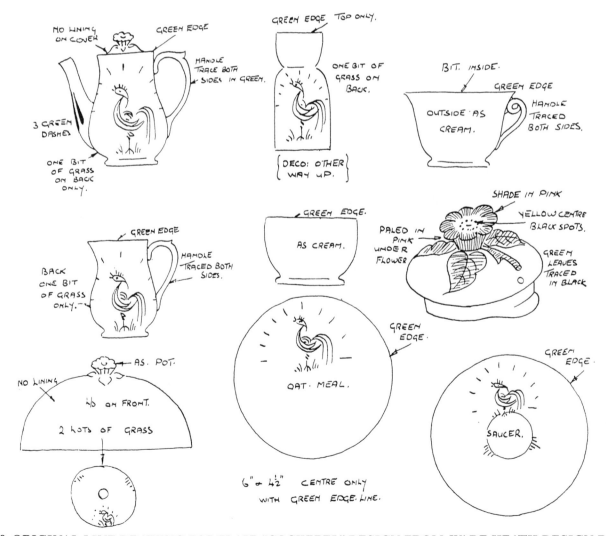

FIG. 99. ORIGINAL LINE DRAWING FOR FLAIR "COCKEREL" DESIGN FROM WADE HEATH DESIGN BOOK.

**FIG. 100.
FLAIR
TABLEWARE.**

VIOLETS
...always attractive, but even more so with the contrasting primrose glaze on the cups, sugar bowls and jugs.

SUMMER ROSE
...the pale pink glaze on the cups, bowls and jugs matches perfectly with the delicate rose sprays—one of the most popular of all WADE sets.

WILD ROSE
...the natural colourings of the rose sprays are enhanced by the pink glaze on the holloware pieces—another favourite.

Additional decorations available in the Flair tableware line were:

"VIOLETS," "SUMMER ROSE," "WILD ROSE," "WOOD MIST" in black (decoration No. 6222/B), red (decoration No. 6223/R), and green (decoration No. 6224/G), "GAIETY," and "HARLEQUIN FRUIT SETS." For illustrations of these decorations see FIG. 100.

WOODMIST (RED)
...the bold red centre leaf motif has a background of pale grey leaves and coloured flowers. The saucers and cup handles are in matching red—also available with predominant colouring in black.

GAIETY
...delicate conventional sprays in pink, blue and grey, with cups, bowl and jugs in turquoise blue glaze—a most pleasing colour combination.

HARLEQUIN FRUIT SETS
...the fruit dishes are in six different lovely pastel colours. With the pale green bowl the whole effect is delightful.

THE FAMILY FOUR
...a 12-piece set specially produced for the small family, for picnics, caravans, etc. One of the most popular and best-selling of WADE lines, and available in any of the patterns illustrated.

REGENCY COFFEE SETS
Mid. 1950'S-1961.

One of Wade Heath's most popular products, this coffee set of fluted Regency shapes was available in seven color combinations: all-gold, black and gold, maroon and gold, pink and gold, primrose and gold, turquoise and gold, and mother of pearl. This set is found with both, Mark Type 10 and Mark Type 19.

The Regency Coffee Set comprised of:

> **Six cups and Saucers**
> **Sugar Bowl**
> **Cream Jug**
> **Coffee Pot**

FIG. 101.

FANTASIA *1961.*

This set of four vases and tray is based on a theme from the Walt Disney movie, "Fantasia."

FIG. 102.

140

BRAMBLE WARE.

This extensive line of tableware was first introduced circa 1950, and given the decoration No. 4890 along with the name "Natural Colored Bramble". This decoration was of underglaze, hand applied "natural" enamel colors on a Cane-colored embossed body. The term "natural" refers to the original decoration (No. 4890) of this pattern where the leaves and berries were colored with their "real life" colors as found in nature. A second decoration, "Autumn Tints" decoration No. 4945 and a third decoration, "Gold Blush," both based on the original "Bramble" molds, were produced and marketed during the same time period as the "Natural Colored Bramble."

Following is a list of items manufactured in the original lines of "Natural Colored Bramble," "Autumn Tints" and "Gold Blush."

> **Covered Cheese (Wedge shape)**
> **Covered Cheese Dish (Oblong shape)**
> **Salad Servers (Fork and Spoon)**
> **Salad Bowl**
> **Tea Pot (two shapes)**
> **Triple Tray**
> **Jug 24s**
> **Jug 30s**
> **Jug 36s**
> **Jug 42s**
> **Cream Jug (large size)**
> **Cream Jug (small size)**
> **Cruet Set**
> **(Covered Mustard, Salt, Pepper and Tray)**
> **Salt and Pepper**
> **Sugar (small size)**
> **Sugar (large size)**
> **Sauce Boat and Stand**
> **Covered Honey Pot**
> **Covered Sugar**
> **Covered Butter**
> **Oval Dish 8″**
> **Oval Dish 10″**
> **Oval Dish 12″**
> **Round Bowl 4″**
> **Round Bowl 5″**
> **Round Bowl 6″**
> **Round Bowl 7″**
> **Round Bowl 8″**
> **Round Bowl 9″**

By 1954, three new items had been added to the original line:

> **Four Pointed Oval Dish 8″**
> **Star Shaped Dish 9″**
> **Pinwheel Shaped Dish 6″**

As the popularity of these two patterns began to diminish in the mid 1950's, new life was given to the "Bramble" line with the introduction of new background colors with the embossed pattern traced in liquid gold. Patterns issued with this type of finish were "Emerald Gold" and "Golden Turquoise" both with decoration No. 5038, "White Matt" with decoration No. 6013 and "Blace Velvet" with decoration No. 6153.

Circa 1953, a number of items from the "Bramble" line were produced with a white background and colored berries and leaves with an all over irridized finish.

No. 465. through No. 483. are all "Natural Colored Bramble" with decoration No. 4890 and with Mark Type 12.

No. 465. BOWL—measures 9″ in diameter.

No. 466. BOWL—measures 6″ in diameter.

No. 467. BOWL—measures 5″ in diameter.

No. 468. BOWL—measures 4″ in diameter.

No. 469. BOWL—measures 8″ in diameter.

No. 470. SALAD BOWL—measures 6½″ in diameter at rim by 4″ high.

No. 471. SALAD SERVERS—measures 8¼″ long and is unmarked.

No. 472. JUG 24s—measures 5¾″ high.

No. 473. CREAM JUG (large size)—measures 3½″ high.

No. 474. JUG 42s—measures 4½″ high.

No. 475. HONEY POT—measures 4¼″ high to top of finial.

No. 476. BUTTER DISH—measures 3½″ high to top of finial.

Note that the covered sugar is identical to the butter dish with the only difference in the lid which has no cut-out for the spoon.

No. 477. SUGAR (small size)—measures 2¾″ in diameter by 1¾″ high.

No. 478. SUGAR (large size)—measures 2¼″ high.

No. 479. CRUET SET with TRAY.

No. 480. OVAL DISH—measures 8″ long by 5″ wide.

No. 481. CHEESE DISH (oblong)—measures 7¼″ long by 3½″ to top of finial. Although this is referred to as a cheese dish in trade literature, it was frequently used as a butter dish.

No. 482. TRIPLE TRAY—measures 8″ by 7¾″.

No. 483. SAUCE BOAT and TRAY—the tray measures 5¼″ long by 4½″ wide and the boat measures 6″ long by 2½″ at the handle.

No. 484. "EMERALD GOLD" FOUR POINTED OVAL DISH—with decoration No. 5038, measuring 8″ long by 5¼″ wide and ink stamped "WADE ENGLAND" on the base.

No. 485. "EMERALD GOLD" TEA POT—with decoration No. 5038, measuring 5¾″ high to top of finial and is marked "WADE EMERALD GOLD ENGLAND".

No. 486. "GOLDEN TURQUOISE" STAR SHAPED DISH—with decoration No. 5038, measuring 9″ in diameter and is marked "WADE GOLDEN TURQUOISE ENGLAND".

No. 487. "GOLDEN TURQUOISE" TEA POT—with decoration No. 5038, measuring 5¾″ high to top of finial and is marked "WADE GOLDEN TURQUOISE ENGLAND".

No. 488. "GOLDEN TURQUOISE" JUG 24s—with decoration No. 5038, measuring 6¼″ high and is marked "WADE GOLDEN TURQUOISE ENGLAND."

No. 489. "EMERALD GOLD" COVERED CHEESE (Wedge Shape)—with decoration No. 5038, measuring 6¼″ long by 4¾″ wide by 3½″ high to top of finial and has Mark Type 10 on the underside of the base.

No. 490. "EMERALD GREEN" JUG 42s—measures 4½″ high and has Mark Type 10 on the base. Note that the gold decoration is missing from this item.

No. 491. "BLACK VELVET" SALT and PEPPER—with decoration No. 6153. Both items measure 2¼″ high and are unmarked.

No. 492. "BLACK VELVET" TEA POT—with decoration No. 6153, measuring 6¾″ high to top of finial and has Mark Type 16 on the base.

No. 493. "BLACK VELVET" JUG 36s—with decoration No. 6153, measuring 5¼″ high and has Mark Type 16 on the base.

No. 494. "BLACK VELVET" SAUCE BOAT and TRAY—with decoration No. 6153. The tray measures 5¼″ long by 4½″ wide and the boat measures 6″ long by 2½″ high at the handle. Both items have Mark Type 16 on the base.

No. 495. "IRRIDIZED" CREAM JUG (large size)—measures 3½″ high and has Mark Type 10 on the base.

No. 496. "IRRIDIZED" SUGAR (large size)—measures 2¼″ high and has Mark Type 10 on the base.

No. 497. "AUTUMN TINTS" OVAL DISH—with decoration No. 4945, measuring 8″ long by 5″ wide and has Mark Type 12 on the base.

No. 498. "AUTUMN TINTS" SUGAR (small size)—with decoration No. 4945, measuring 2¾″ in diameter by 1¾″ high with Mark Type 12 on the base.

No. 499. "AUTUMN TINTS" CREAM JUG (small size)—with decoration No. 4945, measuring 2¾″ high with Mark Type 12 on the base.

No. 500. "AUTUMN TINTS" HONEY POT—with decoration No. 4945, measuring 4½″ high to top of finial with Mark Type 12 on the base.

No. 501. "WHITE MATT" SUGAR (large size)—with decoration No. 6013, measuring 2¼″ high with Mark Type 10 on the base.

No. 502. "WHITE MATT" CREAM JUG (large size)—with decoration No. 6013, measuring 3½″ high with Mark Type 10 on the base.

No. 503. "GOLD BLUSH" PINWHEEL SHAPED DISH—measures 6″ in diameter with Mark Type 12 on the base.

No. 504. "GOLD BLUSH" JUG 36s—measures 5¼″ high with Mark Type 12 on the base.

No. 505. "GOLD BLUSH" OVAL DISH—measures 10″ long by 7″ wide with Mark Type 12 on the base.

SOLID COPPER LUSTRE AND HAND-PAINTED PATTERNS WITH COPPER LUSTRE

CIRCA 1935-1980.

During the 1930's, Wade Heath produced an extensive line of solid copper lustre ware, of which many pieces were not marked or simply marked "Made in England." Circa the late 1940's to the late 1950's, Wade Heath reintroduced much of their pre-war solid copper lustre range, which was marked with the then current Wade Heath backstamp. Between the years 1946 and 1960, Wade Heath also produced a large line of copper lustre ware with a variety of hand-painted decorations. From circa 1950, the number of designs were decreased as the introduction of silk screen type decoration on plain background proved to be more economically viable.

From the early 1960's to the late 1970's, no copper lustre ware, either solid or decorated, was produced. A small line of eight jugs, four sizes of both the Stag and Diamond Jugs was introduced circa the late 1970's, but these did not prove popular with the consumers and the line was withdrawn in 1980.

Following is a list of solid copper lustre ware items produced from the late 1940's to the late 1950's:

Candy Box	
Cigarette Box	
Ash Tray	
Finger Bowl	
Dandy Jug Creamer	(small size)
Dandy Jug Creamer	(large size)
Dandy Jug 42s	4½″ high
Dandy Jug 36s	5″ high
Dandy Jug 30s	5½″ high
Dandy Jug 24s	6″ high
Beer Mug	
Eagle Tea Pot	
Tea Pot Stand	
Dandy Sugar	(small size)
Dandy Sugar	(large size)
Toby Jug (Pirate)	5″ high
Toby Jug (Highwayman)	5″ high
Lattice Jug 30s	6″ high
Lattice Jug 36s	5″ high
Lattice Jug 42s	4½″ high
Nelson Tea Pot 42s	
Nelson Tea Pot 36s	
Nelson Tea Pot 30s	
Nelson Tea Pot 24s	
Dutch Jug 42s	
Dutch Jug 36s	
Dutch Jug 30s	
Dutch Jug 24s	
Diamond Jug 30s	6″ high
Diamond Jug 36s	5½″ high
Diamond Jug 42s	5″ high
Stag Bowl	
Stag Consol Bowl	

Stag Jug 42s	5″ high
Stag Jug 36s	5½″ high
Stag Jug 30s	6″ high
Polka Jug 42s	5″ high
Polka Jug 36s	5½″ high
Polka Jug 30s	6″ high

Measurements given are taken from trade literature and are from the base to the tip of spout. In actuality, these measurements can vary significantly. It can be assumed that the trade literature gave dimensions to the nearest half inch. Dimensions given will be those as noted in the literature.

DECORATION No. 5033 *CIRCA 1951.*

The style of this decoration is referred to as "copper lustre and resist." This method of decoration is time consuming and necessitates considerable artistic ability on the part of the decorator. Needless to say tableware produced by this technique was costly to manufacture and was thus marketed in limited quantities. Tableware with this type of finish is now highly collectible and commands high prices. The process for this type of decoration involves painting the design on a "cane" body with water color which is then glazed and fired. On cooling the design is once again painted over in water color. The piece is then painted all over with copper lustre and fired once more. The copper lustre does not adhere to the design area and peels off, leaving the colored design with the copper lustre background. Decoration No. 5033 was applied to the range of standard Wade Heath tableware shapes. (See FIG. 82).

No. 506. LATTICE JUG 30s—with decoration No. 5033 and Mark Type 10. Decoration No. 5033 was applied to all three sizes of the "Lattice Jugs".

No. 507. STAG JUG 36s—in solid copper lustre with Mark Type 19. This jug is an example of the late 1970's reissue of the "Stag Jug" in solid copper lustre, which included sizes 30s, 42s and a new smaller size, 48s.

No. 508. DANDY JUG 24s—in solid copper lustre with Mark Type 19. The Dandy Jugs were amongst the last solid copper lustre items to be withdrawn around 1960.

No. 509. DIAMOND JUG 30s—with decoration No. 5033 and Mark Type 10. Decoration No. 5033 was applied to all three sizes of the "Diamond Jug".

No. 510. BEER MUG—with "Oak" pattern and Mark Type 10. The mug measures 5″ high.

No. 511. DIAMOND JUG 36s—with "Oak" pattern and Mark Type 10. This decoration was applied to all three sizes of the "Diamond Jug".

Numerous "copper lustre and resist" designs were used during the 1950's. Five additional examples are illustrated in FIG. 103 and FIG. 103a.

5086

6134

6146

6147

FIG. 103.

FIG. 103a. "BARLEY" DESIGN.

"FESTIVAL" *(Decoration No. 5070) 1954.*

The "Festival" decoration is based on molds previously issued, in solid copper lustre, under the name of "Polka," in the 1930's and marked simply "MADE IN ENGLAND." Polka was reintroduced in the late 1940's, again with a solid copper lustre finish with Mark Type 10. It is most probable that this mold shape, along with the "Stag" design molds, were first used at a much earlier date. Examples of these shapes have been seen with molded marks dating from the late 19th century, but it is not clear, due to lack of records, whether these early molds were owned, at that time, by one

of the Wade potteries. A companion set to the "Festival" decoration was also introduced under decoration No. 6192. Decoration No. 6192 had similar colored figures to "Festival" but had an "all-over" light blue background. The "Festival" decoration was given major exposure at the British Industries Fair in 1954. The range consisted of the following items:

Jug 30s	**6″ high**
Jug 36s	**5½″ high**
Jug 42s	**5″ high**
Tea Pot	
Sugar	
Creamer	
Tankard	

No. 512. "FESTIVAL" JUG 36s—with Mark Type 18.
No. 513. "FESTIVAL" JUG 42s—with Mark Type 18.
FIG. 104. "FESTIVAL" TANKARD—measures 4¾″ from base to rim with Mark Type 18.

FIG. 104.

No. 514. POLKA JUG 42s—with Mark Type 10. This solid copper lustre jug was issued in the late 1940's.
No. 515. DANDY JUG 42s—with decoration No. 5033 and Mark Type 10.
No. 516. STAG CONSOL BOWL—in solid copper lustre with Mark Type 13. The bowl measures 11¼″ long by 6″ wide by 4″ high.
No. 517. CIGARETTE BOX—with decoration No. 5033 on the lid only and Mark Type 10 on the base only.
No. 518. POWDER BOWL—with decoration No. 5078 on lid only and Mark Type 13 on the base along with an impressed mark "Made in England". The bowl measures 4¼″ in diameter, at the lid, by 1½″ high. The decoration shows only the pink flower from the two flower (pink and purple) design.

No. 519. CANDY BOX—with decoration No. 5033 on the lid only and Mark Type 10 on the underside of the four-footed base. The box measures 7″ long by 5″ wide by 3½″ high.

No. 520. OVAL DISH—with decoration No. 5033 and Mark Type 10. The dish measures 8″ long by 5″ wide by 1½″ high. This is an additional item to the standard range of tableware.

No. 521. DANDY SUGAR (small size)—with decoration No. 5033 and Mark Type 10.

No. 522. DANDY CREAM (small size)—with decoration No. 5033 and Mark Type 10.

No. 523. DANDY SUGAR (small size)—in solid copper lustre with Mark Type 13.

No. 524. DANDY CREAM (small size)—in solid copper lustre with Mark Type 13.

No. 525. ROUND DISH—with decoration No. 5033 and Mark Type 10. The dish measures 6″ in diameter by 1¼″ high and is an additional item to the standard range of tableware.

No. 526. ROUND DISH—with decoration No. 5033 and Mark Type 10. The dish measures 5″ in diameter by 1″ high and is an additional item to the standard range of tableware.

No. 527. DUTCH JUG 42s—with decoration No. 5086 and Mark Type 3. This decoration was reintroduced after WW II. in red/solid copper lustre combination under the same decoration number. It is believed that both pre-war and post-war decorations were applied to the full range of the standard tableware shapes. (See FIG. 82).

No. 528. DUTCH JUG 42s—with decoration No. 4883 and Mark Type 13. This decoration was available in the standard range of tableware.

No. 529. DUTCH JUG 42s—with decoration No. 4881 and Mark Type 7. This decoration was available in the standard range of tableware.

No. 530. DUTCH JUG 30s—with Mark Type 3. This decoration was available in the standard range of tableware and is not known to have been reproduced after WW II.

No. 531. DUTCH JUG 30s—with decoration No. 4884 and Mark Type 7. This decoration was available in the standard range of tableware.

No. 532. DANDY JUG 30s—with decoration No. 5045 and Mark Type 13. This decoration was available in the standard range of tableware.

No. 533. DANDY JUG 30s—with silk screen decoration applied to a white body with Mark Type 19. This jug was produced in the early 1960's. It is believed that this decoration was applied to a limited range of standard tableware items.

No. 534. DANDY JUG 36s—with Mark Type 13. This decoration was available in the standard range of tableware.

No. 535. DANDY JUG 36s—with decoration No. 4884 and Mark Type 7. This decoration was available in the standard range of tableware

and was in production from the late 1940's to the mid 1950's, therefore, similar shapes will be found with a variety of backstamps.

No. 536. DANDY JUG 36s—with Mark Type 13. This decoration, which has an irridized finish, was available in the standard range of tableware.

No. 537. DANDY CREAM (large size)—with Mark Type 7. This simple decoration of a band and lines below hand-applied leaves is believed to have been one of the first lines of tableware, produced in a limited range when production of tableware resumed after WW II.

No. 538. DANDY JUG 42s—with decoration No. 5024 and Mark Type 16. This decoration of copper lustre traced on a white body was available in the standard range of tableware.

No. 539. DANDY SUGAR (small size)—with decoration No. 5024 and Mark Type 16.

No. 540. DANDY CREAM (small size)—with decoration No. 5024 and Mark Type 16.

No. 541. DANDY CREAM (large size)—with decoration No. 4899 and Mark Type 7. This decoration is similar to No. 4884 but with the solid copper lustre band at the rim and spout replaced by a wash band and two lines. The copper lustre was not applied to the handle which, instead, had a dashed decoration. Decoration No. 4899 was marketed for a number of years from the late 1940's to the mid 1950's and was applied to the standard range of tableware.

No. 542. DANDY SUGAR (small size)—with decoration No. 4899 and Mark Type 13. The band and two lines which appear on the outside of the creamer (No. 541 above) are applied to the inside face of the sugar.

No. 543. DANDY SUGAR (small size)—with copper lustre leaf design and Mark Type 7.

No. 544. DANDY CREAM (small size)—with copper lustre leaf design and Mark Type 7.

FIG. 105. DANDY SUGAR (small size)—with decoration No. 4404 and Mark Type 7.

FIG. 105.

No. 545. DANDY SUGAR (small size)—with decoration No. 6018 and Mark Type 16. This decoration was available in the standard range of tableware.

No. 546. DANDY CREAM (large size)—with decoration No. 6018 and Mark Type 16.

No. 547. DANDY CREAM (small size)—with decoration No. 6018 and Mark Type 16.

No. 548. DANDY SUGAR (large size)—with decoration No. 4879 and Mark Type 7. This decoration was available in the standard range of tableware.

No. 549. DANDY CREAM (small size)—with a "Meadow" type decoration and Mark Type 19. This small line of tableware was in production circa 1960. See decoration No. 6266 for a list of items produced in this line.

No. 550. DANDY SUGAR (small size)—with decoration No. 4882 and Mark Type 7. This decoration was available in the standard range of tableware.

No. 551. DANDY CREAM (small size)—with decoration No. 4882 and Mark Type 7.

No. 552. DANDY CREAM (large size)—with decoration No. 4884 and Mark Type 10.

No. 553. DANDY SUGAR (large size)—with decoration No. 4884 and Mark Type 13. This decoration was available in the standard range of tableware.

DECORATION NO. 6266 *CIRCA 1960.*

With the drop in the number of tableware lines produced by Wade Heath toward the end of the 1950's, a number of standard shapes were dropped and some shapes revised. Few of the earlier lines of tableware included plates and cups and saucers; however, the new, smaller lines of the early 1960's included plates, cups and saucers. The shape of the creamers remained in the "Dandy" shape but the sugars were restyled to be similar to the new "Flair" line of tableware introduced in the early 1960's. Items in this and similar lines were:

    Plate 4½″
    Saucer
    Cup
    Sugar (small size)
    Cream (small size)
    Tea Pot

The lithograph design was complimented by ¼″ black bands placed ⅛″ from the edge of the various items. The tea pot lid had a band up to the handle.

No. 554. SUGAR—similar to decoration No. 6266 with Mark Type 19. The Lithograph decoration is similar to No. 6266 but the black bands are replaced with copper lustre trim.

No. 555. DANDY CREAM (small size)—similar to decoration No. 6266 with Mark Type 19.

No. 556. DANDY SUGAR (small size)—with decoration No. 6050 and Mark Type 13. This decoration was available in the standard range of tableware.

No. 557. DANDY CREAM (small size)—with decoration No. 6050 and Mark Type 13.

TEA POTS *1927-1987.*

No. 558. "POPPY" TEA POT—with Mark Type 20 introduced in October 1984 as part of a tableware line to be sold through the Boots Drug Store chain. Only the tea pot for the tableware line was made by Wade. The tea pot measures 6½″ high to top of finial by 5½″ diameter base. A second size, not illustrated, is made with a similar decoration measuring 5½″ high by 4½″ diameter.

No. 559. PAISLEY DESIGN TEA POT—with decoration No. 6026 and Mark Type 1 which dates the manufacture of the tea pot to the late 1920's. The tea pot measures 6¾″ high to top of handle by 8″ overall. This pattern was produced in lithograph form as an open stock pattern supplied by a lithograph manufacturer to any pottery who cared to use this pattern. This pattern was applied to a teapot in white body. Teapots in red bodies would pre-date the white body.

No. 560. NELSON TEA POT 24s—with decoration No. 4880 and Mark Type 7. This decoration was available in the standard range of tableware.

No. 561. NELSON TEA POT 24s—with decoration No. 6117 and Mark Type 16. This decoration was available in the standard range of tableware.

No. 562. NELSON TEA POT 36s—with decoration No. 4884 and Mark Type 7. This decoration was available in the standard range of tableware.

No. 563. NELSON TEA POT 42s—with decoration No. 4811 and Mark Type 7. This decoration was available in the standard range of tableware.

No. 564. NELSON TEA POT 42s—with decoration No. 6018 and Mark Type 16. This decoration was available in the standard range of tableware.

No. 565. EAGLE TEA POT—with decoration No. 6018 and Mark Type 10. This tea pot measures 6″ high by 10″ overall. This tea pot was an additional item to the standard range of tableware.

No. 566. TEA & WATER POT STAND—with Mark Type 2 measuring 8¼″ long by 7″ wide by 1″ high.

No. 567. HOT WATER POT—with decoration No. 3599 and Mark Type 2. The pot measures 5½″ high by 8″ overall.

No. 568. TEA POT—with decoration No. 3599 and Mark Type 2. The tea pot measures 5½″ high by 9½″ overall. Item No.'s 566, 567 and 568 form a set and were produced in a variety of patterns other than the set illustrated.

SCOTTIE TEA POT *1953-1955.*

This series of four tea pots in two sizes was designed by Georgina Lawton. The only variation between the four designs involved the coloring of the cap-shaped lids with the finials black in each variation.

The four different colored tartan lids were:

> Decoration No. 6045 (black & brown on a light brown background).
> Decoration No. 6046 (black, red & yellow on a light yellow background).
> Decoration No. 6047 (black & white on a blue background).
> Decoration No. 6071 (black, green & orange on a light green background).

No. 569. SCOTTIE TEA POT—with decoration No. 6046 and Mark Type 16 measures 5¼″ high to top of finial by 8″ overall.

No. 570. SCOTTIE TEA POT—with decoration No. 6071 and Mark Type 16 measures 5¾″ high to top of finial by 9″ overall.

Royal Victoria Pottery Decorating Shop. Circa 1951.

Tankards & Souvenirs

by

Wade Heath & Company Ltd.

and

Wade (Ireland) Ltd.

TANKARDS (MID. 1950'S-1986)
AND SOUVENIRS (MID. 1950'S-1961).

From the mid. 1950's Wade Heath & Company Ltd. and later Wade (Ireland) Ltd. produced an extremely popular line of handsome and useful tankards of various colored glazes and decorations. One of the most popular shapes was the "Traditional" shaped tankard. This is easily recognized from similar shaped tankards made by other potteries because of the molded leaf type design at the top of the handle. In later years, a limited number of the "Traditional" style tankards were produced in the Irish pottery with a "D" shaped handle. These tankards can be identified by their backstamp.

The "Traditional" style tankard was made in one pint size (approx. 4¾" high), half pint size (approx. 4" high) and a miniature size (approx. 2" high). Other popular shapes in the tankard line were the "Barrel" and "Plymouth" tankards. Both of these shapes were produced in three sizes. The "Barrel" one pint size is approx. 5" high, the half pint size is approx. 3½" high and the miniature size is approx. 2" high. The tapered "Plymouth" tankard one pint size is approx. 4¾" high, the half pint size is approx. 3¾" high and the miniature size is approx 2" high.

A companion piece to the tankard line was the "Oil Jug" measuring approx. 3½" to tip of spout. It is believed that the "Oil Jug" was produced in only the amber glaze highlighted with silver colored bands and handles. As with the "Traditional" shaped tankard, the "Oil Jug" was produced with a variety of colorful transfer decorations.

The most popular decoration of all time for the amber "Traditional" shaped tankard was a series of Veteran Cars. The series was designed for RICHARD KOHNSTAM LTD., the sole distributors of the Veteran Car Range. These tankards all bear a backstamp "An 'RK' Product by Wade of England." It should be mentioned that all three sizes in this shaped tankard along with the "Oil Jug," "Tire Dishes" and "Cigarette Boxes" were all produced in the Veteran Car Range. Each item is numbered along with the name of the car illustrated. Unfortunately, records only exist of the first five sets issued, but it is believed that there were a further five sets produced.

From the mid 1950's to 1961, the transfer type decoration of the Veteran Cars was applied in black only. This applied to the first five sets. In 1961, the sixth set of three designs were the first to be produced in color. It was at this time that Wade Heath ceased making gift ware items and the tankard molds were transferred to the Irish pottery where production of the tankards continued. No date is available for the end of the Veteran Car Range produced for RICHARD KOHNSTAM LTD., but decorated amber glazed tankards were produced at the Irish pottery until the mid 1980's.

The first five sets, consisted of three designs per set and were issued prior to 1961. Set No. 5 was the first in color and issued in 1961. They were as follows:

SET 1.
Benz 1899, Ford 1912, Darracq 1904.
SET 2.
Sunbeam 1904, Rolls Royce 1907, Baby Peugeot 1902.
SET 3.
De Dion Bouton 1904, Spyker 1905, Lanchester 1903.

SET 4.
Oldsmobile 1904, Cadillac 1903, White Steam Car 1903.
SET 5.
Buggatti, Sunbeam 1914, Itala 1908.

For examples of tankards from the various Veteran Car range, see items in the color section as listed below.

No. 571. OLDSMOBILE—one pint tankard. No. 10 from Series 4.

No. 572. LANCHESTER—one pint tankard. No. 9 from Series 3.

No. 573. DARRACQ—one pint tankard. No. 3 from Series 1.

No. 574. WOLSLEY—one pint tankard. No. 25 from Series 9.

No. 575. HISPANO-SUIZA—one pint tankard. No. 24 from Series 8.

No. 576. SUNBEAM—one pint tankard. No. 15 from Series 5.

No. 577. ALFA ROMEO—one pint tankard. No. 16 from Series 6.

No. 578. 1907 FIAT F2—one pint tankard. No. 21 from Series 7.

No. 579. CADILLAC—one pint tankard. No. 11 from Series 4.

No. 580. BUGATTI—one pint tankard. No. 17 from Series 6.

No. 581. SPYKER—one pint tankard. No. 8 from Series 3.

No.582. ITALA—one pint tankard. No. 13 from Series 5.

No. 583. DE DION BOUTON—one pint tankard. No. 7 from Series 3.

No. 584. 1925 MG—half pint tankard. No. 20 from Series 7.

No. 585. FORD—half pint tankard. No. 2 from Series 1.

No. 586. SUNBEAM—one pint tankard. No. 4 from Series 2.

The "Traditional" and "Plymouth" tankards, in all three sizes, along with the "Oil Jug" have been used as souvenir items. The variety of transfer-applied decorations is considerable. The souvenir tankards are marked with transfer type marks either "Wade England" or "Wade Ireland." Occasionally the word "souvenir" is also included in the backstamp. Examples of the souvenir tankards are shown in the color section.

No. 587. TRAFALGAR SQUARE—one pint souvenir tankard.
No. 588. RYERSON POLYTECHNICAL INSTITUTE—one pint souvenir tankard. (Courtesy—Ryerson Bookstore, Ryerson Polytechnical Institute).
No. 589. PLYMOUTH TANKARD—one pint size souvenir tankard with crest decoration of unknown origin.
No. 590. YEOMAN WARDER—one pint souvenir tankard.
No. 591. THE GENT'S A GOURMET—one pint tankard.
No. 592. RYERSON POLYTECHNICAL INSTITUTE—one pint souvenir tankard. (Courtesy—Ryerson Bookstore, Ryerson Polytechnical Institute.)

No. 593. GOLFERS—one pint tankard with comical crest.

No. 594. DALHOUSIE UNIVERSITY—one pint souvenir tankard.

No. 595. PLYMOUTH TANKARD—one pint size souvenir tankard decorated with map of Newfoundland, Canada.

No. 596. TRADITIONAL TANKARD—half pint size souvenir tankard decorated with Lobster and Trap and the crest of Nova Scotia, Canada.

No. 597. PLYMOUTH TANKARD—half pint size souvenir tankard decorated with the crest of Nova Scotia, Canada.

No. 598. TRADITIONAL TANKARD—half pint size tankard. Souvenir of Great Britain.

No. 599. TRADITIONAL TANKARD—half pint size tankard. Souvenir of Grand Bahama Island.

No. 600. PLYMOUTH TANKARD—half pint size souvenir tankard decorated with the crest of New Brunswick, Canada.

No. 601. BIG BEN—half pint souvenir tankard.

BARREL TANKARDS

Four sizes of the barrel tankards were made with a rich amber glazing contrasting beautifully with the burnished silver of the raised hoops and rope handles. The four sizes are 2″ high miniature, 3¾″ half pint, 5″ one pint, and the 7½″ "jumbo" four pint size.

No. 602. BARREL TANKARD—standard one pint size.

No. 603. BARREL TANKARD—standard half pint size.

MINIATURE OIL JUGS

No. 604. BENZ—oil jug. No. 1 from Series 1 of the Veteran Car Range.

No. 605. BIG BEN—souvenir oil jug.

No. 606. TOWER BRIDGE, LONDON—souvenir oil jug.

No. 607. TRAFALGAR SQUARE—souvenir oil jug.

BUD VASE SOUVENIRS
CIRCA MID 1950'S-1961.

No. 608. BUD VASE—handpainted flower decoration with Mark Type 19. This vase and the following two vases are 4½″ high.

No. 609. BUD VASE—souvenir of London with Mark Type 19.

No. 610. BUD VASE—souvenir of New Brunswick, Canada, with Mark Type 19.

MINIATURE "TRADITIONAL" TANKARDS—ANIMAL SERIES.

No. 611. GIRAFFE.

No. 612. ZEBRA.

No. 613. RHINOCEROS.

No. 614. GAZELLE.

No. 615. ELEPHANT.

No. 616. LION.

MINIATURE "TRADITIONAL" TANKARDS—SOUVENIR.

No. 617. NOVA SCOTIA, CANADA.

MINIATURE "TRADITIONAL" TANKARDS—VETERAN CAR RANGE.

No. 618. ROLLS-ROYCE—No. 5 from Series 2.

No. 619. SUNBEAM—No. 4 from Series 2.

No. 620. SPYKER—No. 8 from Series 3.

No. 621. DARRACQ—No. 3 from Series 1.

SOUVENIR PLATES AND TRAYS
CIRCA 1954-1961.

During the second half of 1950's until 1961, Wade Heath & Company Ltd. produced a large number of decorative gift ware items, many of which were aimed at the souvenir trade. The demand for Wade Souvenir Pottery was worldwide, and new subjects from many countries were added to the range over the years and with the beautiful full color reproduction of typical scenes, animals, etc., these items became best sellers.

Popular shapes used for the gift ware and souvenir items were wall plates, small trays of various shapes, and a small number of vases. A variety of these items are illustrated in the color section.

WALL PLATES.

No. 622. BRITISH COLUMBIA—9½″ diameter plate with Mark Type 19.

No. 623. PROVINCE OF ONTARIO—9½″ diameter plate with Mark Type 19.

No. 624. NIAGARA FALLS—9½″ diameter plate with Mark Type 19.

TIRE DISHES—
VETERAN CAR RANGE.

No. 625. BABY PEUGEOT—No. 6 from Series 2.

No. 626. FORD—No. 2 from Series 2.

FAMOUS SHIP DISHES.

A set of three dishes, from the same mold as the Tire Dishes, features illustrations of the "Sailing Ships" as used for the "Snippets" issued in 1956-1957. Not shown are the "Santa Maria" and the "Revenge".

No. 627. MAYFLOWER—5″ diameter "Tire Dish."

MISCELLANEOUS GIFT WARE.

No. 628. TROOPER—LIFE GUARDS—this 4½″ diameter tray is believed to be from a series. The name and number of items in the series is unknown.

No. 629. DEER & RABBITS—this octagonal shaped tray measures 4⅜″ across and has Mark Type 19. The measurements and Mark Types apply to the following four octagonal dishes.

No. 630. PIPER.

No. 631. MR. PICKWICK—this dish is from a series comprising six different subjects based on characters from the books of Charles Dickens. A second series of similar dishes was based upon characters from *Vanity Fair* by Wm.M. Thackeray. Both sets of dishes were available boxed singly or in pairs, with each dish bearing Mark Type 19 along with a likeness of the author.

Companion pieces to the *Vanity Fair* and Charles Dickens sets were three 4½″ high miniature vases. For shapes see FIG. 106. These vases were also available with colored floral sprays and blue bands at top and bottom.

FIG. 106. VASE SHAPES.

No. 632. STAGECOACH.
No. 633. SCOTTISH DANCER.

The following seven souvenir dishes are all 4¼″ in diameter with tapered edges ¾″ high. Unless noted otherwise the dishes are marked "Souvenirs of London By Wade England."

No. 634. THE WESTBURY HOTEL with Mark Type 19.
No. 635. BIG BEN.
No. 636. TOWER BRIDGE—LONDON.
No. 637. TOWER BRIDGE—LONDON with Mark Type 19.

No. 638. EROS—PICCADILLY CIRCUS.
No. 639. TRAFALGAR SQUARE.
No. 640. BAHAMIAN CONSTABLE with Mark Type 19.

WALL PLATES.

No. 641. NEW BRUNSWICK-CANADA—9½″ diameter plate with Mark Type 19.
No. 642. HISTORIC NOVA SCOTIA—9½″ diameter plate with Mark Type 19.
No. 643. PRINCE EDWARD ISLAND—9½″ diameter plate with Mark Type 19.

POTTERY TRAYS.

The following ten pottery trays all measure 4¼″ by 4¼″ with Mark Type 19 on the base unless noted otherwise.

No. 644. ALEXANDER GRAHAM BELL MEMORIAL MUSEUM.
No. 645. NOVA SCOTIA-CANADA. This tray measures 5¼″ by 5¼″.
No. 646. GREAT BRITAIN.
No. 647. TROPICAL FRUIT GATHERERS— SUGAR CANE.
No. 648. TROPICAL FRUIT GATHERERS— COCONUTS. The "Tropical Fruit Gatherers" set comprised six illustrations available in dishes, boxed singly or in pairs, and in miniature 4½″ high vases. See vase shape type "C" in FIG. 106.
No. 649. FRUITS.
No. 650. BUCKINGHAM PALACE.
No. 651. TRAFALGAR SQUARE.
No. 652. ST. PAUL'S CATHEDRAL.
No. 653. COMIC GOLF SCENE.

The following seven souvenir dishes are all 4¼″ in diameter with tapered edges ¾″ high and all have Mark Type 19 on the underside of the base.

No. 654. NEW BRUNSWICK-CANADA.
No. 655. "THE LOBSTER".
No. 656. CAPE BRETON ISLAND N.S.
No. 657. NOVA SCOTIA — THE GATEWAY TO CANADA.
No. 658. FLOWER SPRAY.
No. 659. KING OF DIAMONDS.
No. 660. QUEEN OF CLUBS. Not shown are the "Queen
     of Hearts" and "King of Clubs".

EMETT DISHES *CIRCA 1960.*

This set of four dishes was sold in gift packs of four or singly decorated with reproductions of Emett's famous cartoons. See FIG. 107.

EMETT DISHES

Everyone knows and loves the ingenious fantasies of Emett, and only WADE have the right to use his delightful creations on pottery.

They are beautifully reproduced in full colour on dainty square dishes and most attractively packed, either singly or in the Presentation Gift Box containing the full set of four designs.

FIG. 107.

Royal Victoria Pottery. Circa 1951.
Product Display.

Royal Commemoratives

by

George Wade & Son Ltd.,

Wade Heath & Company Ltd.

and

Wade (Ireland) Ltd.

ROYAL COMMEMORATIVES
1937-1986.

Since the reign of Queen Victoria, many of the British potteries have produced a number of items, from mugs, jugs to cups and saucers, etc., commemorating royal events such as the jubilee celebrations of Queen Victoria and the coronations of the various monarchs taking the throne after Queen Victoria's death in 1901.

With the death of King George V in 1936, Wade joined, for the first time, the other potteries by producing a medium-sized pitcher to celebrate the coronation of King Edward VIII in May of 1937. This, no doubt, was a decision made due to the popularity of the new king when he had been the Prince of Wales. Unfortunately this coronation was never to take place due to the king's abdication, but this was too late for Wade as they had already begun to issue decorative pitchers with a transfer showing the likeness of King Edward VIII. As soon as the abdication was announced, the various potteries, including Wade, withdrew these commemorative items from circulation. With haste, as the coronation date for the new king, King George VI, had not been changed, Wade designed a new transfer with pictures of King George VI and Queen Elizabeth (the present Queen Mother) to be applied to the items set aside for the coronation commemoratives.

Since 1937, Wade has been producing a variety of items commemorating royal occasions. There have been rather a large number in recent years because of the marriages and births of the growing royal family. Due to the number of items produced for these occasions, a few of the royal commemoratives produced by Wade are still quite easily found e.g. the Silver Wedding dish. Others are extremely hard to find e.g. King Edward VIII items. It has, of late, become the practice for the major potteries to limit the variety and quantity of commemorative items as it has proven that public interest wanes soon after the occasion is celebrated, thus leaving a large surplus of unsold pottery.

No. 661. VASE—issued in 1981 to commemorate the marriage between H.R.H. Prince Charles and Lady Diana Spencer which took place on the 29th July 1981. The vase is 8¾" high and is transfer marked "WADE" on the underside of the base.

No. 662. "BELL'S WHISKY DECANTER"—issued in 1982 to commemorate the birth of Prince William of Wales on the 21st of June 1982. This 50cl size decanter is transfer marked "WADE" on the underside of the recessed base.

No. 663. "BELL'S WHISKY DECANTER"—issued in 1986 to celebrate the 60th Birthday of Her Majesty Queen Elizabeth II on April 21, 1986. This 75cl size decanter is transfer marked "WADE" on the underside of the recessed base.

No. 664. "BELL'S WHISKY DECANTER"—issued in 1986 to celebrate the marriage of Prince Andrew with Miss Sarah Ferguson on the 23rd July 1986. This 75cl decanter is marked as the above decanter. The porcelain Bell's Scotch

Whisky pourer is also made by Wade but is unmarked.

In 1981, a 75cl "BELL'S WHISKY DECANTER" (not shown) was produced by Wade to commemorate the marriage of Prince Charles and Lady Diana Spencer.

The transfer decorations must first be approved by the royal household. They are hand-applied to the decanter after the white porcelain finish has been fired on. The 24 carat gold bands (approx. $5.00 value) are applied next and a second firing takes place. The decanters are then ready for shipping to the distillery. These decanters are issued in a very limited quantity and are shipped to many countries around the world.

No. 665. CORONATION PITCHER—issued in 1936 to commemorate the upcoming coronation of King Edward VIII on May 12th 1937. The transfer decoration was augmented by hand applied color to the handle, spout and base. The pitcher used was from a stock Wade Heath mold No. 113 which is 5⅛" high and has a black "WADEHEATH" ink stamp on the base. See Mark Type 2.

No. 666. CORONATION LOVING CUP—issued in 1937 to commemorate the coronation of King George VI and Queen Elizabeth. The decoration around the likeness of the king and queen (which is a transfer) is molded and hand-painted as are the handles. The lettering around the cup, below the handles, is also a transfer type decoration. The royal monogram, GR is molded on the back of the loving cup entwined with leaves all of which are handpainted. The base of the cup is recessed and holds a musical box which, when the cup is lifted, plays "God Save the King." The cup is 5" high, 4½" diameter at the top and has a black "WADEHEATH WARE" ink stamp on the base similar to Mark Type 4, but without the word England.

No. 667. CORONATION PITCHER—issued in 1937 to commemorate the coronation of King George VI and Queen Elizabeth on May 12, 1937. The transfer decoration, which also includes a picture of the young Princess Elizabeth (the present Queen Elizabeth II) on the back of the pitcher along with the red and blue handpainted decoration is applied to a stock Wade Heath pitcher, mold No. 106 M. It is 5⅝" high and has a black "WADEHEATH" ink stamp on the base. See Mark Type 4.

No. 668. CORONATION PITCHER—issued in 1937 to commemorate the coronation of King George VI and Queen Elizabeth. The transfer decorations are similar to those described above, but this time are applied to a different shape pitcher. This pitcher is a stock "WADEHEATH" item, mold No. 88 M which is 5½" high and has a similar backstamp as described above.

No. 669. CORONATION JUG—issued in 1937 for the coronation as described above. The transfer decoration is the same as the two previous pitchers but applied to a standard "WADEHEATH" tableware jug which is 4⅛" high and bears a black "WADEHEATH" ink stamp on the base. See Mark Type 2.

FIG. 108. CORONATION FRUIT BOWL—issued in 1937 to commemorate the coronation of King George VI and Queen Elizabeth. The·12″ dia. orange mottled brown bowl has Mark Type 6 on the footed base. This bowl was issued in a very limited number of 250, twenty-five of which were issued in a more expensive finish of a cream background with the highlights picked out in gold, these were individually signed by the designer of the bowl, Robert Barlow.

FIG. 108.

No. 670. CORONATION JUG—issued in 1953 to celebrate the coronation of Queen Elizabeth II on June 2nd 1953. The transfer decoration is applied to a stock "WADEHEATH" water jug which is 4″ high at the spout and is transfer marked "WADE REGICOR" on the base. See Mark Type 42.

No. 671. &

No. 672. CORONATION DISH—produced in 1953 to celebrate the coronation of Queen Elizabeth II. This dish is based upon a similar, die pressed mold made by George Wade & Son Ltd. to commemorate the 1937 coronation of King George VI. The center of the 1937 dish was embossed with GVIR, otherwise the dish was identical to the 1953 dish. Around the inside rim of the dish are the names of the major countries of the then British Empire. It is interesting to note that both Canada and Newfoundland were still included on the 1953

dish. This was an oversight on the part of the designer as Newfoundland had become the tenth province of Canada in 1949 so was not, in 1953, a separate country. The dishes measure 4¾″ diameter and are 1⅛″ high. They are mold marked "WADE ENGLAND CORONATION 1953" in the recessed base. The mold number is marked on the underside of the rim, which is No. 5 for the blue dish and No. 6 for the brown dish. As well as the blue and brown dishes illustrated, this dish was also made with a green finish.

No. 673. CORONATION GOBLET—issued in 1953 for the coronation of the present queen. This goblet, decorated only by the royal monogram E II R with a crown above the letters, was the first giftware item to be produced by Wade (Ulster) Ltd. now known as Wade (Ireland) Ltd. The goblet is 4¾″ high and is unmarked. Wade (Ulster) Ltd. also produced a 4½″ high CORONATION TANKARD (See FIG. 112) with the same decoration as the goblet.

FIG. 109. COMMEMORATIVE TANKARD—issued in 1958 with Mark Type 19. The 3¾″ high tankard has a cream background with a thin gold line around the base and a wider gold band around the rim. The wording on the back of the tankard reads: Presented as a memento of the visit of H.M. Queen Elizabeth and H.R.H. Prince Philip to Redbourn Works, 27th June 1958. RTB.

FIG. 109.

154

No. 674, No. 675 &
No. 676. SILVER JUBILEE DISH—issued in 1977 to commemorate the Queen's Silver Jubilee. This dish which was made in the three colors shown was based on the mold used for the Coronation Dish. The center motif and the names of the various countries that once formed the British Empire were deleted. The dish had a two fold purpose: one, it was a giftware item and, secondly, a fund raising item. An inscription is molded onto the underside of the rim which says, "Part of the Proceeds from the Sale of this souvenir will be Donated to the Queen's Silver Jubilee Appeal." The dish is the same size as the Coronation Dish but is mold marked simply "WADE ENGLAND" in the recess in the base.

FIG. 110. SILVER JUBILEE TANKARD—issued in 1977 by Wade (Ireland) Ltd. to celebrate the Silver Jubilee of Queen Elizabeth II. The transfer decoration on the front has a multicolored flower design incorporating the rose, thistle, daffodil and shamrock. There is a second transfer on the back of the tankard of a crown surmounted by 1977 and the words "Jubilee Year" below. The tankard measures 4″ high and is transfer marked "WADE IRELAND" on the base.

No. 677. MINIATURE LOVING CUP—issued in 1981 with an inscription on the back reading: "To Commemorate the Wedding of H.R.H. Prince Charles and Lady Diana Spencer at St. Paul's Cathedral 29th July 1981." The cup measures 2″ high and is transfer marked "WADE MADE IN ENGLAND". See Mark Type 26. A "NAPKIN RING" (not shown) approx. 1¾″ in diameter, was also issued to commemorate this wedding incorporating a similar gold-colored silhouette design as was used for the miniature Loving Cup.

No. 678. BELL—issued in 1981 to celebrate the wedding of Prince Charles to Lady Diana Spencer. The bell measures 5¾″ high by 3½″ diameter at the rim and is transfer marked "WADE" on the inside, upper part of the bell.

No. 679. CANDLESTICKS—issued in 1981 to commemorate the wedding of Prince Charles and Lady Diana Spencer. They measure 5¾″ high and are transfer marked "WADE" on the underside of the base.

FIG. 111. TRINKET BOX—issued in 1981 to commemorate the wedding of Prince Charles and Lady Diana Spencer. The mold used is the same as that used for the Trinket Boxes decorated with pictures of British "Pop Singers" issued in the early 1960's. The two part Trinket Box is 1½″ high with the lid in place and 3½″ across and is mold marked "WADE PORCELAIN MADE IN ENGLAND" on the underside of the base. See Mark Type 25.

FIG. 110.

FIG. 111.

155

Wade (Ireland) Ltd.

IRISH PORCELAIN BY WADE (IRELAND) LTD. *1953-1986.*

Wade (Ulster) Ltd., later known as Wade (Ireland) Ltd. was formed in 1946 to produce die-pressed porcelain insulators and refractories with a workforce of up to 450 operatives. By the end of 1949, the demand for die-pressed insulators decreased so the pottery changed over to the production of turned insulators. These were made on lathes, from solid, extruded wads of clay. As the Irish pottery had little experience in this type of work, an experienced potter, Ernest Taylor, was persuaded to relocate from Stoke-on-Trent to Portadown to oversee the development of the turned insulators.

In 1953, it was decided to expand the production of industrial porcelain to include lines of giftware. This diversification came about when an order for a quantity of Coronation Tankards was placed with Wade (Ireland) Ltd. The Irish Pottery asked Wade Heath Ltd. to supply this order of tankards. But Wade Heath had already produced and sold their quota. The Portadown pottery had no choice but to produce their own tankards. A telephone lathe was modified and six tankard samples were then turned out of solid wads of clay.

To decorate the tankards, Ernest Taylor applied his unique form of decoration, known as knurling, around the tankard. This type of decoration was done by a small, hand-held wheel which had either an embossed or engraved decoration on the rim. This wheel was then applied while the tankard was in the green state and still turning on the lathes. The six samples were then given to the glazing foreman, Cecil Holland, with instructions to glaze two white, two cobalt blue and two Rockingham brown. After three days the fired samples were presented to Straker Carryer, Managing Director of the Portadown pottery, for his approval. Unfortunately Cecil Holland had made an error and produced a grey/blue finish, nothing like the requested colors. The grey/blue glaze was immediately approved. It took two weeks for Cecil Holland to duplicate his mistake and discover which two glazes he had accidentally blended to produce such a unique result.

The glaze finish is obtained by a sequenced application of different colors. Consequently, no two pieces would ever have exactly the same glaze color. Sometimes the result is a grey/blue finish and sometimes a grey/green, depending on the balance of application and the exact firing. There is no official name for this color, but at the Portadown pottery it is referred to as "Irish Porcelain" glaze.

With the success of the 4½″ high Coronation Tankard, (see FIG. 112)

FIG. 112.

the Irish pottery entered the field of giftware items in earnest. Iris Carryer, wife of the Managing Director and daughter of the late Sir George Wade, had extensive experience in the field of ceramics. She was therefore appointed Art Director in charge of all design and development. Under the guidance of Iris Carryer, Wade (Ireland) Ltd. developed many popular designs for goblets, vases, ashtrays, cruets and various-sized tankards, many of which stayed in production from the mid 1950's to 1986, when Wade (Ireland) Ltd. ceased production of giftware.

However, Wade (Ireland) Ltd. will commence production of Fine Porcelain Tableware in 1988, under the "Irish Porcelain" brand name.

Because so many items have been in production for a great number of years, it is difficult, if not impossible, to give exact production dates. A large selection of backstamps, both embossed and transfer-applied, have been used over the years. It is only from these that one is able to obtain an idea of the date an item was produced. For Irish porcelain items shown in the color section, reference should be made to the section on Mark Types. The items illustrated are noted with their Mark Type, but it is possible that a number of similar items may be found with a different Mark Type. This would occur when a mold was remade and the current backstamp was applied to the new mold. Similar mold shapes are to be found decorated with a variety of colorful transfer type decorations, many of which have been used since the mid 1950's. An example of porcelain made by Wade (Ireland) Ltd. in its early years is a 3½″ high covered Preserve Jar shown in FIG. 113.

G. Anthony J. Wade presenting a retirement gift to Cecil Holland. 1983.

FIG. 113.

FIG. 114.

IRISH PORCELAIN *1953-1986.*

For a number of years Wade Heath & Company Ltd. had been producing a range of amber glaze tankards. In 1960-1961, when Wade Heath ceased production of tableware, all tankard molds were transferred to Ireland. It is therefore possible to find the amber tankards with both an English and Irish backstamp.

No. 680. ONE PINT TANKARD—shape No. I.P.2 with Mark Type 28. This tankard measures 6¼" high.

CELTIC PORCELAIN
CIRCA MID 1960'S.

An attractive special range manufactured in limited quantities. The panels used for this set were taken from the Book of Kells, a beautiful manuscript book illustrated by Irish monks many long years ago. Interestingly, no one at Wade (Ireland) Ltd. remembers for what purpose these items were made.

No. 681. SERPENT URN—shape No. C.K.3 with Mark Type 34. This urn measures 11½" high.

No. 682. SERPENT URN—shape No. C.K.5 with Mark Type 34. This urn measures 5¾" high.

FIG. 114. SERPENT BOWL—shape No. C.K.6 with Mark Type 34. The bowl measures 4¾" in dia. by 2" high.

Other items in the "SERPENT" set were:
C.K.1—Serpent Jar
C.K.2—Serpent Dish
C.K.4—Beard-pullers Jar

No. 683. IRISH COFFEE MUG—shape No. I.P.44 with Mark Type 28. This mug measures 5" high. The Irish coffee mug is sometimes referred to as "Coffee Goblets" and was available in a gift pack of two goblets.

No. 684. HALF PINT TANKARD—similar to shape No. WH.2 with Mark Type 37. The tankard, which measures 4½" high, was a special order in the white glaze with a personalized crest of unknown origin.

No. 685. ONE PINT TANKARD—similar to shape No. I.P.10 (Tyrone Tankard) with Mark Type 35. The tankard, which measures 6⅜" high, was a special order as for item No. 684.

No. 686. MUSICAL TANKARD—shape No. I.P.5 ink stamped "Made in Ireland." The tankard measures 5½" high and was first introduced in the late 1950's.

No. 687. CANDY BOX—shape No. I.P.92 with Mark Type 29. The candy box measures 5" long by 4" wide by 1¾" high.

No. 688. IRISH PORCELAIN ADVERTISING SIGN. The sign measures 4" wide by 5½" high and is unmarked. This piece was not a retail item.

No. 689. VASE with Mark Type 30. This vase measures 4" high and is believed to have had a short production run in the mid 1950's to early 1960's.

No. 690. HALF PINT TANKARD—shape No. I.P.1 and Mark Type 28. This tankard measures 4¼" high.

No. 691. LARGE GOBLET—shape No. I.P.11 with Mark Type 28. This goblet, which was discontinued in the late 1970's, measures 4¼" high.

No. 692. LARGE CRINKLED ASHTRAY—shape No. I.P.622 with Mark Type 41. This ashtray measures 6" in diameter by 1¼" high. Companion piece to this ashtray is the "SMALL CRINKLED ASHTRAY," shape No. I.P.607.

No. 693. THISTLE ASHTRAY—shape No. I.P.628 with Mark Type 41. This ashtray measures 6" overall by 1¼" high.

No. 694. LARGE SQUARE ASHTRAY—shape No. I.P.626 with Mark Type 29. This ashtray measures 6" long by 5" wide by 1¼" high.

No. 695. BUTTERDISH—shape No. I.P.75 with Mark Type 38. The dish measures 5" in diameter by 1" high at the rim.

COUNTRYWARE *1973-1984.*

This line of amber glazed kitchenware was also manufactured, near the end of production, in a two green pattern. This pattern was made in very limited quantities, and little was exported. The range was designed by Kilkenny Design, Ireland—a design centre sponsored by the Irish Government.

No. 696. COUNTRYWARE LARGE STORAGE JAR— shape No. KD.2 with Mark Type 36. The jar measures 5½" high by 4" diameter.

No. 697. COUNTRYWARE COVERED MUSTARD POT —shape No. KD.6 with Mark Type 36. The pot measures 2½" high by 2½" diameter.

No. 698. COUTRYWARE SMALL STORAGE JAR— shape No. KD.3 with Mark Type 36. The jar measures 4¼" high by 4" diameter.

No. 699. COUNTRYWARE SOUP BOWL—shape No. KD.8 with Mark Type 36. This bowl measures 5" in diameter by 2" high.

Other items in the "COUNTRYWARE" set were:
KD.1—3½ pint Casserole (7) KD.7—Pepper Mill (6)
KD.4—Salt (4)   KD.9—2 pint Casserole (1)
KD.5—Pepper (5)

No. 700. CHILD'S TANKARD—shape No. I.P.4 with Mark Type 28. The tankard measures 3" high.

No. 701. MINIATURE TANKARD—shape No. I.P.614 with Mark Type 28. The tankard measures 2" high.

No. 702. MINIATURE TYRONE TANKARD—shape No. I.P.9 with Mark Type 28. The tankard measures 3" high.

No. 703. MINIATURE SUGAR—shape No. I.P.72 with Mark Type 28. The sugar measures 2¼" diameter by 1½" high.

No. 704. MINIATURE CREAM—shape No. I.P.73 with Mark Type 28. The creamer measures 2" high.

No. 705. JARDINIERE—shape No. C.302 with Mark Type 30. The Jardiniere measures 8½" overall by 4" high at the handle.

No. 706. JARDINIERE—shape No. unknown. This piece measures 5¾" overall by 2½" high at the handle and has Mark Type 28 on the base.

No. 707. DONKEY AND CART VASE—shape No. C.338 with Mark Type 31. The vase measures 6¼" overall by 4" high. Two variations of this vase exist. The earlier version has a space between the base and the underside of cart and spaces between the end of each shaft and the donkey's neck. The later version is solid in both areas described for the earlier version.

No. 708. CIGARETTE LIGHTER—shape No. I.P.95 with Mark Type 28. The lighter is 4" high and was discontinued in the late 1970's.

No. 709. EGG CUP—shape No. unknown. This piece measures 2¼" high by 2" diameter and has Mark Type 28 on the base. It is believed this item was discontinued in the early 1970's.

No. 710. IRISH PORCELAIN ADVERTISING SIGN— the sign measures 4¼" high by 3⅜" wide and is unmarked. This piece was not a retail item.

No. 711. PIPE ASHTRAY—shape No. I.P.623 with Mark Type 29. This ashtray measures 6" in diameter by 1" high.

No. 712. DONNEGAL CUP & SAUCER—shape No. M336 and M337. The cup has an embossed Mark Type 40 and the saucer has a similar mark but impressed. The cup measures 2¾" high by 3¼" diameter and the saucer is 5½" in diameter.

RAINDROP DESIGN TABLEWARE

No. 713. RAINDROP SUGAR—shape No. C.310 with Mark Type 33. The sugar measures 2" high.

Other items in the "RAINDROP" set were:
C.305—1 pint Jug   C.309—Tea Strainer
C.306—¾ pint Jug   C.311—Creamer
C.307—½ pint Jug   C.312—Tea Pot
C.308—1 pint Coffee Pot

No. 714. IRISH COOKING POT—shape No. I.P.603 with Mark Type 28. The pot measures 2" high.

No. 715. FOOTED BON BON DISH—shape No. I.P.602 with Mark Type 28. The dish measures 2⅝" in diameter by 1½" high.

No. 716. PRESERVE JAR—shape No. I.P.23 with Mark Type 28. The dish measures 4" high to top of finial by 2¾" diameter.

No. 717. PINTRAY—shape No. I.P.619 with Mark Type 41. The tray measures 3" in diameter.

No. 718. TRIANGULAR ASHTRAY—shape No. I.P.612 with Mark Type 41. The ashtray measures 4" at its widest point.

No. 719. SHAMROCK ASHTRAY—shape No. I.P. 609 with Mark Type 41. The ashtray measures 3½".

Other "ASHTRAYS" include:
I.P.611—Small Square Ashtray
(with indents at each corner)
I.P.627—Rose Ashtray (with two offset indents)
I.P.634—Hexagonal Ashtray (with three indents)

FIG. 115. CUP & SAUCER—shape No. I.P.100 and I.P.101. This occasional cup and saucer was manufactured circa 1960. The cup measures 2⅞″ high by 2⅜″ dia. at the rim and has Mark Type 28 on the base. The saucer is 5″ in dia. and has an embossed mold Mark Type 29.

EGG CODDLERS *CIRCA 1965-1986.*

Two sizes of egg coddlers were manufactured as part of the giftware range. The double egg coddler is 4″ high and the single egg coddler is 2¾″ high. Both coddlers measure 2½″ in dia. at the lid. Both size coddlers have Mark Type 28 on the base. Circa 1968 a special order was placed by A.S. Cooper of Bermuda who specifically requested their name be impressed on the double coddlers for their order. This item bears Mark Type 39.

See item I.P.631 (Single Egg Coddler) and item I.P.632 (Double Egg Coddler) in FIG. 116.

"MOURNE" RANGE
CIRCA MID 1970'S.

For a very short time Wade (Ireland) Ltd. manufactured a short line limited to sixteen porcelain tableware items under the name of the "Mourne" Range. The glaze used for this line is quite different from the regular "Irish Porcelain" glaze. The distinguishing features of the "Mourne" glaze are orange/red flower decorations on a predominantly greenish/grey background.

No. 749. "MOURNE" RANGE (see color section). Items in the range were:

C.345 Vase 4″	C.353 Preserve Jar with Lid
C.346 Vase 3¾″	C.354 Square Dish 5½″
C.347 Vase 7½″	C.355 Butterbox with Lid
C.348 Candy Box	C.356 Cream Jug
C.349 Dish	C.357 Sugar Bowl
C.350 Vase 6⅝″	C.358 Salt
C.351 Half pint Tankard	C.359 Pepper
C.352 One pint Tankard	C.360 Dish (footed)

FIG. 116. REPRODUCTION OF WADE (IRELAND) LTD. CATALOG CIRCA 1979.

I.P.42   I.P.43   I.P.44   I.P.72/73   I.P.75   I.P.76

I.P.92   I.P.93   I.P.94   DISCONTINUED   I.P.95   I.P.602   I.P.604-5

I.P.603   I.P.609   I.P.611   I.P.612

I.P.606C   I.P.622   I.P.607   I.P.609P   I.P.614   I.P.619

I.P.619L   S.11   I.P.623   I.P.626   I.P.627

I.P.628   I.P.631   I.P.632   C.302   C.305   C.306   C.307

C.308   C.309   C.310-311   M336/7

C.312   C.338   S.2   S.8   DISCONTINUED   S.9   M344

WADE (IRELAND) LTD. Irish Porcelain

FIG. 116. *cont.*

161

The items illustrated in this catalog are:

I.P.1	Half pt. Tankard
I.P.2	One pt. Tankard
I.P.3	Stein Tankard
I.P.4	Child's Tankard
I.P.5	Musical Tankard
I.P.6	Half pt. Knurled Tankard
I.P.8	Half pt. Tyrone Tankard
I.P.9	Min. Tyrone Tankard
I.P.10	One pt. Tyrone Tankard
I.P.10A	Small Goblet
I.P.12	Straight sided Goblet
I.P.23	Preserve Jar
I.P.34	Violet Bowl
I.P.41	6″ Killarney Urn
I.P.42	4½″ Killarney Urn
I.P.43	Min. Killarney Urn
I.P.44	Irish Coffee Mug
I.P.72/73	Indv. Cr & Sugar
I.P.75	Butter Dish
I.P.76	Nut Bowl
I.P.92	Candy Box
I.P.93	Barrel Vase
I.P.94	Biscuit Barrel
I.P.602	Ftd. Bon Bon Dish
I.P.603	Irish Cooking Pot
I.P.604-5	Salt and Pepper
I.P.606C	Cruet set on Stand complete
I.P.607	Crinkled edge Butter Dish
I.P.609	Shamrock Ashtray
I.P.609P	Shamrock Ashtray & Pixie
I.P.611	Square Ashtray
I.P.612	Triangle Ashtray
I.P.614	Min. Tankard
I.P.619	Butterpat
I.P.619L	Leprechaun Pintray
S.11	Leprechaun
I.P.622	Large crinkled Ashtray
I.P.623	Pipe Ashtray
I.P.626	Large sq. Ashtray, Shamrock
I.P.627	Large dia. Ashtray, Rose
I.P.628	Large rd. Ashtray, Thistle
I.P.631	Single Egg Coddler
I.P.632	Double Egg Coddler
C.302	Jardiniere
C.305	One pt. Jug, Raindrop
C.306	¾ pt. Jug, Raindrop
C.307	Half pt. Jug, Raindrop
C.308	One pt. Coffee Pot
C.309	Tea Strainer
C.310-311	Sugar and Cream
C.312	Tea Pot
C.338	Donkey and Cart
S.2	Lucky Leps. Box of 24
S.8	Lucky Leps. on Pig's back
M.336/7	Donegal Cup & Saucer
M.344	Donegal Plate, 6″

NEW SHAMROCK RANGE
1982-1986.

FIG. 117. TABLEWARE.

FIG. 117.

1. SR05 Tea Pot
2. SR04 Coffee Pot
3. SR08 Tea/Coffee Cup
4. SR06 Sugar & Cream Set
5. SR07 Salt & Pepper Set

FIG. 118. VASES.

FIG. 118.

1. SR09 Bud Vase
2. SR10 Round Vase
3. SR11 Oval Vase
4. SR20 Shamrock Cooking Pot
5. SR19 Shamrock Urn

FIG. 119. MISCELLANEOUS ITEMS.

FIG. 119.

1. SR01 Half pint Tankard
2. SR02 One pint Tankard
3. SR17 Large Ashtray with Gold Rim
4. SR18 Small Ashtray without Gold Rim
5. SR12 Candlestick

FIG. 120. BELLS OF IRELAND.

FIG. 120.

1. SR03/3 Bunratty Castle
2. SR03/4 Spinning Wheel
3. SR03/1 Blarney Castle
4. SR03/2 Ross Castle
5. SR03/7 Christmas Bell
6. SR03/5 Shamrocks
7. SR03/8 Thatched Cottage

FIG. 121. IRISH GOBLETS.

FIG. 121.

1. SR14/1 Blarney Castle
2. SR14/4 Spinning Wheel
3. SR14/8 Thatched Cottage
4. SR14/2 Ross Castle
5. SR14/3 Bunrattey Castle
6. SR14/5 Shamrocks

FIG. 122. IRISH COFFEE MUGS.

FIG. 122.

1. SR16 Irish Coffee (Gift Pack of Two)
2. SR13 Decanter

IRISH SOUVENIRS AND FIGURINES.

FLYING BIRDS *1956-1959.*

A set of three wall decorations in the shape of "Flying Birds" produced in distinct colorings of green/white, green/yellow, beige/grey and beige/blue. See FIG. 123.

FIG. 123.

In the late 1950's, a second set of "Flying Birds" was issued for a brief period. The birds of set one have their wings pointed towards the tail, and the back facing away from the wall. The birds in the second set have the wings pointing up, alongside the head, with the breast and feet facing away from the wall.

GIFTS FROM OLD IRELAND *1959.*

A 1959 Wade catalog illustrates three gift ware items consisting of a small comical "Elephant," a wide eyed "Pig" and a "Cottage." The cottage remained in the line until the mid 1980's, but it is believed the elephant and pig had only a short run. See FIG. 124.

FIG. 124.

LEPRECHAUN PINTRAYS
CIRCA 1956-1986.

Three miniature Leprechauns, Tailor, Cobbler and Crock of Gold, in a variety of color combinations mounted on the Butterpat shape No. I.P.619 but with the addition of the Leprechaun the shape number was changed to I.P.619L. See also "LUCKY LEPRECHAUNS."

No. 720. LEPRECHAUN PINTRAY—shape No. I.P.619L with Mark Type 32. This tray features the "Tailor Leprechaun."

No. 721. LEPRECHAUN PINTRAY—shape No. I.P.619L with Mark Type 32. This tray features the "Cobbler Leprechaun."

IRISH CHARACTER FIGURES
CIRCA EARLY 1970'S-1986.

This set of nine figurines based on characters from typical Irish songs and folk tales is ink-stamped "MADE IN IRELAND" on the underside of the base. Some figures have the name of the character molded into the front of the base.

No. 722. DANNY BOY—shape No. S.16 measuring 4″ high.

No. 723. MOTHER MacCREE—shape No. S.19 measuring 2½″ high.

No. 724. MOLLY MALONE—shape No. S.17 measuring 3¼″ high.

No. 725. KATHLEEN—shape No. S.18 measuring 3½″ high.

No. 726. EILEEN OGE—shape No. S.25 measuring 3¾″ high.

No. 727. PHIL THE FLUTER—shape No. S.20 measuring 3¾″ high.

No. 728. PADDY REILLY—shape No. S.26 measuring 3¾″ high.

No. 729. ROSE OF TRALEE—shape No. S.24 measuring 4″ high.

No. 730. PADDY MAGINTY—shape No. S.21 measuring 3¼″ high.

LUCKY LEPRECHAUNS
CIRCA 1956-1986.

In the mid 1950's, Wade (Ireland) Ltd. began marketing souvenirs based on the famous Irish Folk People, the Leprechauns. These figurines were made in a variety of shapes and sizes from 1½″ high to 4″ high. The larger figures were issued individually as well as applied to bookends. The miniature "Lucky Leprechauns" were issued featuring the "Little People" in various poses, plying their various trades. These miniature Leprechauns were marketed in boxes of three, individually mounted on the standard Butterpat (see LEPRECHAUN PINTRAYS) or applied to the Oak Leaf Dish. This Oak Leaf Dish was also made by George Wade & Son Ltd. but without the Leprechaun. The English-made dishes were made with Mark Type 25 and the Irish dishes with Mark Type 31. Miniature Leprechauns were also issued under the name "Lucky Fairyfolk" in 1956, featuring the figurines riding an Acorn, a Pig and a Rabbit.

FIG. 125.

No. 731. **LARRY**—shape No. S.22. This figurine is 4″ high and is found either unmarked or with an ink stamp "Made in Ireland" on the underside of the base.

No. 732. **LESTER**—shape No. S.22. this figurine is similar in shape and size to "Larry" with the only apparent difference in the coloring. "Larry" and "Lester" were also applied as decoration to bookends.

No. 733. **LUCKY LEPRECHAUN**—shape No. S.11. This figurine measures 2¾″ high and has a ribbed effect on the underside of the base similar to the later Wade England figurines.

No. 734. **LEPRECHAUN ON A PIG'S BACK**—shape No. S.8. The figurine measures 1¾″ high by 1¼″ long and may be found unmarked or ink stamped "Made in Ireland."

No. 735. **LUCKY LEPRECHAUN WITH CROCK OF GOLD**—shape No. S.2. The figurine is 1½″ high and may be found unmarked or ink-stamped "Made in Ireland."

No. 736. **LUCKY COBBLER LEPRECHAUN**—shape No. S.2. The figurine is 1½″ high and may be found unmarked or ink-stamped "Made in Ireland."

No. 737. **LUCKY TAILOR LEPRECHAUN**—shape No. S.2. The figurine is 1½″ high and may be found unmarked or ink-stamped "Made in Ireland."

No. 738. **COTTAGE**—shape No. S.6 and Mark Type 31. The cottage is 2¾″ long by 1½″ wide by 2″ high.

No. 739. **LEPRECHAUN LEAF DISH**—shape No. S.3 with Mark Type 31.

No. 740. **SHAMROCK ASHTRAY & PIXIE**—shape No. I.P.609P with Mark Type 29.

FIG. 126. LEPRECHAUN AND COTTAGE—shape No. S.9. This combination of shape S.6 and S.2 is mounted on a base in the shape of Ireland and was in production between 1960-1970.

FIG. 126.

BALLY-WHIM IRISH VILLAGE
1984-1987.

With the popularity of the English Village series, "Whimsey-on-Why," Wade (Ireland) Ltd. decided to introduce a series of miniature houses which would be typical of houses found in an Irish village. To date only one set of eight houses has been produced although Wade literature does note that more will follow.

As production of all giftware items was discontinued at the Irish pottery in 1986, the molds for "Bally-Whim" were transferred to Stoke-on-Trent, where production of the Irish Village will continue. Each miniature house is mold-marked "Wade Ireland" in a recess on the underside of the base. Each model bears its number in the series enclosed in a circle located at either the rear or on the corner of the miniature house.

No. 741-1. **UNDERTAKER'S HOUSE**—measures 2″ high by 1½″ long by ¾″ wide.

No. 742-2. **MOORE'S POST OFFICE**—measures 1½″ high by 1″ long by ⅝″ wide.

No. 743-3. **BARNEY FLYNN'S COTTAGE**—measures 1⅛″ high by 1¾″ long by ¾″ wide.

No. 744-4. **KATE'S COTTAGE**—measures 1⅛″ high by 1¾″ long by ¾″ wide.

No. 745-5. **THE DENTIST'S HOUSE**—measures 2″ high by 1¾″ long by 1″ wide.

No. 746-6. **MICK MURPHY'S BAR**—measures 1¾″ high by 1½″ long by ¾″ deep.

No. 747-7. **W. RYAN'S HARDWARE STORE**—measures 1½″ high by 1½″ long by ¾″ wide.

No. 748-8. **BALLY-WHIM HOUSE**—measures 2″ high by 3¼″ long by 1¼″ wide.

IRISH PORCELAIN SONG FIGURES *1962-1986.*

Unlike the "Irish Character Figures" which were produced in the 1970's and early 1980's, the "Irish Porcelain Song Figures" were very much a prestige line of most carefully manufactured (slip cast) and hand painted figurines. Eight of the figurines measure approx. 6″ high and are marked "Irish Porcelain—Made in Ireland" along with the name of the figurine and the name of the designer. The remaining three figurines in the series are approx. 9″ high and are only marked "Irish Porcelain Figures—Made in Ireland." For the complete range of the Irish Porcelain Song Figures see the color section. The list of figurines as they appear in the series is as follows:

No. 750. SONG FIGURES (see color section). Figures in the set were:
 1. C.503 Little Crooked Paddy
 2. C.500 Phil the Fluter
 3. C.501 Widda Cafferty
 4. C.510 The Bard of Armagh
 5. C.505 The Star of the County Down
 6. C.504 The Irish Emigrant
 7. C.506 Molly Malone
 8. C.502 Micky Mulligan
 9. C.508 Mother MacCree
10. C.507 Dan Murphy
11. C.509 Eileen Oge

Wade (PDM) Ltd.

INTRODUCTION

During the 1950's, the fairly extensive tableware lines produced by the Royal Victoria Pottery, had developed into functional and more simple designs. With increased competition in traditional tableware by the larger potteries, Wade Heath gradually dropped its tableware lines from production in favor of growing orders for advertising ware.

By 1962, Wade Heath had completely ceased production of table/ornamental ware in preference to the more profitable advertising and contract orders. Today, these form the backbone of Wade Heath's present business.

In the early 1950's, when Wade Heath began producing advertising ware in large quantities, the company entered into a contract with Reginald Corfield (Sales) Ltd. They collaborated with Wade Heath in the design, production and distribution of the advertising ware. This association lasted from the early 1950's, until 1969, when Wade Heath decided to form its own design and marketing company. This new member of the Wade Group was incorporated in August of 1969, under the name WADE (PDM) LIMITED.

Between the early 1950's and the present time, six transfer type backstamps have been used to mark the large variety of advertising items produced by Wade Heath. The six marks or backstamps, as they are sometimes called, are illustrated in the section on "Mark Types" in this book. Collectors will find these marks a good means of identifying the general time period of production.

A description of the various types and finishes of typical jugs and ashtrays made by Wade Heath for Wade (PDM) Ltd. is illustrated below in FIG. 127.

EASY CLEAN—means an easy-to-clean ashwell area with or without ash-rests and is very suitable for the application of transfers to the inside walls and ashwell areas.

OVERHANG LIP—where the top rim has a return lip, with or without rests, affording a greater inside ash area.

TWO-TONE—achieved by spraying on to an actual glaze to which transfer prints can then be applied. If "color" is used and not a glaze, transfer application to that area is usually not possible.

SPUN SHAPES—restricted to basic round shapes and dish production. These items are spun on a rotating wheel using malleable clay, the alternative production being liquid clay poured into a two part casting mold.

ICE CHECK—incorporated into the pouring spout of a water jug and is partly applied by hand.

RECESSED HANDLES—an attractive alternative to protruding handles on water jugs, giving a slimmer appearance.

TWO PART LID AND BASE—where the lid and base to an ashtray or ice bucket are separately cast allowing a two-tone glazed finish if required. Also the underside of the lid can carry a foam rubber pad for protection when fitted to the base.

TRANSFER—decoration of all ware by application of a ceramic transfer which is then fired. The size and shapes can be varied and the inclusion of gold highlighting along with the use of large colored panel prints is also possible.

The measurements given are to the highest point of the item described e.g. the top of spout for a jug.

ADVERTISING WATER JUGS.

No. 751. J&B SCOTCH WHISKY—water jug with ice check spout and overall glaze. The jug is 6⅛" high and is marked "WADE PDM" in yellow. See Mark Type 46. The jug illustrated was made in 1970 and is still in production today. However, jugs made after 1980 will have Mark Type 47.

EASY CLEAN   OVERHANG LIP   TWO-TONE   TWO-PART UNIT   SPUN ASHTRAY   SPUN DISHES

OVERALL GLAZE   TWO-TONE   ICE CHECK   RECESSED HANDLE   RELIEF MOULDING   TRANSFER LIMITS

FIG. 127. FINISHES AND TYPES OF ASHTRAYS AND JUGS.

No. 752. BORZOI VODKA—water jug with ice check spout, overall glaze finish with applied transfer decoration. The jug, which was produced in 1973, is 6¼″ high and has a green "WADE PDM" transfer Mark Type 46.

For this illustration, illustration No. 773 (Beefeater Gin water jug) and FIG. 131 (Beefeater Gin ashtray) the co-operation of "James Borrough PLC" is appreciated.

No. 753. CARLING BLACK LABEL—water jug with ice check spout and an overall glaze finish with applied transfer decoration. This jug was produced circa 1976/1978 is 6½″ high and has a green "WADE PDM" transfer Mark Type 46 on the base.

No. 754. QUEEN ANNE SCOTCH WHISKY—water jug with ice check spout and overall glaze finish with applied transfer decoration. The jug, produced in the late 1950's is 5⅛″ high and has a white "WADE REGICOR" transfer Mark Type 43 on the base. For this illustration and illustration No. 801 (Hudson's Bay Scotch Whisky ashtray) the co-operation of "Hill Thompson & Co. Ltd." is appreciated.

No. 755. DEWAR'S WHITE LABEL SCOTCH WHISKY—water jug with ice check spout and overall glaze finish with applied transfer decoration. The jug was issued between 1973-1977 and is 6¾″ high with a green "WADE PDM" transfer Mark Type 46 on the base.

No. 756. TEACHER'S SCOTCH WHISKY—water jug with ice check spout and overall glaze finish with applied transfer decoration. This jug was first issued in 1980 for Wm. Teacher & Sons Ltd., a distillery that was established in 1830. The jug is 5⅛″ high and has a red "WADE PDM" transfer Mark Type 47 on the base.

No. 757. TEACHER'S SCOTCH WHISKY—water jug with ice check spout and overall glaze finish with applied transfer decoration. This water jug was produced in 1972/1973 and is 5″ high with a green "WADE PDM" transfer Mark Type 46.

For this illustration and illustrations No. 756 (Teacher's Scotch Whisky water jug) and No. 804 (Teacher's Highland Cream Scotch Whisky ashtray) the co-operation of "Wm. Teacher & Sons Ltd." is appreciated.

No. 758. WHITE HORSE SCOTCH WHISKY—water jug with ice check spout and an overall glaze finish with applied transfer decoration. The back of this jug has an attractive transfer of a white horse 3½″ high by 3½″ long. This water jug was produced in 1980 and is 5½″ high with a red "WADE PDM" transfer Mark Type 47.

No. 759. WHITE HORSE WHISKY—water jug with ice check spout and an overall glaze finish with similar applied transfer decoration on both sides. The jug was produced between 1968-1970 and is 5¼″ high with a red "WADE REGICOR"

transfer Mark Type 45. For this illustration and illustrations No. 758 (White Horse Scotch Whisky water jug) and No. 787 (White Horse ashtray) the co-operation of "White Horse Distillers Ltd." is appreciated.

No. 760. WHYTE & MACKAYS SCOTCH WHISKY—water jug with ice check spout, no handle, has an overall glaze finish with applied transfer decoration. The jug is 7¼″ high by 3″ diameter and was first issued in 1973/1974 and is still in production. The jug illustrated has a "WADE PDM" transfer Mark Type 46 but jugs of this design made after 1980 will have the Mark Type 47.

The co-operation of "Whyte & Mackay Distillers Ltd." is appreciated.

No. 761. KING GEORGE IV OLD SCOTCH WHISKY—water jug with ice check spout and an overall glaze finish with a similar applied transfer decoration on both sides. This jug measures 4½″ high and was made circa 1962, with the "WADE REGICOR" transfer Mark Type 44. It was followed by a revised "WADE REGICOR" Mark Type 45 until 1970 and a "WADE PDM" Mark Type 46 until 1974.

No. 762. STAR BEERS—water jug without ice lip, with an overall glaze finish and a similar transfer decoration on both sides. The jug is 4″ high, was made circa mid 1950's, and bears a black "WADE REGICOR" transfer Mark Type 42.

No. 763. OLD PARR SCOTCH WHISKY—water jug with ice check spout and an overall glaze finish with transfer decoration on both sides. The jug illustrated is 5¼″ high, was produced in 1970, and has a green "WADE PDM" transfer Mark Type 46. This jug is still produced in this shape but the wording has been changed from time to time.

The co-operation of "MACDONALD GREENLEES LIMITED" is appreciated.

No. 764. DUNCAN MACGREGOR SCOTCH WHISKY—water jug with ice check spout, overall glaze finish and similar transfer decorations on both sides. The jug is 5¾″ high, was made circa the mid 1970's, and has a green "WADE PDM" transfer Mark Type 46.

No. 765. V-J DRY GIN—water jug without ice check spout, with overall glaze finish and similar transfer decorations on both sides. The jug is 4½″ high by 3¾″ square and was produced between 1970-1980. The jug has a green "WADE PDM" transfer Mark Type 46 on the base.

For this illustration and illustration No. 764. (Duncan MacGregor Scotch Whisky water jug) the co-operation of "Bass Export Limited, Glasgow, Scotland" is appreciated.

No. 766. MINSTER GINGER ALE—water jug with recessed handle and without ice check spout and a glaze finish with similar transfer decorations on both sides. The jug is 4⅝″ high and was produced in 1966 for Minster (Soft Drinks) Ltd., a subsidiary of Britvic Soft Drinks as part of a matching utility set for the licensed trade. The jug is marked with a green "WADE REGICOR" transfer Mark Type 44.

The co-operation of "Britvic Soft Drinks Limited" is appreciated.

No. 767. AMBASSADOR DELUX SCOTCH WHISKY—water jug with ice check spout and glazed finish. Transfer decorations of similar design are on both sides. The jug is 5¼″ high and was produced between 1968-1970 and is marked "WADE REGICOR" on the base.

The co-operation of "Hiram Walker & Sons (Scotland) PLC" is appreciated.

No. 768. KING GEORGE IV OLD SCOTCH WHISKY—water jug with ice check spout and glazed finish. Similar applied transfer decorations are on both sides. The jug, which is 4¾″ high was issued between 1957-1960, and has a green "WADE REGICOR" transfer Mark Type 43 on the base.

No. 769. TIA MARIA—water jug with recessed handle and without an ice check spout. The jug is overall glazed with similar transfer decoration on both sides and is 4½″ high with a green "WADE PDM" transfer Mark Type 46 which dates production of this jug between 1970-1980.

No. 770. BOMBAY LONDON DRY GIN—easy clean type ashtray with an overall glaze and similar applied "lettering" transfer decoration on two sides. Not shown here are two transfer decorations in green and gold of a head and shoulders likeness of Queen Victoria placed between the "lettering" transfers. The ashtray, issued circa 1980, is 6″ in diameter at the base and 2½″ high tapering to 5⅜″ diameter at the rim. It has the "WADE PDM" Mark Type 47 in red on the underside of the base.

No. 771. BOMBAY LONDON DRY GIN—water jug without an ice check spout was issued circa 1980. The jug is 6″ high, and has an overall glaze and similar transfer decorations appearing on both sides. The mark on the base is a red "WADE PDM" Mark Type 47. This jug was first issued in January 1974 when an order for 2,500 jugs was supplied to New York. The mark on the 1974 issue was "WADE PDM" Mark Type 46.

No. 772. BOMBAY LONDON DRY GIN—two-part unit ice bucket issued circa 1980 with a red "WADE PDM" Mark Type 47 on the base. The bucket is 6½″ high and has an overall glaze with the transfer decoration appearing on both sides. No. 770 (Bombay London Dry Gin ashtray), No. 771 (Bombay London Dry Gin water jug) and No. 772 (Bombay London Dry Gin ice bucket) are shown by permission,

"COPYRIGHT OF THE BOMBAY SPIRITS COMPANY LIMITED."

No. 773. BEEFEATER GIN—water jug issued in 1974 and has a black "WADE PDM" Mark Type 46 on the base. The jug is 5¾″ high and has an overall glaze finish and a similar transfer decoration on both sides.

No. 774. BELL'S OLD SCOTCH WHISKY—decanter first made in the 750ml size by Wade in 1965. The two-tone decanter with hand applied gold trim has paper labels on both sides and is 10″ high to the top of the stopper. As with all the Bell's decanters, it is marked in black "WADE" on the underside of the base.

No. 775. DEWAR'S SCOTCH—water jug with ice check spout and an overall glaze, measures 6½″ high and has similar applied decorations on both sides. The jug was issued between 1968-1970 and has a "WADE REGICOR" Mark Type 45 on the base.

FIG. 128. DEWAR'S SCOTCH WHISKY—overhang lip type ashtray, 4¾″ in dia. by 1½″ high with Mark Type 42. The ashtray has a yellow body with black and red lettering.

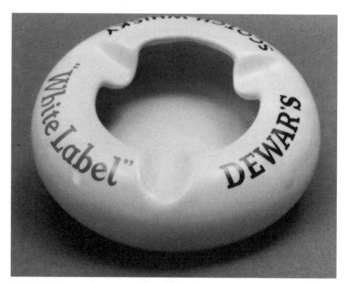

FIG. 128.

No. 776. DEWAR'S SCOTCH WHISKY—easy clean type ashtray is 6½″ long by 4¾″ wide by 1¾″ high and has an overall glaze finish with similar transfer decorations on both sides. The ashtray was issued between 1966-1969 and has a red "WADE REGICOR" Mark Type 43 on the recessed base.

This illustration, illustration No. 775 (Dewar's Scotch water jug), No. 755 (Dewar's White Label Scotch Whisky water jug) and FIG. 128 (Dewar's Scotch Whisky ashtray) are reproduced by courtesy of "John Dewar & Sons Ltd. Scotch Whisky Distillers".

No. 777. TANQUERAY ENGLISH GIN—ashtray with an overall glaze and transfer lettering was issued in 1979 and has the "WADE PDM" Mark Type 46 on the base. The ashtray measures 7″ long by 5¼″ at the widest point.

The co-operation of "Tanqueray Gordon & Co. Ltd." is appreciated.

No. 778. MACKINLAY'S OLD SCOTCH WHISKY—water jug with an ice check type spout, overall glaze finish and relief molding with transfer decoration. The jug is 6¼″ high with a red "WADE REGICOR" transfer Mark Type 43 on the base. This jug was issued in the mid 1960's.

No. 779. PUSSER'S RUM—stoneware flagon first produced in 1981. This stoneware container is handcast with three decorative transfers fired onto its ceramic surface. The one illustrated is the Pusser's brand label. A second transfer shows a picture of "Jolly Jack Pusser" which is a likeness of the figurehead from HMS DERING, a Royal Navy brig launched in 1844. The third transfer incorporates Admiral Nelson's message to the British Fleet at the battle of Trafalgar in 1805 that read, by the use of signal flags, "ENGLAND EXPECTS THAT EVERY MAN WILL DO HIS DUTY." This 1.0 litre size flagon is 7″ high by 6¼″ diameter and is transfer marked "WADE MADE IN ENGLAND". A miniature version of this shaped flagon is also available but with altered decoration.

For this illustration and illustration No. 838 the co-operation of "Pusser's Ltd." is appreciated.

No. 780. BELL'S OLD SCOTCH WHISKY—decanter in the 375 ml size was first made by Wade in 1965. The design and decoration is similar to that described for No. 774. This decanter is 7¾″ high.

No. 781. KING GEORGE IV SCOTCH WHISKY—octagonal water jug without ice check spout. The jug has an overall glaze finish with transfer decoration on both sides and with the wording "KING GEORGE IV" Old Scotch Whisky under the spout. The jug is 4⅜″ high, has a black "WADE REGICOR" Mark Type 42 on the base, and was produced in the early 1950's.

No. 782. KING GEORGE IV SCOTCH WHISKY—octagonal overhang lip type ashtray and a companion piece to the jug described above. The finish, decorative transfers and marking on the base are as described for No. 781. above. The ashtray is 2″ high by 4⅛″ long by 3¼″ wide.

This illustration and illustrations No. 781 (King George IV Scotch Whisky octagonal water jug), No. 761 and No. 768 (King George IV Scotch Whisky oval water jugs) are shown by permission of "The Distillers Agency Ltd."

No. 783. JOHNNIE WALKER—square ashtray produced circa 1971 in limited quantities in this color. The easy clean type ashtray is 6½″ square at its widest point by 1⅝″ high and has a green "WADE PDM" Mark Type 46 on the base.

No. 784. JOHNNIE WALKER—water jug with ice check spout and overall glaze finish with similar transfer decorations on both sides. The jug is 5¼″ high and was first produced circa early 1960's with "WADE REGICOR" Mark Type 43, then circa 1967, with "WADE REGICOR" Mark Type 44. The glaze was changed to white in 1972, with the "WADE PDM" Mark Type 46.

No. 785. CAPTAIN MORGAN—boat-shaped ashtray produced circa 1961. The ashtray has a two-tone glaze finish with transfer decoration and measures 7¾″ long by 4¼″ at its widest point by 2⅛″ high at the bow. The "WADE REGICOR" Mark Type 43 is placed on the underside of the tray.

"CAPTAIN MORGAN is the registered trade mark of Seagram United Kingdom Ltd."

No. 786. BELL'S OLD SCOTCH WHISKY—decanter in the quarter bottle size first produced in the early 1970's. The design and decoration is similar to that used for No. 774. The decanter is 6⅜″ high.

No. 787. WHITE HORSE—ashtray with a single glaze finish and transfer type decoration was first produced in the early 1960's and bears the "WADE REGICOR" Mark Type 43. The ashtray is 5½″ square at its widest point by 1″ high.

No. 788. MOUNT GAY BARBADOS RUM—overhang lip type ashtray was produced on one occasion in 1973 and bears a green "WADE PDM" Mark Type 46 on the base. The ashtray measures 5⅛″ square by 2⅛″ high. The applied transfer decoration appears on all four sides.

The co-operation of "Mount Gay Distillers Ltd." is appreciated.

No. 789. MACKINLAY'S SCOTCH WHISKY—overhang lip type ashtray produced circa mid 1950's, bearing the "WADE REGICOR" Mark Type 42. The ashtray is 7¼″ long by 5⅛″ wide at its widest point by 1½″ high.

For this illustration and illustration No. 778 (MACKINLAY'S OLD SCOTCH WHISKY water jug) the co-operation of "CHARLES MACKINLAY & Co. Ltd." is appreciated.

No. 790. CUTTY SARK SCOTCH WHISKY—easy clean type ashtray was produced circa 1968 and has the "WADE REGICOR" Mark Type 45 on the base. This ashtray is no longer in production having been replaced by a yellow ashtray design. The overall glaze finish has applied transfer decorations on both sides with small white boats appearing below the cigaret rests.

171

The tray is 5″ in diameter by 1½″ high.

"CUTTY SARK" is the registered trade mark of Berry Bros. & Rudd Ltd., London, England.

No. 791. BELL'S OLD SCOTCH WHISKY—miniature 50ml decanter was first introduced in 1979, and measures 4¼″ high completing the family of four different sized decanters. The design and decoration is similar to that for No. 774.

For this illustration and illustrations No. 774, No. 780 and No. 786 (Bell's Old Scotch Whisky Decanters) the co-operation of Arthur Bell & Sons plc. is appreciated.

FIG. 129. B.O.A.C.—water jug with ice check spout and recessed handle. The 5¼″ high jug has an overall grey/blue glaze on the outside and white glaze on the inside. The transfer type decoration is in black and white and the lettering is white. The jug bears Mark Type 42 on the base. Also produced for B.O.A.C. in the period early 1960's-1971, were the following items:

Large Round Ashbowl, Pottery Dish, One pint Tankard, and a Half pint Tankard.

FIG. 129.

ASHTRAYS.

No. 792. BRITISH AIRWAYS—two-tone spun ashtray produced in 1973. The ashtray is 8½″ in diameter by 1⅞″ high and bears the "WADE PDM" Mark Type 46. The red/blue wording "British Airways" appears four times around the vertical side of the tray.

The co-operation of "British Airways Plc." is appreciated.

No. 793. JOHNNIE WALKER—easy clean type rectangular ashtray produced circa 1962. This ashtray with an overall glaze finish and transfer decoration is 9″ long by 7″ wide by 1½″ high and has a red "WADE REGICOR" Mark Type 43 on the base.

No. 794. JOHNNIE WALKER—easy clean type oval shape ashtray produced circa 1962. The finish to this ashtray is similar to the one described above and measures 10¼″ long by 6″ wide by 1¾″ high and has a green "WADE REGICOR" Mark Type 43 on the base.

No. 795. VAUX—easy clean ashtray with relief molding produced between 1970-1980 and has a green "WADE PDM" Mark Type 46 on the base. The ashtray is 7″ long by 6½″ wide overall by 1¾″ high.

No. 796. J&B SCOTCH WHISKY—easy clean type ashtray with an overall glaze finish and transfer decoration on each side. This ashtray is a companion piece to the J&B Scotch Whisky water jug No. 751 and has a black "WADE PDM" Mark Type 46 on the base. The ashtray measures 6″ long by 2½″ wide by 1½″ high.

For this illustration and illustration No. 751 (J&B Scotch Whisky water jug) the co-operation of "Justerini & Brooks Ltd. the proprietors of J&B rare Scotch Whisky" is appreciated.

No. 797. GREENALL WHITLEY—easy clean type spun ashtray produced in 1979 and bears a "WADE PDM" Mark Type 46 on the base. The overall glaze finish ashtray has a transfer type decoration and is 8″ in diameter by 1¾″ high.

The co-operation of "Greenall Whitley PLC" is appreciated.

No. 798. PRESIDENT SCOTCH WHISKY—overhang lip type ashtray with transfer type decoration. The ashtray illustrated was produced between 1970-1980, and has a green "WADE PDM" Mark Type 46 on the base. It is probable that this shape ashtray was in production as early as 1953, in which case it would have a "WADE REGICOR" backstamp. This ashtray is 7″ long by 4″ wide by 1½″ high.

The co-operation of "MACDONALD GREENLEES LIMITED" is appreciated.

No. 799. ILLINI—easy clean type ashtray with an overall glaze finish and transfer decoration. This ashtray was issued in a limited quantity by special order of the University of Illinois. Issued in 1980, the ashtray has a red "WADE PDM" Mark Type 47 on the base and is 7″ in diameter by 1½″ high.

No. 800. JOHNNIE WALKER SCOTCH WHISKY—easy clean type ashtray was made circa 1962 and has a green "WADE REGICOR" Mark Type 43 on the base. The ashtray has an overall glaze finish with transfer type decoration and measures 5⅛" square by 1⅝" high.

This illustration and illustrations No. 783, No. 784, No. 793 and No. 794 (Johnnie Walker ashtrays and water jug) are shown by permission, "© John Walker & Sons Limited."

No. 801. HUDSON'S BAY SCOTCH WHISKY— overhang lip type ashtray was produced in the late 1960's and has a red "WADE REGICOR" Mark Type 45. The ashtray is 6¼" in diameter by 2¾" high. The ashtray has an overall glaze finish with applied transfer lettering appearing three times on the overhang lip and a different style transfer appearing three times around the vertical sides located under the lip indents.

No. 802. BANKS—overhang lip type ashtray produced between 1968-1970 for the Banks Brewery. The ashtray is 4¾" in diameter at the base by 1⅝" high and has a red "WADE REGICOR" Mark Type 45.

No. 803. TETLEY BITTERMEN—menu holder was first produced in the mid 1960's. However, the one illustrated was made in the early 1970's, and has the "WADE PDM" Mark Type 46 on the base. The menu holder measures 2½" by 2¼" at the base by 1¾" high. The solid ceramic holder has an overall glaze finish with a similar transfer decoration on both sides.

The co-operation of "Joshua Tetley & Son Limited, the Leeds based brewers who are part of Allied Lyons" is appreciated.

No. 804. TEACHER'S HIGHLAND CREAM SCOTCH WHISKY—overhang lip type ashtray produced in the early 1980's, and bears a red "WADE PDM" Mark Type 47. The ashtray measures 6" in diameter at the base by 1¾" high. The applied lettering transfer decoration appears five times around the vertical edge.

No. 805. JOHN BULL—easy clean type ashtray produced in 1980 to promote John Bull Bitter Ale. Bearing the "WADE PDM" Mark Type 47, the triangular-shaped ashtray has an overall glaze finish with transfer lettering decoration appearing on the three sides and a trade mark decal, showing the picture of John Bull appearing three times under the molded indents. The ashtray measures 7" at its widest point at the base by 1⅞" high.

The co-operation of "IND COOPE LIMITED, the Romford based brewers who are part of Allied Lyons" is appreciated.

No. 806. BLACK & WHITE SCOTCH WHISKY—easy clean type ashtray produced between 1970-1980 and has a green "WADE PDM" Mark Type 46 on the base. The overall glaze finish ashtray is 5" in diameter by 1⅝" high. The white lettering transfer type decoration appears three times around the vertical edge.

No. 807. PARKINSON'S DONCASTER—spun dish type ashtray produced circa mid 1950's to promote the production of their "Old Fashioned Humbugs," a popular type of candy. The ashtray which measures 5⅜" in diameter by 1" high has an overall glaze finish with a transfer type decoration and has the "WADE REGICOR" Mark Type 42 on the base.

No. 808. EMBASSY HOTELS—spun type scatter dish/ ashtray was first commissioned circa 1976. The ashtray illustrated was made in the early 1980's, bears the "WADE PDM" Mark Type 47 and measures 4¾" in diameter by ⅞" high. The overall glaze finish ashtray shows a transfer type decoration of the Embassy Hotels logo.

Embassy Hotels retains the ownership and copyright of the Trade Mark.

No. 809. CARLSBERG—pressed type ashtray was produced in 1972 and bears the "WADE PDM" Mark Type 46. The ashtray is 5½" square by 1¼" high having an overall glaze finish with a transfer type decoration.

"Carlsberg" is a Registered Trade Mark of United Breweries International Ltd."

No. 810. BLACK & WHITE SCOTCH WHISKY—easy clean type ashtray produced in 1970, with an overall glaze finish, hand applied gold trim and transfer type lettering decoration appearing on all four sides. The ashtray, which measures 5" square by 1¼" high, has a red "WADE REGICOR" Mark Type 45 on the base.

This illustration and illustration No. 806 (Black & White Scotch Whisky ashtray) are "Reproduced by kind permission of James Buchanan & Company Limited."

FIG. 130. BULMERS WOODPECKER CIDER—easy clean type ashtray produced in 1977 with an overall yellow glaze with red and white lettering. The ashtray measures 5½" wide by 6¾" long by 1½" high and has Mark Type 46 on the base.

FIG. 130.

FIG. 131. BEEFEATER GIN—pressed ashtray. This square ashtray measures 5½″ by 1¼″ high and bears Mark Type 46. The ashtray has a white background with lettering in red and black as is the head and shoulders of the Beefeater.

FIG. 131.

GILBEY'S WINE BARRELS
CIRCA 1953.

In the early 1950's, W&A Gilbey Limited, Wine Shippers & Distillers since 1857, commissioned Wade Heath to produce a limited number of miniature wine barrels. These miniature barrels are based on the Pottery Barrels as used in Public Houses in the 19th Century. Messrs. W. & A. Gilbey Ltd., the famous Wine Merchants commissioned Wade Heath to assist in producing these as a Christmas gift line. The public was so charmed with their Victorian elegance that the production of these barrels was extended long beyond the original planned period of issue. It is probable that these barrels were in production until the late 1950's.

Due to the popularity of these porcelain barrels, the initial issue of Sherry, Gin, Scotch and Port were extended to include Rum, Cognac and Irish Whisky and maybe others. Two sizes of barrels were produced with the larger size issued, in limited numbers, as table lamps. The large size oval-shaped barrels measure 5¾″ high by 4½″ long at the oval base. The smaller size barrels measure 4¾″ high by 3⅝″ long at the base. Both size barrels bear Mark Type 17. (Royal Victoria Pottery).

The co-operation of "W&A Gilbey Ltd." is appreciated.

No. 811. COGNAC BARREL LAMP—large size.
No. 812. PORT BARREL—large size.
No. 813. IRISH BARREL—large size.
No. 814. SCOTCH BARREL—large size.
No. 822. SHERRY BARREL—small size.
No. 823. GIN BARREL—small size.
No. 824. SCOTCH BARREL—small size.
No. 825. PORT BARREL—small size.

ROTHMAN'S TANKARD

No. 815. ROTHMAN'S OF PALL MALL—tankard produced circa the mid 1970's. The transfer decoration is applied to a standard large size Wade tankard measuring 4¾″ high with a "WADE PDM" Mark Type 46 on the base. The decoration on the back of the tankard tells a story as follows:

"THE ROTHMAN'S COACH"
Every day from Pall Mall through the West End of London along the Mall and Carlton House Terrace, Rothmans still deliver their famous cigarettes to select Clubs and Embassies by coach and footmen. This time-honoured custom is a tradition of the House of Rothman.

The illustration of this tankard is "Reproduced by permission of Rothmans Cigarettes."

BASS PROMOTIONAL ITEMS.

In 1777 William Bass established a brewery in Burton-upon-Trent, a town already famous at that time due to brewing waters rich in minerals. Water for Bass beers is still drawn from wells situated on the company's own land in the area. Brewers already established in the area included Benjamin Printon and Samuel Sketchley, who both established breweries in 1741, Benjamin Wilson in 1742, and William Worthington in 1744. Worthington & Co. was later to become part of the Bass Brewery and beer is still marketed under the Worthington name.

A descendent of Wm. Bass, Roger Bass, married Anne Worthington, which established ties between the two brewing companies. At this time Michael Thomas Bass II, eldest brother of Roger, was running the brewery, and by his death, in 1884, had turned the company into one of the greatest breweries in the world.

With the introduction of the Trade Marks Registration Act of 1875, a member of the Bass staff was the first person to enter the Registrar's office to insure that a label incorporating the Red Triangle, already associated with Bass products, would be the first trade mark to be registered officially. This mark can still be seen on Bass products today.

Bass PLC is today made up of a large number of breweries which have amalgamated between 1777 and 1967. Amongst these breweries taken over during the years were Worthington & Co. Ltd. in 1927, Mitchells and Butler Ltd. in 1961, and Charrington United Breweries Limited in 1967, when the company name was changed to Bass Charrington Limited and later to Bass Public Limited Company.

The famous beers and lagers which now come from Bass include Worthington E, Draught Bass, Carling Black Label Lager, Worthington Bitter, Bass Blue Triangle and Worthington White Shield.

No. 816. BASS EXPORT ALE—spun ashtray produced in 1969-1970, and marked with the "WADE REGICOR" Mark type 45. The ashtray measures 9" in diameter by 1½" high. This ashtray is no longer in production.

No. 817. BASS—pressed ashtray first produced in 1985, and is still made today. The square ashtray measures 6¼" by 1⅛" high and bears the "WADE PDM" Mark Type 47. The ashtray has an overall glaze finish with transfer type decoration.

No. 818. STONE'S BEST BITTER—easy clean type ashtray was produced in 1978, and has the "WADE PDM" Mark Type 46 on the base. The ashtray measures 8¼" long by 5" wide by 1½" high. The overall glaze finished ashtray is decorated with transfer type decals which appear on all four sides as well as the central decal shown in the picture.

No. 819. WORTHINGTON E—relief molded water jug without ice check spout was issued in 1977 and has the "WADE PDM" Mark Type 46 on the base. The jug measures 5½" high by approx. 7" from spout to handle. The reverse side of the "E" shaped jug has the word "Worthington" applied backwards to conform to the reverse shape of the letter "E".

No. 820. BASS JUG—which is a reproduction of a 1910, Minton jug made for the Bass bicentenary celebrations in 1977, but it was probably on sale as early as 1975-1976. The item is still available for sale in the Bass Museum in Burton-upon-Trent. The jug measures 6⅞" high and bears the "WADE PDM" Mark Type 46 on the base.

No. 821. GREAT STUFF . . . BASS—easy clean type ashtray first produced circa 1976; however, the ashtray illustrated was made after 1980, and bears the "WADE PDM" Mark Type 47. The ashtray is 7" square at the base by 2⅛" high. The overall glaze finish ashtray has two types of transfer decorations each appearing twice on the sloped sides of the ashtray.

For illustrations of BASS Waiter Trays see FIG. 135 items B, C, E and H.

"The Publishers and authors acknowledge that Bass Public Limited Company or its subsidiaries are the proprietors of all copyright trade mark and all other rights associated with these illustrations and the items depicted therein."

BOTTLE POURERS.

Amongst the many products made by George Wade & Son Ltd. for distributions through WADE (PDM) Ltd. are a number of different shaped bottle pourers. The pourers consist of two parts: the porcelain die-cast body which is usually highly decorated with transfer type decorations (or hand painted to special order) and the nickel plated copper tubing which is not made by George Wade but supplied by a small locally based company called "Frank Thornton". The porcelain portion of the pourer is not marked other than a reserved line number impressed into the underside of the pourer.

Two examples of bottle pourers. The 'Burroughs' pourer is hand painted porcelain, and the 'Gordons' pourer is a combination of metal and porcelain with a transfer fired on the porcelain button.

(Screen Printing and Point of Sale News, March 1966)

Following are a few examples of the many different pourers produced:

No. 826. McCALLUMS WHISKY—measures 1⅝" in diameter.

No. 827. MARTELL COGNAC—measures 1½" high by 1¾" across the face.

No. 828. KISKADEE—measures 2⅜" high by 1⅜" across the face.

No. 829. SMIRNOFF VODKA—measures 1½" in diameter.

No. 830. CROFT ORIGINAL CREAM SHERRY—measures 1½" high by 1¾" across the face.

No. 831. VAT 69—measures 1½" in diameter.

No. 832. FAMOUS GROUSE—measures 1½" high by 1⅞" across the face.

GUINESS PROMOTIONAL FIGURINES 1968.

In December 1968, Guinness Brewing commissioned George Wade to produce four promotional figurines based on characters featured in the "Guinness Book of Advertising." The order was for 3,000 sets of the four figurines and 8,000 singles (2,000 each of the four). These figurines have proven to be highly collectible and due to the limited issue, are hard to find and thus command a high price.

None of the figurines are marked with a Wade backstamp or mark but all have "GUINNESS" mold-marked on the front of the base. However, the hand painted underglaze finish is unmistakably "WADE". The illustrations of the figurines and the reproduction of excerpts from the Guinness Book of Advertising are "Reproduced by kind permission of Guinness Brewing".

No. 833. TONY WELLER—holding a glass of Guinness. This figurine is based on an illustration by "Phiz" for The Pickwick Papers by Charles Dickens (1837). The figurine measures 3″ high by 1¾″ across the base.

No. 834. TWEEDLEDUM AND TWEEDLEDEE—both holding a glass of Guinness. This figurine of the twins is based on characters from *Alice's Adventures in Wonderland* by Lewis Carroll which in turn was based on a press advertisement from 1958 celebrating the 7th anniversary of Guinness, which had acquired control of Callard and Bowser. The figurine measures 2⅞″ high by 2¼″ across the base.

No. 835. MADHATTER—a figurine again based on a character from *Alice's Adventures in Wonderland* which, in turn, was based on an advertisement by Antony Groves-Raines for a 1954, edition of *The Illustrated London News*. The figurine measures 3¼″ high by 1½″ across the base.

No. 836. WELLINGTON BOOT—a figurine based on a contemporary caricature of the Duke of Wellington after the Battle of Waterloo and first used as a Guinness advertisement in 1933. The figurine measures 3½″ high by 1¾″ oval shaped base.

Confectionately yours

Alice could not help pointing her finger at Tweedledum and saying, "First Brother!"

"Nohow!" Tweedledum cried out briskly.

"Next Brother!" said Alice, passing on to Tweedledee. But he only shouted out "Contrariwise!"

"Look before you leap to conclusions," said Tweedledum. "Just because we're alike . . ."

"We might be no more alike," broke in Tweedledee, "than a glass of Guinness and a packet of Butter-Scotch—and *still* belong to the same family."

"But," began Alice, "Guinness is brewed—"

"Exactly," said Tweedledee, "Guinness's brood includes Callard. And Bowser, of course."

"By adoption, you know," said Tweedledum gravely.

"But Guinness is tall, rich and handsome," Alice ventured to object.

"Callard and Bowser sweets are small, rich and toothsome," said Tweedledum. "There's a strong likeness, if you look."

"Goodness!" said Alice.

"Precisely," said Tweedledee.

Issued jointly by

GUINNESS and CALLARD & BOWSER

Guinness, brewers of stout since 1759, seven years ago acquired control of Callard & Bowser, makers of fine Butter-Scotch and other confectionery since 1837.

FIG. 132. EXTRACT FROM THE GUINESS BOOK OF ADVERTISING.

A Soldier at Waterloo

"WHEN I was sufficiently recovered to be permitted to take some nourishment, I felt the most extraordinary desire for a glass of Guinness, which I knew could be obtained without difficulty. Upon expressing my wish to the doctor, he told me I might take a small glass. . . .

"It was not long before I sent for the Guinness and I shall never forget how much I enjoyed it. I thought I had never tasted anything so delightful. . . . I am confident that it contributed more than anything else to the renewal of my strength."

From the Diary of a Cavalry Officer, June 1815, after being severely wounded at the Battle of Waterloo.

Ethel M. Richardson, "LONG FORGOTTEN DAYS." (Heath Cranton, 1928).

NOTE.—An interesting point about this extract is that before it came to light, the earliest known reference to the export of Guinness was in 1816, the year after Waterloo. The fact that Guinness "could be obtained without difficulty" in Belgium in 1815 shows that export must actually have begun some time before this.

FIG. 133. EXTRACT FROM THE GUINESS BOOK OF RECORDS.

LABATT'S TANKARD

No. 837. LABATT'S 50—tankard produced circa early 1970's as a promotional item for a brand of beer produced by John Labatt Limited, Canada's largest brewery. The transfer decoration is applied to a standard large size Wade tankard is 4¾″ high and marked "WADE IRELAND" on the base.

"Labatt's 50" is a Registered Trade Mark of John Labatt Limited whose co-operation is appreciated.

NELSON'S SHIP DECANTER

No. 838. NELSON'S SHIP DECANTER—first produced in January 1983 in a 1 litre size. This decanter is looked upon as the flagship of the Pusser's rum containers.

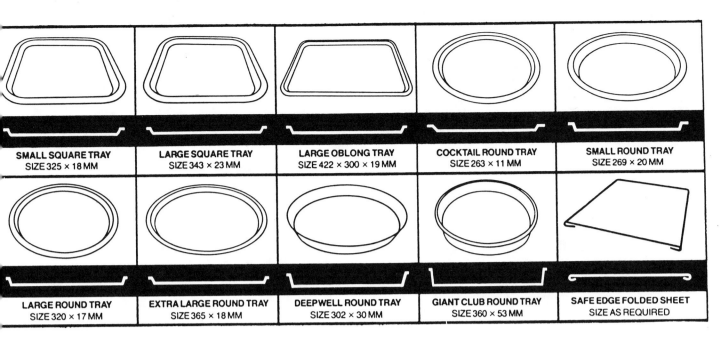

SMALL SQUARE TRAY SIZE 325 × 18 MM	LARGE SQUARE TRAY SIZE 343 × 23 MM	LARGE OBLONG TRAY SIZE 422 × 300 × 19 MM	COCKTAIL ROUND TRAY SIZE 263 × 11 MM	SMALL ROUND TRAY SIZE 269 × 20 MM
LARGE ROUND TRAY SIZE 320 × 17 MM	EXTRA LARGE ROUND TRAY SIZE 365 × 18 MM	DEEPWELL ROUND TRAY SIZE 302 × 30 MM	GIANT CLUB ROUND TRAY SIZE 360 × 53 MM	SAFE EDGE FOLDED SHEET SIZE AS REQUIRED

FIG. 134. STANDARD SHAPES OF WAITER TRAYS.

WAITER TRAYS *1970-PRESENT.*

In 1970 Wade (PDM) Ltd., in conjunction with their associates Avon Tin Printers, began offering a large range of tin "Waiter Trays" as a point-of-sale item to advertise their clients products. The trays were designed by Wade (PDM) Ltd. and produced by Avon Tin Printers using high quality off-set litho printing onto the metal trays. This made a bright eye-catching addition to the already popular ceramic advertising items. The trays are all marked "Made in the United Kingdom—a Wade (PDM) Ltd./Avon Product".

FIG. 134 illustrates a number of shapes of standard tin plate pressings.

Illustrated below are nine typical examples of Wade/Avon Waiter Trays.

FIG. 135. A. GORDON'S GIN—small round tray (10½" dia. by ¾" high). The tray was produced in 1974 and has an all over yellow color with red and black lettering.

B. EXTRA LIGHT BY BASS—deepwell round tray (12" dia. by 1¼" high). This tray, introduced in 1973, has an all over light blue color with red lettering.

C. TOBY BITTER—small round tray (10½" dia. by ¾" high). The tray was introduced in 1977 and has an all over medium blue color with white lettering.

D. TETLEY BITTERMEN—small round tray (10½" dia. by ¾" high). The tray has a white rim with a black well, white lettering, flesh-colored hand and a glass of beer in its natural color.

E. WORTHINGTON E small—round tray (10½" dia. by ¾" high). This tray, introduced in 1977, has a dark blue rim with a white vertical edge with a dark blue well and white lettering.

F. MARSTON'S—small round tray (10½" dia. by ¾" high). This tray, introduced in 1976, has a medium blue rim with a white vertical edge and multicolored well. For this illustration the cooperation of "Marston, Thompson & Evershed p.l.c." is appreciated.

G. MORLAND—large square tray (13½" square by 1" high). This tray was produced in 1973, for the oldest independent brewery in the U.K. which was established in 1711. It has a black rim with a white vertical edge, dark green well with white lettering.

H. STONES BEST BITTER—small square tray (12¾" square by ¾" high). This tray, introduced in 1976 has a gold-colored rim and vertical edge with a multicolored well.

J. SPRINGBANK SCOTCH WHISKY—small square tray (12¾" square by ¾" high). This tray, produced in 1972, has a black rim with a white vertical edge and multicolored well.

Distilled by "J.&A. Mitchell & Co., Ltd. Springbank Distillery, Campbeltown, Argyll, Scotland".

FIG. 135. WAITER TRAYS.

Miscellaneous Items

by

The Wade Group of Companies

FIG. 136. VASE—The vase is 7″ high with decoration No. 3405 and Mark Type 1A. The streaked decoration is of green and orange. (Wade & Co.)

FIG. 137. JUG—The jug is 6½″ high with decoration No. 3404 and Mark Type 2A. The streaked decoration, from top to base is of orange, green and blue. (Wade Heath & Co. Ltd.)

FIG. 138. JUG—The 1930's original shape No. 154 (see No. 388 in color section.) The pitcher is 9″ high and has Mark Type 6 on the base and produced in a variety of color combinations. (Wade Heath & Co. Ltd.)

FIG. 139. JUG—The jug is 11¾″ high with decoration No. 4486, shape No. 164 and Mark Type 7. This jug is marked "Sample". It is known that this shape and decoration was in production in 1936 but had a limited distribution. (Wade Heath & Co. Ltd.)

FIG. 140. MEDALLION JUG—This jug is 6½″ high with Mark Type 10. This jug was also produced in 6″ and 5″ high sizes. This jug, originally produced in the late 1930's, was also used by George Wade & Son Ltd., as a container for handmade china flowers. (Wade Heath & Co. Ltd.)

FIG. 141. SQUIRREL BUTTER DISH—This dish is similar to No. 273 and produced in the same time period. (George Wade & Son Ltd.)

FIG. 142. TIRE DISH—Veteran Cars series 2 (No. 4) illustrating a 1904 Sunbeam. The dish is 5″ in dia. (Wade Heath & Co. Ltd.)

FIG. 143. PLYMOUTH TANKARD WITH SPOUT—a variation on the standard 3¾″ high, half pint Plymouth tankard with Mark Type 19. (Wade Heath & Co. Ltd.)

FIG. 144. SANDEMAN DECANTER—8½″ high figural port container with Mark Type 19. Produced between 1958-1961 for George G. Sandeman & Co., Ltd. (Wade Heath & Co. Ltd.)

FIG. 145. TOWER STOUT HORS D'OEUVRE DISH/ TOOTHPICK HOLDER—10″ high to top of handle by 8½″ dia. produced in 1968. (Wade Heath & Co. Ltd./Reginald Corfield (Sales) Ltd.)

FIG. 146. McCALLUM'S ASHTRAY—4¾″ in dia. with overall brown glaze marked "Wade Regicor England." (Wade Heath & Co. Ltd./Reginald Corfield (Sales) Ltd.)

FIG. 147. NUT BOWL—shape No. I.P.76 with Mark Type 28. The bowl is 6½″ in dia. by 2″ high. (Wade (Ireland) Ltd.)

FIG. 148. FRUIT BOWL—shape No. I.P.74 with Mark Type 30. The bowl was produced in the early 1960's and measures 5″ in dia. by 2″ high. (Wade (Ireland) Ltd.)

FIG. 149. ROSE DISH—shape No. I.P.625 with Mark Type 29. The dish is 5½″ long and was produced in the late 1950's-early 1960's. (Wade (Ireland) Ltd.)

FIG. 150. COVERED PRESERVE JAR—shape No. C.316, designed by James Borsey, and bears a mark very similar to Mark Type 33. This 4½″ high jar was produced in the late 1960's. (Wade (Ireland) Ltd.)

FIG. 151. MINIATURE TYRONE TANKARD—shape No. I.P.9S with an all over design produced in the late 1950's. The tankard is 4″ high and has Mark Type 28. (Wade (Ireland) Ltd.)

FIG. 152. LEPRECHAUN ON A TOADSTOOL—Shape No. C340, produced for a short period in the early 1960's. The figurine measures 4½″ high and is transfer marked "Made in Ireland" on the base.

FIG. 153. VASE—This vase is similar to No. 661 but with a larger and more elaborate decoration.

FIG. 154. TOADSTOOL MONEY BANK—introduced in 1987, this money bank is unmarked and measures 5½″ high by 6″ wide with a plastic plug in the base. (George Wade & Son Ltd.)

FIG. 155. KENNEL MONEY BANK—introduced in 1987, this money bank is unmarked and measures 4½″ high by 5¼″ long by 3″ wide with a plastic plug in the base. (George Wade & Son. Ltd.)

FIG. 156. FAWN MONEY BANK—introduced in 1987, this money bank has Mark Type 19 and measures 5¼″ high by 5″ long with a plastic plug in the base. (George Wade & Son Ltd.)

FIG. 157. NEW WHIMTRAY—introduced in 1987, this Whimtray measures 4½″ long by 3½″ wide and is produced in blue, black and green colors. The set consists of the OWL, SQUIRREL, PONY, PUPPY, and the DUCK as illustrated. All figurines are from the current Whimsie-Land series. All trays are mold marked "WADE ENGLAND." (George Wade & Son Ltd.)

FIG. 158. WHIMSEY-ON-WHY VILLAGE SET 5—This set of four houses was issued in 1987. The houses continue with the same system of numbering as the earlier sets. A. SCHOOL TEACHER'S HOUSE (No. 33), B. FISHMONGER'S (No. 34), C. POLICE STATION (No. 35), and D. LIBRARY (No. 36.) (George Wade & Son Ltd.)

FIG. 136.

FIG. 137.

FIG. 138.

FIG. 139.

FIG. 140.

FIG. 141.

FIG. 142.

FIG. 143.

FIG. 144.

FIG. 145.

FIG. 146.

FIG. 147.

FIG. 148.

FIG. 149.

FIG. 150.

FIG. 151.

FIG. 152.

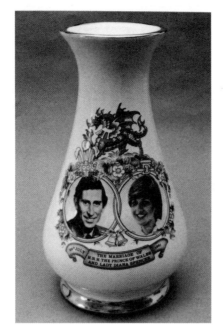

FIG. 153.

FIG. 154.

FIG. 155.

FIG. 156.

FIG. 157.

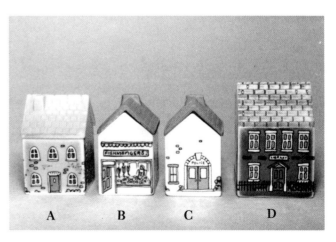

FIG. 158

INDEX

ADDIS SHAVING MUGS MID 1960'S TO PRESENT 115
ADVERTISING WATER JUGS...168
ANIMAL FIGURES BY WADE HEATH & COMPANY LTD. AND GEORGE WADE & SON LTD.
   MID 1930'S-1960 28
ANIMAL FIGURES CIRCA 1937-1939. (Underglaze Finish) 22
ANIMAL FIGURES and FIGURINES CIRCA LATE 1940'S-LATE 1950'S. (Underglaze Finish) 23
ASHTRAYS 172
AQUA DISHES SET 1. 1958-1960 111
AQUA DISHES SET 2. 1960 111
AQUARIUM SET CIRCA 1975-1980 27
BALLET CIRCA LATE 1950'S 110
BALLY-WHIM IRISH VILLAGE 1984-1987 165
BARGE POSY BOWL 1954 109
BARREL TANKARDS...149
BASKET WARE "2" CIRCA MID 1950'S 137
BASKET WARE (Decoration No. U 4804) CIRCA 1946 131
BASS PROMOTIONAL ITEMS 174
BISTO-KIDS CIRCA MID 1970'S 26
BLUE BIRD DISH 1958-1959 111
BLUE BIRD TREE TRUNK POSY VASE 1957-1959 111
BOTTLE POURERS 174
"BOULDRAY" TRAY CIRCA LATE 1960'S TO EARLY 1970'S 115
BRAMBLE WARE 140
BRIDGE POSY HOLDER 1954-1958 107
BUDDIES CIRCA 1960 133
BUD VASE SOUVENIRS CIRCA MID 1950'S-1961 149
CANADIAN RED ROSE TEA PROMOTION 1967-1973 96
CANADIAN RED ROSE TEA PROMOTION 1971-1979 98
CANADIAN RED ROSE TEA PROMOTION 1981 99
CANADIAN RED ROSE TEA PROMOTION 1982-1984 100
CANADIAN SALADA TEA PROMOTION 1984 101
CANADIAN RED ROSE TEA PROMOTION 1985-1986 103
CANDLEHOLDERS 1965-1982 117
CAMEO DISHES 1965 113
CAPRI (Decoration No. 6057) 1953 135
CAT AND PUPPY DISHES 1974-1981 84
CELTIC PORCELAIN CIRCA MID 1960'S 158
CHAMPIONSHIP DOGS 1975-1981 86
CHERUB BOWL 1957-1959...110
CHEVALINE POSY BOWL 1955-1959 108
CHILD STUDIES 1962 26
CHIMPANZEE POSY VASE 1959-1960 112
CHINA FLOWERS 21
CIRCUS ANIMAL SET 1978-1979 104
COUNTRYWARE 1973-1984 159
COVERED HEDGEHOG DISH 1961 113
COVERED SHORE CRAB DISH 1960 112
CRANKY TANKARDS 1947-EARLY 1950'S 129
"C" SHAPED POSY LOG 1954-1959 108
DECORATION No. 5033 CIRCA 1951 142
DECORATION No. 6266 CIRCA 1960 145

DECORATIVE PLATES CIRCA 1951-1960 133
DISNEY "BLOW-UPS" 1961-1965 83
DISNEY MONEY BOXES 1962 82
"DISNEYS" 1981-1987 83
DOG DISH CIRCA 1957 109
DOG MODELS CIRCA 1927-EARLY 1930'S (Cellulose Finish) 13
DOG PIPE RESTS 1973-1981 87
DOGS AND PUPPIES SERIES 1969-1982 84
DRUM BOX SERIES 1956-1959 29
EGG CODDLERS CIRCA 1965-1986 160
EARTHENWARE FLOWERS 19
EMETT DISHES CIRCA 1960 151
EMPRESS (Decoration No. 5082) CIRCA LATE 1940'S-LATE 1950'S 131
EVERLASTING CANDLES 1953-1954 134
FAMOUS AIRCRAFT TRAYS 1959 112
FAMOUS SHIP DISHES 150
FANTASIA 1961 140
FARMYARD SET 1982-1983 104
FAWN DISH CIRCA MID 1960'S 113
"FESTIVAL" (Decoration No. 5070) 1954 143
FIGURINES BY GEORGE WADE & SON LTD. 1927-1940 24
FIGURINES BY GEORGE WADE & SON LTD. 1956-1987 26
FIGURINES, ANIMAL FIGURES AND ASHTRAYS BY GEORGE WADE & SON LTD. 1956-1987 29
FIGURINES CIRCA 1927-LATE 1930'S (Cellulose Finish) 12
FLAIR TABLEWARE CIRCA EARLY 1960'S 138
FLYING BIRDS 1956-1959 164
GIFTS FROM OLD IRELAND 1959 164
GILBEY'S WINE BARRELS CIRCA 1953 174
GOTHIC 128
"GRAPE" DECORATION TABLEWARE CIRCA 1953 132
GUINESS PROMOTIONAL FIGURINES 1968 175
HANNA-BARBERA CARTOON CHARACTERS CIRCA 1959-1969 31
HAPPY FAMILIES 1962-1965 86
HAPPY FAMILIES 1978-1986 86
"HARLEQUINS" 1957-1958 109
HARMONY TABLEWARE CIRCA 1957-EARLY 1960'S 136
"HAT BOX" SERIES 1956-1965 82
HONEY POTS CIRCA 1939 AND 1946 129
HORSE SETS 1974-1981 87
IRISH CHARACTER FIGURES CIRCA EARLY 1970'S-1986 164
IRISH PORCELAIN SONG FIGURES 1962-1986 166
IRISH PORCELAIN 1953-1986 158
IRISH SOUVENIRS AND FIGURINES 164
KOALA BEAR TREE TRUNK POSY VASE 1957-1959 111
K.P. FOODS LIMITED—POTATO CHIP PROMOTION 1983 103
LARGE ANIMAL FIGURES AND FIGURINES CIRCA 1935-1939 (Underglaze Finish) 15
LARGE ANIMAL FIGURES AND FIGURINES CIRCA 1935-1939 (Underglaze Finish) 16
LARGE MERMAID POSY BOWL 1955-1959 108
LARGE TRADITIONAL POSY BOWL 1955-1959 108
LATTICE WARE (Decoration No. 6191) CIRCA LATE 1950'S 137
LEAF DISH 1957-1959 110
LEAF DISH 1957-1958 110
LEAF DISH 1958-1959 110
LEPRECHAUN PIN TRAYS CIRCA 1956-1986 164
LESNEY TRAY CIRCA 1968-1975 118
LUCKY LEPRECHAUNS CIRCA 1956-1986 164
MABEL LUCIE ATTWELL CHARACTERS 1959 26
MAN IN BOAT 1978-1984 117
"MEADOW" DECORATION TABLEWARE CIRCA 1951-1960 133

MINIATURE ANIMAL FIGURES CIRCA EARLY 1930'S-1939 (Underglaze Finish) 14
MINIATURE "TRADITIONAL" TANKARDS—ANIMAL SERIES 149
MINIATURE "TRADITIONAL" TANKARDS—SOUVENIR 149
MINIATURE "TRADITIONAL" TANKARDS—VETERAN CAR RANGE 149
MINIKINS SETS 1956-1959 30
MISCELLANEOUS GIFT WARE 150
MISCELLANEOUS PREMIUMS MID 1960'S 96
MODE CIRCA LATE 1950'S EARLY 1960'S 135
MODE SHAPE CIRCA 1953-EARLY 1960'S 135
MODE WARE (Decoration No. 6105) 1953 135
"MOURNE" RANGE CIRCA MID 1970'S 160
NEW SHAMROCK RANGE 1982-1986 162
NODDY SET 1958-1960 29
NOVELTY ANIMAL FIGURES 1955-1960 28
NURSERY FAVOURITES 1972-1981 85
NURSERY RHYME FIGURINES BY WADE HEATH & COMPANY LTD CIRCA 1949-1958 24
NUT TRAYS CIRCA 1939 AND 1946 130
OVENWARE CIRCA 1939 135
PAINTED LADIES 1984-1986 106
"PEERAGE" TRAY CIRCA LATE 1960'S TO EARLY 1970'S 115
PEGASUS POSY BOWL 1958-1959 109
PEONY (Decoration No. 4871) 127
PET DISH—CAIRN TERRIER 1979-1982 113
PET DISH—FAWN 1979-1982 113
PET—FACE DISHES SET 1. 1959-1960 112
PET—FACE DISHES SET 2. 1960 112
PITCHERS BY WADE HEATH & COMPANY LTD. CIRCA 1934-1955 120
PORCELAIN NOVELTIES 1954 107
POTTERY TRAYS 150
PREMIUMS AND PROMOTIONAL ITEMS 96
QUACK QUACKS CIRCA 1936-1939 AND CIRCA 1953-LATE 1950'S 135
RABBIT BUTTER DISH 1955-1959 108
RAINDROP DESIGN TABLEWARE 159
REGENCY COFFEE SETS MID. 1950'S-1961 140
RITA (Decoration No. 6056) 1953 135
ROMANCE RANGE 1983-1985 116
ROYAL COMMEMORATIVES 1937-1986 153
SAFARI SET 1976-1977 104
SCALLOPED DISHES 1954-1962 (1971-1984) 109
SCOTTIE TEA POT 1953-1955 146
SEA-GULL BOAT 1961 117
SEA LION CORKSCREW 1960 81
SILHOUETTE SERIES 1962 113
SMALL MERMAID POSY BOWL 1955-1959 108
SMALL TRADITIONAL POSY BOWL 1955-1959 108
SNIPPETS 1956-1958 26
SNOWHITE AND THE SEVEN DWARFS 1981-1986 27
SOLID COPPER LUSTRE AND HAND-PAINTED PATTERNS WITH COPPER LUSTRE CIRCA 1935-1980 . . .142
SOUVENIR DISH CIRCA 1957 109
SOUVENIR PLATES AND TRAYS CIRCA 1954-1961 149
SPIRIT CONTAINERS CIRCA 1961 82
STRAIGHT POSY LOG WITH SQUIRREL 1954-1959 107
"S" SHAPED POSY LOG 1954-1959 108
"S" SHAPED POSY LOG WITH RABBIT 1954-1959 108
STARFISH TRAY 1959-1960 112
ST. BRUNO PIPE TOBACCO PROMOTION 1986 103
SURVIVAL SET 1984-1985 104
TABLEWARE CIRCA LATE 1930'S-1960 127
TANKARDS (MID. 1950'S-1986) AND SOUVENIRS (MID. 1950'S-1961) 148

TEA AND DINNER WARE ORB SHAPE CIRCA EARLY 1950'S 133
TEA POTS 1927-1987 145
THE BRITISH CHARACTER SET CIRCA 1959 27
THE CONNOISSEUR'S COLLECTION 1978-1982 94
THE TORTOISE FAMILY 1958-TO DATE 31
"THE WORLD OF SURVIVAL" SERIES 1978-1982 93
THOMAS THE TANK ENGINE AND FRIENDS 1985-1987 118
TIRE DISHES—VETERAN CAR RANGE 149
"TOM AND JERRY" 1973-1979 81
TOM SMITH & CO. LTD. PARTY CRACKERS 1967-1985 103
TORTOISE ASHBOWLS 1965-1984 29
TREASURE CHEST COVERED DISH 1961 113
"TREASURES"—THE ELEPHANT CHAIN 1956 31
T.T. TRAY 1959-1960 112
TV PETS SERIES 1959-1965 81
U.S.A. RED ROSE TEA PROMOTION 1983-1985 101
U.S.A. RED ROSE TEA PROMOTION 1985 102
VIKING SHIP POSY VASE 1959-1965 112
VILLAGE STORES 1982-1986 114
WADE HEATH ANIMALS 1937-1959 29
WADE FLOWERS CIRCA 1930-1939 18
WAGON TRAIN DISHES 1960 118
WAITER TRAYS 177
WALL PLATES 149
WALL PLATES 150
WESTMINSTER PIGGY BANK FAMILY 1983 TO PRESENT 116
WHIMSIES 1953-1959 90
WHIMSIES 1971-1984 91
WHIMSIE-LAND BRITISH WILDELIFE 1987 88
WHIMSIE-LAND FARMYARD 1985 88
WHIMSIE-LAND HEDGEROW 1986 88
WHIMSIE-LAND PETS 1984 88
WHIMSIE-LAND SERIES 1984 TO DATE 88
WHIMSIE-LAND WILDLIFE 1984 88
WHIMSIE-ON-WHY VILLAGE SETS 1980 TO PRESENT 106
WHIMTRAYS 1958-1965 114
WHIMTRAYS 1971-1987 115
WHOPPAS 1976-1981 87
WILDLIFE SET 1980-1981 104
"WILDFOWL" 1960 113
ZAMBA 1957 110
ZOO LIGHTS 1959 81